HOW ARMIES GROW

HOW ARMIES GROW

The Expansion of Military Forces in the
Age of Total War 1789–1945

Editor
Matthias Strohn

CASEMATE
Oxford & Philadelphia

Published in Great Britain and the United States of America in 2019 by
CASEMATE PUBLISHERS
The Old Music Hall, 106–108 Cowley Road, Oxford OX4 1JE, UK
and
1950 Lawrence Road, Havertown, PA 19083, US

Hardback Edition: ISBN 978-1-61200-601-7
Digital Edition: ISBN 978-1-61200-602-4

A CIP record for this book is available from the British Library

Printed and bound in the United Kingdom by TJ International

Typeset in India for Casemate Publishing Services. www.casematepublishingservices.com

For a complete list of Casemate titles, please contact:

CASEMATE PUBLISHERS (UK)
Telephone (01865) 241249
Email: casemate-uk@casematepublishers.co.uk
www.casematepublishers.co.uk

CASEMATE PUBLISHERS (US)
Telephone (610) 853-9131
Fax (610) 853-9146
Email: casemate@casematepublishers.com
www.casematepublishers.com

Front cover image (top): Detail of a painting of the battle of Hanau (1814) by Horace Vernet
Front cover image (bottom): Tank units taking part in a parade for Adolf Hitler's 47th birthday in 1936 (Bundesarchiv Bild 102-17612)

Contents

List of Contributors

Alexander A. Falbo-Wild is a historian and professional military educator based in Maryland. He is the Chief Archivist for the Witte Memorial 29th Division Archive and Maryland Museum of Military History. He is also a Historian in Residence at Marine Corps University (MCU) History Division and the Chairman for the Western Front Association's East Coast Branch (USA). From 2014–17, he was a Teaching Fellow at Case Method Project at MCU where he instructed US Marines in military history and decision making. His most recent monograph, entitled *Supporting Allied Offensives*, was published by the US Army's Center of Military History.

Dr Tim Gale was awarded his PhD by the Department of War Studies, King's College London for his work on French tank development and operations in the First World War. He has contributed chapters on the subject to numerous academic books. His book *The French Army's Tank Force and the Development of Armoured Warfare in the Great War1* (Ashgate/Routledge) was published in 2013 and was followed by *French Tanks in the Great War* (Pen & Sword, 2016). He is Assistant Secretary-General of the British Commission for Military History.

Dr Robert Johnson is the Director of the Changing Character of War (CCW) Centre at the University of Oxford and a Senior Research Fellow at Pembroke College. His primary research interests are in the history of strategy and war, and their contemporary applications. He is the author of *True to Their Salt: Partnering Indigenous Forces* (2017), *The Great War and the Middle East* (2016) and *The Afghan Way of War* (2011), as well as several other works on armed conflicts in the Middle East, Asia and Europe. He has worked as an advisor to senior military officers, including the Resolute Support Mission in Afghanistan, where he assisted in the development of the Afghan national army. Rob Johnson is a Fellow of the Royal Historical Society. Under his leadership, CCW has become well known for its track record in outstanding research and the utility of blending ideas, theory, and practice in current strategic and security policy.

Dr Alexander Jones is a Senior Lecturer in the Department of War Studies, Royal Military Academy Sandhurst. He was awarded his DPhil from the University of Oxford in 2016 for his research on the role and organisation of the Territorial Army between the world wars. An active infantry reservist for many years, Dr Jones has previously served operationally with the British Army in Afghanistan.

Dr Paul Latawski is a Senior Lecturer in the Department of War Studies, Royal Military Academy Sandhurst. Before coming to RMAS he lectured at the School of Slavonic and East European Studies (SSEES), University of London where he was also an Honorary Visiting Fellow. He was also an Associate Fellow at the Royal United Services Institute for Defence Studies (RUSI), London. In 2012 he was made a Senior Research Fellow in Modern War Studies with the Humanities Research Institute, University of Buckingham. He completed his Ph.D. at Indiana University USA specialising in Central and Eastern Europe with particular emphasis on modern Poland. His official research work includes: post 1945 British contingency operations, the changing character of armed conflict and the historical evolution of British Army doctrine. His area studies specialist research includes the operational history of the Polish Armed Forces in the West and Polish resistance to occupation 1939–45.

Major General Dr Andrew Sharpe has commanded on operations in all ranks from second lieutenant to brigadier during 34 years of military service and nine operational tours. He was the Deputy Commandant of the UK Joint Services Command and Staff College and the Director of the UK Higher Command and Staff Course. He left the British Army as a Major General, completing his military career as the Director of the UK MoDs independent think tank – the DCDC. For three years, he ran the UK Chief of Defence Staff's Strategic Advisory Panel. Dr Sharpe is the Director of the British Army's Centre for Historical Analysis and Conflict Research and a Senior Mentor on the British Army's generalship programme. In addition, as an independent consultant, he has partnered with governments, international organisations and businesses to provide strategic, operational and leadership advice, support and mentoring. He holds various fellowships at King's College London, the University of Exeter and in Cambridge; and he lectures and advises widely and internationally on strategy, leadership, risk and operational art. He is the Chairman of The Poppy Factory. He has an MA in International Studies from King's College London, and a PhD in Politics and International Studies from Trinity College Cambridge.

Dr Matthias Strohn, M.St., FRHistS is the Head of Historical Research at the British Army's Think Tank, the Centre for Historical Analysis and Conflict Research. In addition, he is a Reader in Modern War Studies at the Humanities Research Institute at the University of Buckingham. Previously, he worked in the Department of War Studies at the Royal Military Academy Sandhurst. He holds a commission in the German Army and is a member of the military attaché reserve, having served in London, Paris and Madrid. He has published widely on 20th-century German and European military history.

Dr Claus Telp was awarded his PhD by the Department of War Studies, King's College London for his work on Frederician and Napoleonic warfare. His book *The Evolution of Operational Art from Frederick the Great to Napoleon: 1740–1813* (Frank Cass) was published in 2005. He is currently Senior Lecturer in the Department of War Studies, Royal Military Academy Sandhurst.

Colonel Martin Todd is a serving General Staff officer. He commanded The Queen's Royal Lancers and was later Assistant Director of the Army's Centre for Historical Analysis and Conflict Research 2016–18. Currently he is studying for a PhD in Politics and International Studies at Cambridge.

Editor's Acknowledgments

To write a book is never a one-man's task alone. This applies in particular to anthologies such as the one that you are holding in your hands now, and I would like to take the opportunity to express my gratitude to the people who made this book possible.

First and foremost, I would like to thank the contributors. Without their dedication, this book would not have been produced. Their professionalism made my job as editor very easy indeed. In particular I would like to thank the Chief of the General Staff of the British Army, General Sir Mark Carleton-Smith, who found the time to write the foreword to this book.

Also, I would like to thank Casemate Publishing and the team that has worked with me on this book, in particular Clare Litt, Isobel Nettleton and Ruth Sheppard. I have worked with the team on a number of projects and their professionalism, dedication and ability to move things along when needed is second to none.

The idea for the book was developed out of a research project that the Centre for Historical Analysis and Conflict Research conducted for the British Army. Turning this internal project into a book required a lot of work and, first and foremost, time. I am very grateful to CHACR and its director, Major-General (retired) Dr Andrew Sharpe, for giving me the opportunity to produce the book. The entire team at CHACR supported the endeavour from start to finish and it is fair to say that the final product was a team effort. The conceptual component of fighting power is vital for any army and it is re-assuring to see that the British army invests in this area and encourages independent thought and advice from the CHACR.

As usual, I promised my family that with this book everything would be different: This time there would be no night shifts and I would not neglect my wife, Rocio, and the children. As usual, I failed to deliver. It is too easy to take family support for granted when one hides in one's study, but I hope you know how grateful I am to you all. Without Rocio's on-going support, I would not be where I am today.

As said above, the idea for the book developed out of a project for the British Army and some of the original parameters are still visible in the book: It predominately concentrates on land forces and the selection of case studies focuses on armies and countries that are of direct relevance to a western military power. This, and the limitations on page numbers, meant that some hard choices had to be made when selecting the case studies. I hope that you, the reader, will approve of the selection made.

Matthias Strohn
June 2019

CHACR

The Centre for Historical Analysis and Conflict Research (CHACR) is a 'think-tank' based in Robertson House, the former British Army Staff College, in Camberley. It was established on behalf of the British Army in 2016 to help to strengthen the conceptual component of fighting power and to offer independent and objective views to inform future force development. It is designed to appraise the Army of wider thinking in order to challenge convention and inform strategic decision making. It is not, therefore, a vehicle to portray the Army's own thinking; on the contrary, it is a vehicle to bring varied views together to stimulate the Army's thinking.

Foreword

The Chief of the General Staff, General Sir Mark Carleton-Smith,
KCB CBE ADC Gen

The commander of every army is faced, and has always been faced, with two questions that often sit in conflict with each other. The first, and pressing, question is: 'How do I best address the problems that immediately face me?' The second, perhaps less pressing but nonetheless important, question is: 'How do I remain capable of addressing the other problems that may face me in the future?'

In a 21st-century western democracy, the first question is ever more complex in its components. The Cold War of the 20th-century was waged by the presence of credible war-fighting heavy divisions and corps arrayed in central Europe, but it was fought by light infantry, training teams, guerillas and proxies scattered across the globe. The grand strategic backdrop of the 21st century is such that war-fighting heavy capabilities retain their relevance, if nothing else for deterrence and insurance reasons; and the ability to war-fight, at scale, will always remain the benchmark against which friends, allies, observers, commentators and potential enemies will default when they measure an army. But the armies of democracies must always also secure and retain a political, legal and public 'license to operate' by having, and demonstrating, real utility to the politicians and polity that they serve. In this respect, they must be able to operate, with demonstrable effect, below the threshold of war-fighting. They must be able to help a nation to compete effectively in the 'constant competition' of international strategy. Thus, they must be able to convert their military capability and capacity into demonstrably positive campaign outcomes, preferably in support of like-minded allies. And, at the same time, whether or not they are engaged in an easily identifiable campaign abroad, they must create, sustain and deliver a credible asymmetric advantage in the land domain as that constant competition below the threshold of war-fighting is waged. Addressing this requirement constitutes the army chiefs' first, and pressing, question.

Yet still, the second question retains its importance, despite the unrelenting demands of the first. All armies have to structure and operate to deal with the requirements of the first question, but responsible armies must also do their best to retain their ability to adjust and adapt, often rapidly and unpredictably, to address the demands of the second question. While they concentrate on the problems in hand, they must prepare for the contingencies that they may face. And, in this respect, this book poses a vital question.

At the very least, we have to think about these problems and work through, mentally, to the potential solutions. At best, we use that thinking to inform our strategic and force development behaviour. And the 'we' I refer to here are not just the military professionals, but also if this thinking is to have traction, as you will quickly see in the pages of this book, it must also include the politicians, polity and public that those military professionals serve. For that reason, I commend this book not only as essential reading to military professionals but also to anyone with a stake, or indeed an interest, in defence.

CHAPTER I

Reconstitution in History

An Overview

Dr Paul Latawski

Historical Models for Growing Armies

In surveying the historical models employed since the French Revolution for growing armies, it is not the intention here to consider them in detail because the case studies explored in the chapters of this book will do so. Rather, the aim is to identify what this author views as the broad approaches to growing armies that developed from 1789 to 1945. The approaches adopted for growing armies were very much linked to the character, conduct and requirements of war in a given period of history. Differing military traditions and threat perceptions also drove the adoption of new military ideas for increasing the size of armies but also constrained change from traditional military patterns. War or major domestic upheavals could act as a catalyst for change as could enduring threats or rivalries. Even if historically it can be argued that there were distinctive approaches, or schools, that emerged for growing armies, methods employed could and did converge between contending schools of thought.

Nineteenth century

In the course of the 19th century following the French Revolution, the rise of the idea of the 'nation in arms' drove the creation of mass armies through conscription that fuelled the ability to wage war on a large scale. The industrial revolution later in the century provided the means of equipping the mass army with materiel, swiftly mobilising it, transporting it to theatres of operation and sustaining it by rail.[1] Initially, conscription was introduced in 1793 to serve the immediate needs of France. The revolutionary government adopted it to meet the threat of the conservative powers in Europe that were seeking to snuff out the revolution. Conscription in revolutionary France was thus born of the marriage of ideology and practical need. By the time of the Consulate and Empire, conscription was an established mechanism for raising military manpower. France conscripted just under two million men into its army between 1800 and 1814.[2] The idea of 'universal obligation' of military service, however, was already established in the 18th century.[3] What happened in the case of France was that conscription was now seen as a duty of citizenship, rather than being 'based on civic inequality' in the societies of the conservative continental monarchical powers.[4] What the French Revolution led to was a change in political motivation and the scale for mobilising human resources to deliver larger armies.

The introduction of conscription would eventually spread to other major continental European powers. Although the French model was grounded in the notion of a nation-in-arms that postulated universal military service as a responsibility of citizenship, conscription was not without its voluntary aspect. Where conscription was introduced in the 19th century, opt-out mechanisms lingered for some time before universal obligation became the norm. For example, in France through most of the 19th century there existed a system of '*le remplacement*' that for a price allowed individuals to avoid military service. Roughly, a quarter of the annual military intake was *remplacement*s between 1835 and 1856.[5]

The porous nature of conscription systems did not last. During the last third of the 19th century, conscription was made universal by major continental powers such as France and Germany. Conscription linked to a reserve system provided the basis of an effective model for enlarging armies in the event of war. In this model, the peacetime army led by a regular professional leadership cadre became a training machine for short-term conscripts. Upon completion of mandatory military service, the conscript was assigned to a reserve unit. Thus, at the onset of war, this pool of trained conscripts could be mobilised. It was a system that made armies of France and Germany 'a vast training school for reserves'.[6] This conscript-reserve model allowed for an enormous build-up of trained military manpower for mobilisation in wartime. For example, the estimated mobilised strength of the Imperial German Army in 1880 was 1.7 million, in 1895 2.3 million and in 1900 3.0 million.[7] Stocks of weapons also had to be amassed if these burgeoning mass armies were to be fully prepared for war. Detailed military planning for war had a significant role with the conscript-reserve model. Mobilisation became an important factor if the large conscript based armies were to be effectively prepared and deployed at the onset of war.[8] This was the system possessed by two of the major protagonists, France, and Germany, at the outbreak of World War I.

While the conscript-reserve model evolved in continental Europe, the trajectory of development of other 19th-century states was very different. What Theodore Ropp called the 'Anglo-American military tradition' produced a very different structure from which to grow an army.[9] Britain and the United States had small volunteer regular armies augmented by volunteer militias. Expansion of the volunteer regular-army-militia model generally involved seeking more volunteers or mobilising the militia in times of conflict. For example, the United States Army expansion to fight the Mexican War drew on both militia and volunteers.[10] With Britain shielded by the Royal Navy and the United States by the broad expanse of the Atlantic, this model proved adequate as neither state required the raising of a mass army for a conflict with a major power. The Crimean War for Britain (1853–56) and the Mexican-American War (1846–48) for the United States qualified as limited wars. Only the United States had occasion to raise a mass army to fight a civil war against the southern rebellion. When manpower requirements forced the United States government to introduce the draft during the Civil War, the legal provisions provided a wide scope for exemption and 'substitution' so much so that only 6 per cent of the 2,666,999 soldiers brought into the Union Army were in military service as a result of the draft.[11] The volunteer regular army-militia model remained intact despite the unprecedented requirements for manpower in the Civil War.

The two broad models from which to grow armies in the 19th century were the product of very different trajectories of military development. The continental European model of short-term conscription linked to reserves was an outgrowth of the major political and social change triggered by the French Revolution. Its evolution was driven forward by great-power competition and the perceived need to raise and equip large mass armies in wartime. More isolated from the threat of powers with large mass armies, the volunteer regular army-militia model of the Anglo-American tradition remained adequate as a base of expansion. Both of these models shared a common feature insofar as expansion took place not in peacetime but was triggered by the outbreak of war. Both models, however, either through voluntary participation or by conscription maintained a reserve force in peacetime to provide a basis for expansion. The immediacy of threat was low and hence the expansion of armies in the Anglo-American tradition could proceed safely after the outbreak of hostilities. Even in the case of the continental powers who adopted the conscription-reserve model, mobilisation for war was complex and took time. The approach taken for expanding the 19th-century army was more reactive than pre-emptive insofar as it did not take place until the outbreak of war.

The World Wars

World War I and World War II in the first half of the 20th century brought a mixture of traditional approaches, convergence and new challenges to the problem of growing armed forces. The outbreak of World War I signified something of an apogee in the development of the conscription-reserve-mobilisation model. Taking France and Germany as examples, the outbreak of war saw impressive numbers of reservists mobilised in a matter of weeks. Between 2–16 August 1914, France mobilised 3.6 million men, while Germany took just 12 days to mobilise 3.5 million men.[12] In a triumph of planning and organisation, France and Germany utilised, respectively, 10,000 and 20,000 trains to assemble their expanded armies for war.[13] In contrast, Britain's entry into the war saw a more modest expansion of its army at the onset of World War I. When the United States later entered the war on 6 April 1917, it was in the words of an official history of mobilisation 'completely unprepared to give immediate military assistance to the Allies'.[14] The existing volunteer regular army-militia model was clearly unable to meet the exigencies of war, although significant reforms had been launched on the eve of the American entry into the war.

World War I made voracious demands for military manpower. During the four years of war, millions of men were called to the colours, as shown in Table 1.1, with a selection of the major powers.

Table 1.1 Manpower mobilised (1914–18)[15]

Country	Number of men mobilised
France	8,700,000
Britain	6,000,000
Germany	13,000,000
United States of America	3,800,000

For France and Germany, existing conscription systems provided a reliable source of manpower for armies facing unprecedented demands. The scale of military expansion was such that both Britain and the United States, with their strong tradition of the volunteer regular army-militia model, had to resort to conscription. In Britain, the growth of the army by seeking volunteers persisted and not until 1916 was conscription introduced.[16] Britain was unique in two respects, in raising its forces both in terms of the high percentage of volunteers and the fact that the Dominions and Empire also supplied large numbers of troops. By the end of the war, 2.4 million had enlisted as volunteers and 2.5 joined as conscripts.[17] Similarly, the United States adopted conscription with the Selective Service Act of 1917 and by the end of the war drafted 2.8 million men.[18] Conscription was important not only for meeting military manpower requirements but also for ensuring that skilled elements of the industrial work force were exempted from military service to meet the needs of the wartime economy.[19]

Any assumptions that the clash of arms that began in August 1914 would be of short duration faded with the inability of any of the belligerents to reach an early decision in the conflict. The onset of a long and costly conflict in terms of manpower also indicated that growing an army was not simply about the numbers of soldiers who could be mobilised. War in the wake of the industrial revolution and changing technology now meant that parallel to manpower mobilisation had to be economic mobilisation to support the vastly expanded wartime armies. All the major combatants had to increase the production of weapons and munitions to equip the large armies, replace materiel losses and introduce new technologies in an attempt to gain ascendency on the battlefield. The importance of firepower on the battlefield saw vast increases in the employment of artillery and expenditure of munitions. The capacity of the major combatants for economic mobilisation was a significant factor in shaping the outcome of the war. The long-term effects of economic mobilisation could also be damaging, even to the victorious power (Britain and France), as it led to weakened financial power and increased national debt.[20]

In the aftermath of World War I, the victorious powers retained the pre-war pattern for growing armies. For Britain, the post-war period saw a return to the volunteer regular army-militia model and an extension of global commitments particularly in the Middle East. The shift, however, was not immediate because conscription was retained until March 1920.[21] Nevertheless, the British focus shifted back to the wider global imperial realm to the detriment of the more vital arena of security in Europe.[22] The 'Report of the Committee on the Lessons of the Great War (Kirke Report)' published in 1932 identified some of the challenges that a return to the traditional volunteer regular army-militia model would entail for Britain should the army have to be expanded for a major continental war and suggested mitigating measures.[23] Nevertheless, global commitments shaped priorities and when linked to a prolonged period of austerity of resources for the British Army meant that addressing the growing threat posed by Nazi Germany was belated and mired in a protracted military and political debate in government.[24]

For France, the conscription-reserve-mobilisation model remained extant as the basis for growing the French Army in event of war. World War I, however, had resulted in an enormous cost, both in terms of lost lives and materiel damage. This costly experience did not shake the French commitment to the 'nation in arms', but low birth rates caused by wartime losses and inadequate training of reservists meant significant manpower limitations in both quantitative and qualitative terms.[25] This reality underpinned a defensive strategy built upon an extensive reliance on the Maginot Line system of fortifications. Moreover, France's continuing ability to mobilise substantial amounts of military manpower was undermined by weaknesses in doctrine and tardiness in embracing changes in warfare.[26]

Germany, defeated in World War I, was subjected to major limitations on its armed forces by the Versailles peace treaty. The Treaty of Versailles effectively set out to dismantle the conscription-reserve-mobilisation model and, in doing so, eliminate the means for Germany to grow its army rapidly. This was achieved by limiting the army to 100,000 men, no conscription, no reserves and 25-year enlistment periods for officers, as well as proscribed numbers and types of weapons.[27] The interwar German Army, the Reichwehr, from its creation attempted to lay the groundwork for future expansion. The military architect of a new model of expansion for the treaty limited German Army was General Hans von Seeckt. By adopting qualitative personnel policies, practising deception and evasion of the Versailles treaty requirements, and pursuing covert arms development, Seeckt laid the groundwork for future expansion and military modernisation between 1920 and 1926.[28] Seeckt's approach in developing a qualitatively strong officer and non-commissioned officer corps is held out as something of a model for preparing military leadership cadre as the framework around which to build a larger force. Recruiting from elements in society that were politically conservative, Seeckt's policies for recruitment in certain parts of German society aimed to keep out the influence of socialist ideologies from the Reichwehr.[29] Militarily more significant was his effort to make the *Reichwehr* a *Führerheer* or army of leaders, where each rank would be capable to fill the next post up in an expanded German army.[30] Alongside the qualitative approach to the development of leadership cadre was a strong interest in doctrine development.[31] Seeckt's qualitative expansion model did, however, have its limitations. Reichwehr studies conducted on expansion of the German Army in 1928 and 1933 concluded that a force of 16 and 21 divisions could be built on the existing manpower base without diluting combat effectiveness of personnel.[32]

With Adolf Hitler coming to power in 1933 and the launching of an open attempt to rebuild German military strength, the qualitative approach associated with Seeckt was swept away for a return to the conscription-reserve-mobilisation model for the newly renamed *Wehrmacht*. Whatever the expansibility of the inherited work of Seeckt, Hitler's effort was an attempt to build a large pool of trained manpower though conscription that was reintroduced in 1936. With only three years before Hitler launched his aggression against Poland, growing the German Army suffered from what proved to be a very short timeline to the outbreak of war.

Accompanying the return of the conscription-reserve-mobilisation model was economic mobilisation at an unsustainable pace that meant the *Wehrmacht* would have to go to war sooner rather than later as the over-heating economy could not be 'kept spinning indefinitely'.[33] Despite its early efforts at economic mobilisation, the interwar disarmament of Germany meant that production of equipment lagged behind wartime requirements. Early successes of the German Army brought large amounts of captured equipment and productive capacity in occupied Europe. Economically, however, this was not an effective solution to German capability shortfalls. During the war, the German Army became a two-tier force; one part mechanised and modern and the other part horse drawn and little different from the Kaiser's army.[34] When manpower expansion and economic mobilisation are taken together, it is clear the Versailles restrictions and the belated manpower expansion and economic mobilisation represented significant hurdles that were never completely overcome in Nazi Germany's war effort.

The United States army was the last major state to begin growing its army before the outbreak of the World War II. As late as 1939, the strength of the US army stood at just over 188,000.[35] Like Britain, the United States retained the volunteer regular army-militia model. The regular army was the foundation for the expansion of the manpower base with regular personnel providing the key trainers and leaders in the rapidly expanding force. The mobilisation of the National Guard and reserves augmented this pool of trainers and allowed the regular element to be spread more widely in the expanding force.[36] The rate of expansion, however, did cause problems in officer selection and promotion. The US army faced a dilemma of not wanting to over-promote unsuitable regular officers while having to encourage and promote new talent entering the enlarged force.[37] Apart from building leadership cadre, volunteer enlistments were not going to meet US army manpower needs. The passage of the Selective Service Act in September 1940 led to the first peacetime conscription in United States history. By June 1941, the size of the US army reached 1.4 million men.[38] Also aiding army expansion were large stocks of stored equipment that saw use in training and were an important capability bridge until wartime production delivered more modern equipment in large quantities.[39] Learning from its earlier experience in World War I, the United States government ensured that economic mobilisation proceeded swiftly and would see the American economy deliver '40 percent of the world production of munitions' during World War II.[40]

World War II represented the largest expansion of armies to fight a conflict that was truly global in scale. The war also represented something of an apogee in the two broad models surveyed in this section, namely the conscription-reserve-mobilisation model and the volunteer regular army-militia model. The prelude to the war saw a convergence between the two models insofar as Germany experienced the challenges of having to grow a force from a small volunteer professional army, while Britain and the United States relied on their limited reserve forces and an early introduction of conscription to grow their base force. As can be seen in Table 1.2, World War II resulted in very large manpower mobilisation among the major combatants.

Table 1.2 Manpower mobilised (1939–45)[41]

Country	Number of men mobilised
France	2,680,000
Britain	4,683,000
Germany	18,200,000
United States of America	11,877,000

The ability of the major combatants to mobilise their economies remained a significant factor in shaping the growth of armies during the war. The long-term effects of economic mobilisation did serious damage to some of the combatants (such as Britain) because the war 'overtaxed its economic strength'.[42] For Germany, the economic consequences were nothing short of a self-made catastrophe.[43] Only the United States emerged economically stronger with a position that gave it a post-war dominance. The wartime economies also drove significant technological advances. The most significant of these would lead to the advent of the nuclear age with the utilisation of atomic bombs by the United States late in the war. This development would have a profound impact on how to grow armies after 1945.

Conclusion: Factors Shaping Reconstitution

On the surface, the overview of this historical period suggests that the two models built around the combination of conscription-reserve-mobilization and volunteer regular army-militia were very much products of conditions that no longer prevail and little from this historical legacy can be applied to the problem of reconstitution today. In fact, this period does yield some recurring factors that shaped reconstitution, and even if they cannot be seen as some historically derived template, they raise important questions to be considered in any reconstitution process.

The first of these factors was the relationship of reconstitution to the security environment. A common historical denominator of efforts to grow armies was that they were a response to the then prevalent security environment and the threats it generated. Determining, however, when threats reach a level that is sufficient to warrant growing an army was not always clear. While a potential adversary mounting an aggression provided an unambiguous signal that the time for reconstitution had arrived, the threats in the security environment were at times more opaque, making trigger points for reconstitution difficult to identify.

The human resource dimension of reconstitution was another important thread running through the 1789–1945 period. Reconstitution required not only a quantity of soldiers but was also shaped by their quality. The factor that underpins quantity in reconstitutions was the existence of trained reserves which was characteristic of both the conscription-reserve-mobilization and volunteer regular army-militia models. Whether reserves provided a larger deployable force or were the basis for developing a much larger force, they were an important factor in the reconstitution process as the quantity element.

The qualitative factor was found in the regular leadership cadre of both officers and non-commissioned officers. While the interwar German Reichwehr may have been unique in developing the quality of its leadership cadre specifically to facilitate expansion of the German army, the leadership cadre of the largely conscript based or volunteer regular armies had much the same role in the process of reconstitution. This professional leadership cadre embodied the qualitative element by delivering training, designing doctrine and providing the necessary capacity for planning and organisation.

Similarly, possession of retained stocks of military equipment that was more than necessary to meet the needs of a regular force and its reserves has been an important factor in reconstitution. The fact that both Britain and the United States had quantities of stored equipment had a significant role in reconstitution in the run-up and early years of World War II. War reserves of equipment are not fashionable today in the age of just-in-time logistics and accounting systems that focus on short-term financial costs and not long-term investment in security. Such investment requires more resources. The inescapable historical lesson is that for reconstitution to take place the state must provide increased financial resources to make it possible.

Notes

1 Michael Howard, *War in European History* (Oxford: Oxford University Press, 1977), pp. 75–93 and Maj. Gen. J. F. C. Fuller, *The Conduct of War* (London: Minerva Press, 1961), pp. 77–94.

2 Jean Delmas et al., *Histoire Militaire de la France 2 – 1715 à 1871* (Paris: Presses Universitaires de France, 1992), pp. 307–8.

3 Lars Mjøset and Stephen Van Holde, "Killing for the State, Dying for the Nation: An Introductory Essay on The Life Cycle of Conscription into Europe's Armed Forces" in Lars Mjøset and Stephen Van Holde (eds), *The Comparative Study of Conscription in the Armed Forces* (Amsterdam: JAI, 2002), p. 4.

4 Hew Strachan, *European Armies and the Conduct of War* (London: George Allen and Unwin, 1983), p. 57.

5 Delmas et al., *Histoire Militaire de la France 2 – 1715 à 1871*, pp. 412–13.

6 Strachan, *European Armies and the Conduct of War*, p. 109.

7 David Stone, *Fighting for the Fatherland: The Story of the German Soldier from 1648 to the Present Day* (London: Conway, 2006), p. 446.

8 Theodore Ropp, *War in the Modern World* (London: Collier Books, 1969), p. 200.

9 *Ibid.,* p. 76.

10 Marvin A. Kreidberg and Merton G. Henry, *History of Mobilization in the United States Army 1775–1945*, DA Pamphlet 20–212 (Washington DC, Department of the Army, 1955), p. 78.

11 *Ibid.,* p. 108 and see also pp. 103–9.

12 Jean-Baptiste Duroselle, *La Grande Guerre des Français 1914–1918* (Paris: Perrin, 1998), p. 74 and Alexander Watson, *Ring of Steel: Germany and Austria-Hungary at War 1914–1918* (London: Allen Lane, 2014), p. 73.

13 David Stevenson, *The History of the First World War 1914–1918* (London: Allen Lane, 2004), p. 49.

14 Kreidberg and Henry, *History of Mobilization in the United States Army 1775–1945*, p. 374.

15 William Serman and Jean-Paul Bertaud, *Histoire Militaire de la France 1789–1919* (Lille: Fayard, 1998), p. 720.

16 F. W. Perry, *The Commonwealth Armies: Manpower and Organisation in Two World Wars* (Manchester: Manchester University Press, 1988), pp. 16–19.

17 Stevenson, *The History of the First World War 1914–1918*, pp. 201–2.

18 Kreidberg and Henry, *History of Mobilization in the United States Army 1775–1945*, p. 253 and p. 277.

19 Stevenson, *The History of the First World War 1914–1918*, p. 198.

20 Robert A. Doughty, *Pyrrhic Victory: French Strategy and Operations in the Great War* (Cambridge, Massachusetts: Harvard University Press, 2005), pp. 508–9 and G. C. Peden, *Arms, Economics and British Strategy: From Dreadnoughts to Hydrogen Bombs* (Cambridge: Cambridge University Press, 2007), pp. 96–97.

21 Brian Bond, *British Military Policy between the Two World Wars* (Oxford: Clarendon Press, 1980), p. 21.

22 Michael Howard, *The Continental Commitment* (London: Temple Smith, 1972), pp. 128–36.

23 'Report of the Committee on the Lessons of the Great War (Kirke Report)', The War Office, October 1932, in *The British Army Review Special Edition*, April 2001.

24 Bond, *British Military Policy between the Two World Wars*, pp. 312–36.

25 Robert Allan Doughty, *The Seeds of Disaster: The Development of French Army Doctrine 1919–1939* (Hamdon, Connecticut: Archon Books, 1985), pp. 22–23.

26 *Ibid.*, pp. 178–79 and Guy Pedroncini et al., *Histoire Militaire de la France 3 – 1871 à 1940* (Paris: Presses Universitaires de France, 1992), pp. 339–41.

27 Treaty of Peace between the Allied and Associated Powers and Germany (Treaty of Versailles), Part V, Military, Naval and Air Clauses, 28 June 1919 in J. A. S. Grenville, *The Major International Treaties 1914–197* (New York: Stein and Day, 1975), pp. 68–69.

28 See James S. Corum, *The Roots of Blitzkrieg: Hans von Seeckt and German Military Reform* (Lawrence, Kansas: University Press of Kansas, 1992) and Barton Whaley, *Covert German Rearmament, 1919–1939: Deception and Misperception* (Frederick, Maryland: University Publications of America, Inc., 1984).

29 Carl Hans Herman, *Deutsche Militärgeschichte* (Frankfurt am Main: Bernard & Graefe Verlag für Wehrwesen, 1966), pp. 368–69.

30 Corum, *The Roots of Blitzkrieg*, p. 69.

31 *Ibid.*, pp. 122–43.

32 Wilhelm Deist, *Germany and the Second World War: Volume I The Build-up of German Aggression* (Oxford: Clarendon Press, 1990), pp. 383–84, p. 388.

33 Adam Tooze, *The Wages of Destruction: The Making and Breaking of the Nazi Economy* (London: Allen Lane, 2006), p. 213.

34 R. L. DiNardo, *Mechanized Juggernaut or Military Anachronism?* (Mechanicsburg, PA: Stackpole Books, 1991), pp. 127–33.

35 Mark Skinner Watson, *Chief of Staff: Prewar Plans and Preparations* (Washington DC: Historical Division, Department of the Army, 1950), p. 16.

36 *Ibid.*, pp. 187–89.

37 *Ibid.*, pp. 242–77.

38 *Ibid.*, p. 16.

39 Constance McLaughlin Green, Harry C. Thomson and Peter C. Roots, *The Ordnance Department: Planning Munitions for War* (Washington DC: Historical Division, Department of the Army, 1950), pp. 74–75.

40 James A. Huston, *The Sinews of War: Army Logistics 1775–1953* (Washington DC: Office of the Chief of Military History, United States Army, 1966), p. 490. Regarding lessons learned for economic mobilisation, see: Kreidberg and Henry, *History of Mobilization in the United States Army 1775–1945*, pp. 493–540.

41 John Ellis, *The World War II Databook,* (London: BCA, 1993), pp. 227–28. The figures for Germany are taken from Rüdiger Overmans, Deutsche militärische Verluste im Zweiten Weltkrieg (Munich: Oldenbourg, 2004) p. 215.

42 W. K. Hancock and M. M. Gowing, *British War Economy* (London: His Majesty's Stationary Office, 1949), p. 555.

43 Tooze, *The Wages of Destruction: The Making and Breaking of the Nazi Economy*, pp. 671–72.

CHAPTER 2

Phoenix from the Ashes

The Defeat of Prussia and the Prussian Reforms (1806–14)

Claus Telp

The Catastrophe of 1806

Since the Peace of Basle in 1795 had ended Prussian participation in the wars against revolutionary France, the Prussians had undertaken a number of modest reforms in response to weaknesses identified in 1792–95. Officer education was improved, the treatment of private soldiers became more humane, additional light infantry battalions were established and a general staff was created. However, since the Prussian army had emerged with credit from the war against the armies of revolutionary France, there seemed no urgent need for more fundamental reforms of army and state.[1]

It turned out that the years 1795–1806 represented a missed opportunity for Prussia to ready itself for the military whirlwind that Napoleon was about to unleash in October 1806. In this fateful campaign, glaring weaknesses at all levels became undeniable.[2]

The government failed to settle for a determined conduct of war as the influence of the 'war party' and 'peace party' at court waxed and waned. As late as the eve of the battle of Jena, the king was still hoping for a negotiated peace. The absence of a single-minded pursuit of military victory was also reflected in the penny-pinching, late and incomplete mobilisation of the army, whose training had been undercut by economy measures for years.

During the campaign, the Prussian army performed poorly. Problems with an inefficient and slow supply system undermined morale and discipline, poor reconnaissance left the army commanders unaware of French movements, unclear chains of command and personality clashes undermined the command and control of the three Prussian field armies, poor staff work resulted in confusion and delays, and a long baggage train and leisurely marches prevented timely reaction to French moves. The hastily improvised organisation into all-arms divisions, commanded by generals unfamiliar with this type of formation and 'supported' by inexperienced and poorly trained staff, merely caused confusion rather than aiding operational manoeuvres or combined arms tactics.

In battle, Prussian troops fought bravely and generally demonstrated tactical competence at the unit level but performed poorly in combined arms combat. The officer corps was dominated by poorly educated and overaged officers. About 56 per cent of infantry officers and 70 per cent of cavalry officers were more than 50 years old.[3] Training suffered from an obsession with military paraphernalia and adherence to scripted reviews, which were impressive to watch but did not represent realistic preparation for battle. Quiet garrison life left officers and troops alike unfamiliar with the unavoidable friction of campaigning.

After the crushing double defeat of Jena and Auerstedt on 14 October 1806, vigorous French pursuit soon turned retreat into rout. Whilst some surviving fragments of the army conducted a fighting retreat, overall the Prussian army had little fight left in it. Most fortresses readily surrendered rather than making any attempt to resist; and larger formations, which had escaped form the double defeat, notably forces retreating under the command of Prince Hohenlohe which readily surrendered at Prenzlau to a handful of French hussars, demonstrated that, overall, the spirit of many senior officers had been broken. The stubborn defence of Kolberg, the continued resistance of regular and irregular forces in parts of Silesia, and the credible performance of Prussian forces at Eylau demonstrated that Prussia could have continued resisting French occupation to some extent, but overall, the population rapidly accepted French domination whilst local government willingly collaborated with the new masters. Clearly, the patriotic bond linking king, army and people was brittle.

The Reform Programmes

The rapid and comprehensive collapse of Prussia in the face of French invasion shook the elites to the bone. Although Russian diplomatic intervention saved Prussia from total destruction as a state, the Treaty of Tilsit of 9 July 1807 and the Treaty of Paris of 8 September 1808 reduced Prussia to the status of a mere satellite. The urgent requirement for fundamental reform was now undeniable in the face of total defeat and the narrowly averted demise of Prussia. This was the hour of reformers, such as Scharnhorst, who had been frustrated by conservativism before 1806.

The most remarkable aspect of the Prussian reforms in the years after 1806 is their scope. The catastrophe of 1806 was not understood as a purely military disaster that merely required military reforms of a technical nature. Rather, in the eyes of the reformers, the events of 1806 had demonstrated fatal flaws in Prussian state and society, as well as the army. All of these had to be addressed in a radical and comprehensive manner to ensure Prussia's survival in the long term. The Prussian monarchy had to be reinvented if it was to regain great-power status. The aim of the reformers, therefore, was not to liberate the Prussian people, but to rebuild Prussia in a way that would permit the House of Hohenzollern to maintain its position in a changing world. The intended result of the reforms would be a country united by a common administration, uniform laws and taxes, personal liberty, equal rights and duties. On the firm basis of this national community (uniting king, army and people), a rejuvenated monarchy could prosper.

In order to create the 'new' Prussia, a number of secondary aims had to be achieved. First, the state apparatus of power and the range of control had to be expanded by creating an effective central government and administration that would overcome feudal and provincial privilege. Second, the inflexibility of the Prussian *Ständestaat* (corporative state) had to be overcome by creating opportunity for social mobility. Third, the backward economy had to be freed of its shackles to become vibrant and productive. A rejuvenated society and economy would then provide the necessary preconditions for the reborn political and military strength of the Prussian state. Fourth, the Prussian army had to be turned into a force equal to the military challenge posed by Napoleon and his army.

The driving force behind the civil reforms was the central state bureaucracy headed by ministers Stein and Hardenberg.[4] The failure of the traditional alliance between king and nobility in 1806 presented an opportunity for reform-minded bureaucrats to gain the approval of the king, still stunned by defeat, for ambitious political, social and economic reforms.

Stein's programme, laid down in the *Nassauer Denkschrift* (Nassau Memorandum) of 1807, resumed and expanded on his pre-1806 reform attempts. Central government had to be overhauled. Instead of a motley of state and provincial institutions, functional ministries had to be created to govern and administer a uniformly organised national territory. The propertied classes should take part in administration and local government in order to bridge the gulf between people and state, to turn the passive subject into an active citizen. Giving the propertied and educated classes a stake in the state should foster patriotic loyalties.

Furthermore, the participation of the educated strata would tap into a vast pool of experience and talent, mobilising intellectual and spiritual forces, which had hitherto been merely engaged in private pursuits, for the benefit of the state. Public participation in local government would also provide the people with an opportunity to voice grievances, thus permitting a timely response to domestic discontent.

In the countryside, the serfs should be liberated from the nobility's iron grip by gaining ownership of the soil they tilled in order to pave the way for progress in agriculture. Replacing the lords' patrimonial justice with state courts would contribute to the liberation of the serfs and at the same time strengthen the authority of the central bureaucracy. The Poles, in addition, should be granted cultural autonomy in order to win their allegiance. In the towns, meanwhile, the guild monopoly had to be broken to unshackle market forces and innovative practices.

True to the overriding priority of making the people of Prussia identify with their monarchy, state schools were to instil patriotism and monarchic loyalty from a tender age, producing young men willing to serve their king.

Hardenberg's programme had much in common with Stein's proposals. He largely shared Stein's views on personal liberty, public participation in government, *laissez-faire* in economic policy, agricultural reform and state control of schools. Hardenberg paid particular attention to breaking provincial privilege and identity in favour of a unified state by introducing a universal tax code, a universal body of law and by strengthening the central bureaucracy.[5]

Military Reforms

Frederick William III put the military reforms into the hands of the Military Reorganisation Commission (*Militärreorganisationskommission* or MRK), established on 25 July 1807. It was headed by Major-General Scharnhorst and included a number of field grade officers, some of whom would subsequently attain prominent positions in the army, notably Gneisenau, Grolman and Boyen.[6] The composition of this commission is striking for two reasons: most of its members were of relatively junior rank and some of its most prominent members, Scharnhorst, Gneisenau and Grolman, just like Stein and Hardenberg in the civil sphere, hailed from outside Prussia and were thus innocent of vested interests. The king's obvious trust in these relatively young, quasi-foreign 'upstarts' must have been irritating to higher-ranking native Prussian officers.

The circle of reformers was not limited to the commission. Experts such as the light infantry officers Yorck and La Roche-Aymon, for instance, contributed their knowledge and ideas in their fields of expertise.[7] Nor were military reforms exclusively of interest to the officer corps. Stein and Hardenberg also took a keen interest in military reforms and maintained a lively correspondence with Scharnhorst and Gneisenau. The latter, in turn, held strong opinions about matters in the field of civil reforms. Since the leading civil and military reformers were broadly in agreement on many points, though, civil-military friction among them was limited.

As a guideline for the commission's work, Frederick William had drafted a list of 19 items he wished to see considered. The list included a wide range of points, such as the punishment of unworthy officers, changes in the selection and promotion process, opening officer rank to commoners, a reform of the recruitment system, a higher degree of manpower mobilisation, a reform of military punishment, an overhaul of military administration, an improved balance of infantry, artillery and cavalry in large formations, the establishment of army corps, the reduction of baggage, enhanced mobility of field artillery, militarisation of the artillery train and training in marksmanship. Prince August of Prussia also contributed to military reform plans. His Soissons Memorandum was based on a thorough analysis of Prussian weaknesses and French strengths. The prince suggested a reform of military administration, universal conscription, the end of aristocratic privilege in favour of meritocracy, motivation by appeals to patriotism, honour instead of coercion, realistic exercises and combined-arms tactics. Operational flexibility should be improved by reduction of baggage and the adoption of either a modified system of rear supply or living off the country according to circumstances.

Though analysis of French superiority could not fail to influence the reformers, Scharnhorst and the other reformers did not draw all their recommendations from the French example.[8] They could also hark back to Prussian tradition such as the Brandenburg peasants' guerrilla warfare against the Swedish invaders in 1675 or the old canton laws of Frederick William I. To some extent Scharnhorst deliberately dressed up modern French ideas as ancient Prussian tradition in order to gain acceptance in conservative circles. The emerging Prussian system of universal military service, in particular, showed this amalgam of Prussian tradition and French example.

The main reform projects in the sights of the commission were universal military service, spiritual mobilisation, changes to the composition and education of the officer corps, a reorganisation of the general staff and military administration, and a revamping of training, tactics, organisation and logistics.

Universal military service obligations had existed in Prussia since the times of Frederick William I but, due to an increasing number of exemptions and a strong reliance on foreign mercenaries, military service had become increasingly selective. With universal conscription, this was bound to change: the citizen, and this meant every able-bodied male, was to be the born defender of his country. Conscription, the cornerstone of military reforms, was meant to build a nation or, in Carl von Clausewitz's words, to become the school of the nation. Although the army had never been a foreign body in the Prussian population, taking into account that a large percentage of the Prussian population consisted of soldiers and cantonists (local conscripts) and their families, there had been a rift: the Prussian people were effectively divided into those liable to service, broadly the serfs, and those exempted, broadly the professions and townspeople. Whilst civil reforms would reconcile state and people, conscription and meritocracy would strengthen the bond between army and people.

In military as in civil reform, the basic idea was to ask the population to take an active part in the affairs of their state, in war, in peace, in politics and in defence. In the case of conscription, the logic of the military and civil reform efforts would converge: conscription would harmonise relations between army and people, whereas the bond between state and people would make conscription tolerable. A reform of military justice, which had, until then, granted the army the status of a state within the state, delivered its share in redefining the relationship between army and population. There was to be one law for one people. Taken together, these efforts should create a nation waging a national war with a national army for a national purpose.

Conscription, however, was meant to be more than a by-product of nation building. It fitted in with the efforts of Prussian reformers such as Scharnhorst and Knesebeck, in the period before 1806, to counter the threat of the French mass armies by creating a Prussian mass army.[9] Ideological considerations apart, this mass army could not be a mercenary army simply because Prussia could not afford it. Therefore, some form of conscription was necessary to reconcile military demands with economic constraints. Combined with the thrust of the civil reforms, conscription seemed an admirable solution: it would help building the nation, provide Prussia with a mass army and was affordable.

In order to render conscription acceptable to the hitherto exempt classes, well-to-do townspeople in particular, it was necessary to improve the image of the Prussian army, whose soldiers were considered ne'er-do-wells, living in constant fear of the corporal's stick; a picture which was rather bleaker than reality. Taking into account the attitudes of the exempt classes, though, a reform of the system of military discipline and motivation was necessary. The soldier should be motivated by the example of his officers, by patriotism, personal honour, and – as a consequence of the meritocratic principle – by ambition. Punishments considered dishonouring should disappear. Flogging was replaced by arrest. Repeat offenders who had proven themselves unworthy of the national cockade could be demoted to second-class soldiers, remaining subject to physical punishment. This honourable army would be fit to receive the sons of society's higher strata.[10]

Apart from efforts to mobilise Prussian manpower, the reformers also tapped into spiritual forces. Patriotism and meritocracy were to motivate the national army. Supporting the effort to foster nationalism by conscription was Gneisenau's proposal to militarise the schools. Schools should teach mathematics for military purposes, introduce military discipline, drill and physical training. Apart from providing useful pre-military training, which would shorten the recruit's training time in case of mobilisation, schools would light the flame of patriotism and virtue in young Prussians, an idea echoed by Stein.[11]

The theme of virtue was generally popular among the reformers. Ancient beliefs that God would help the virtuous became a Prussian military tradition. Over 100 years later, German soldiers still marched into battle with the words 'God is with us' on their belt buckles. The Prussian perception of Paris as the new Babylon and the French as morally depraved stood in the same tradition. In the same vein, it was no coincidence that a clandestine Prussian patriotic organisation, popular with officers and officials, called itself the League of Virtue (*Tugendbund*). The same spirit can also be found in increased emphasis on the personal integrity of officers. Regimental courts of honour for disreputable behaviour were not only a reaction to the premature surrenders of 1806 but also an instrument of maintaining the moral purity of the officer corps. The latter was important for discipline and morale: an untainted officer was more likely to inspire his men and command their respect, both necessary demands if discipline was to be based increasingly on positive motivation.

The emphasis Prussian reformers placed on spiritual mobilisation was reflected in the variety of proposals to this end. They suggested that the names of those fallen in action would be read out in church, distinguished soldiers and warrior widows would sit on the front benches, whereas cowards would be placed on the back benches. The names of deserters would be read out from the pulpit to shame their families. True to the reformers' crusading spirit, the church generally played an important role in contingency plans. Gneisenau's suggestion that clerics should supervise local administration in times of war in order to ensure whole-hearted patriotism reminds one of the representatives on mission during the wars of the French revolution.

In order to further boost the willingness of the population to play an active role in war, Gneisenau went so far as to suggest that the king should promise his people a constitution. He also suggested creating a new aristocracy based on conspicuous bravery similar to Napoleon's imperial service aristocracy. Aristocrats who showed less than total devotion to king and country were to lose their titles.[12]

Besides conscription, the reform of the officer corps, its selection and education, was the second cornerstone of military reform. Officer rank was now to be open to commoners. In peacetime, selection of officers from among the officer candidates, as well as promotion, was to be largely dependent on military education and technical prowess. In war, bravery and proven ability would be the relevant criteria. Seniority was discounted. Colonels were to be selected for merit only. The age hierarchy among generals was abolished. As in the armies of the French Revolution, meritocracy was to mobilise the nation's human resources by paving the way for talent and ambition. The expected increase in military skill and daring would, hopefully, result in enhanced tactical and operational prowess.

Military schools were reformed. The *Kriegsschulen* (military academies) in Berlin, Königsberg and Breslau trained ensigns for the officer's examinations in a nine months course. Emphasis was, as usual with Scharnhorst's institutions, on independent thinking rather than rote learning. The higher classes of the *Allgemeine Kriegsschule* in Berlin offered engineer, artillery, and prospective staff officers who had passed the entry exam a three-year course comprising French, mathematics, geometry, artillery science, tactics, strategy, geography, physics, chemistry, statistics, military history, engineering and a course on staff work. Officers of all arms were trained in artillery science in order to increase understanding for this particular arm and facilitate all-arms combat.

Not only was theoretical officer training improved, care was taken to accustom the officer to independent command of mixed formations. La Roche-Aymon, like Scharnhorst, stressed the importance of officers learning to think independently, to make quick decisions and cope with rapidly changing conditions. For this purpose, he suggested to hold contested manoeuvres and mock battles, to conduct marches and build bivouacs under wartime conditions.

Overall, it was hoped that a corps of young, vigorous and independently thinking officers would lead the troops and serve on staffs by the time the next war broke out. The end of seniority, the introduction of meritocracy and improved education were to transform the officer corps in a way conducive to the successful execution of all-arms combat as well as operational manoeuvres.[13]

An important aspect of the reform of the officer corps was the reform of the general staff. The brightest officers would be selected for general staff duties from the graduates of the *Allgemeine Kriegsschule*. The nature of the general staff was most clearly expressed in Grolman's memorandum, which clearly showed the influence of Scharnhorst, his mentor. Grolman considered the general staff a multi-functional organisation; an institution for learning, teaching, planning, advising and command. In peacetime, the general staff would gather information of military relevance, produce and update maps, prepare for mobilisation and produce campaign plans. Staff officers would conduct staff rides through Prussian and adjacent territories, study the lay of the land, and retrace historical campaigns and battles, thus building an intimate understanding of possible future theatres of war. They would also prepare and take part in large-scale military exercises. During the winter months, general staff officers were to study military history and military sciences, and keep abreast of military developments in other countries, thus making them subject-matter experts fully conversant with the most current ideas and practices. The officers would then disseminate their theoretical insights and practical experience throughout the army. To prevent the general staff from turning into an ivory tower, officers were to alternate postings and tasks among the central general staff in the ministry of war, corps or brigade staffs, troop command and staff rides. Ideally, they should gain some familiarity with all arms. By their presence in the troop staffs of the field army, they could tutor their fellow officers and build a personal relationship with the corps and brigade commanders. The general staff would thus resemble an octopus, with the main body in Berlin and the tentacles extending deep into the army. The intention was to train more general staff officers than necessary for the needs of this institution, in order to raise the standard of professionalism in the army in general. In times of war, general staff officers in general headquarters, in corps and brigade staffs, would draft operations' plans, plan marches and bivouacs, advise the commander, organise logistical support, receive reports and analyse intelligence, maintain correspondence with their counterparts in other troop staffs, disseminate orders and supervise administration.

Devolving responsibility to corps and army commanders would provide flexibility. The role of the general staff officer was to ensure coordination by advising the commander on the basis of principles shared by all general staff officers. Since the new generation of general staff officers had been trained by Scharnhorst, they would rely on common procedures and share a common understanding of the art of war.

With increasing distances and army size, this approach was more viable than Napoleon's system of centralised command and control, aided by a general staff that was no more than a glorified secretariat.[14]

In the context of civil reforms, central ministries were created. One of those was the Ministry of War. Until that point, the various functions associated with army organisation, administration, supply and mobilisation had been spread across a tangle of institutions. Scharnhorst became the first minister for war. The new ministry, the *Kriegsdepartement*, was to consist of two departments, the General Military Office (*Allgemeines Kriegsdepartement*) and the Military-Economic Office (*Militär-Ökonomie Departement*). The new organisation was more efficient and more responsive than the old system. This was important not only because Prussia had to make the most of its very limited remaining resources, but also because mobilisation against a potential French invasion had to be very rapid. Part of the drive towards improved army administration was the abolition of *Kompaniewirtschaft*; the inefficient, embezzlement-prone system by which company commanders were given a lump sum to pay and equip their men. From now on, a paymaster regulated and supervised financial matters in the regiments.

How did the reformers envisage the reborn Prussian army to operate during campaigns and fight in battle? La Roche-Aymon realised that French military superiority rested not only on all-arms tactics but also on a higher operational rate of advance. He identified two causes for this high tempo: independence from rear supply and corps organisation. He also rightly observed that the advance in several corps on parallel axes of advance facilitated surprise by confusing the enemy concerning one's intentions and point of maximum effort.

Frederick William agreed with copying the French practice of operating with corps advancing on parallel axes but was less sanguine than La Roche-Aymon about the Prussian army's ability to outmanoeuvre the wily Napoleon. Instead, the Prussian army should rely on superior numbers. As long as quantitative superiority was not achieved, the Prussian army ought to avoid a major clash. Once numerical superiority was achieved, however, the enemy was to be completely annihilated (*vollends vernichten*).[15]

Enhancing operational manoeuvres required, among other matters, a review of the Prussian system of supply and transport. Although reliance on rear supply from magazines, which had hamstrung army command and left soldiers hungry in 1806, was not discarded, it was at least improved. Instead of having long supply columns shuttling between field army and depots, each brigade should have a train of 32 wagons carrying bread for four days and a train of 34 wagons carrying flour for another four days; a reduction of the logistical 'tail' but still more vehicles than the Grande Armée had in 1806. The bakery train was reduced in the hope that use could be made of civilian ovens in the theatre. To ease the problem of ammunition supply and reduce the number of ammunition vehicles, the new musket had circumspectly been designed to fire French, Austrian and Russian ammunition.

Efforts were made to shorten the baggage train: each company now had only one packhorse for officer baggage. Each battalion had three wagons for baggage, uniforms, shoes and ammunition. Subalterns lost their riding horses. The substitution of tents by coats also contributed to the reduction of baggage. Compared to 1806, the number of horses and amount of baggage had been significantly curtailed.[16]

Prussian tactical inferiority had been identified as one cause of Prussia's defeat. All-arms combat was considered the key to improved tactical performance. Tactical organisation changed accordingly. Originally, the reformers had intended to establish all-arms divisions combined in army corps of two divisions (called 'brigades') of two infantry regiments, 12 squadrons and, in war, one battery of foot and one of horse artillery each, and a corps artillery reserve of one 12-pounder battery of foot artillery and a further battery of horse artillery. Line infantry regiments now had two grenadier companies, two musketeer battalions of four companies each and one light infantry battalion. This organisation provided for much closer cooperation between light and line infantry than previously.

The regulations suggested a standard battle order for the brigade, loosely modelled on the French *ordre mixte* of units deployed in a mix of skirmisher, line, and column formation, but this was only a recommendation. Brigade commanders were repeatedly encouraged to adjust tactics to local conditions. This emphasis on discretion tallied with Frederick William's demand to decentralise tactical command in pursuit of tactical flexibility.

Although only the light battalion, the third rank of the two musketeer battalions, and the grenadier companies were thoroughly trained in skirmishing, the infantryman's training was ideally to be universal, with each infantryman able to fight in line or open order as the situation required. Realising that open-order combat called for intelligent, motivated soldiers with initiative and a basic sense of tactics, much attention was devoted to the training of skirmishers. The light infantry now received, for the first time, regulations which were suited for this arm. The guidelines for the training of light infantry and the third rank were particularly detailed and progressive. Regulations reflected French practice, such as bringing artillery forward into the skirmish line to pour canister fire into the enemy ranks from close range or using skirmishers creeping up to enemy fortifications in order to snipe at gun crews.

In order to furnish musketeer officers with the necessary knowledge for skirmishing, they would serve a short apprenticeship with the regiment's light battalion. In line with the emphasis on marksmanship, an improved musket was introduced to facilitate aimed shooting. Proficiency on the battlefield was to be complemented by other relevant military skills. La Roche-Aymon's manual for light troops, for instance, did not only discuss light-infantry and cavalry tactics but also emphasised the importance of proper reconnaissance and reports, both necessary to provide the general staff and formation staffs with timely and accurate information.[17]

Reflecting the new spirit of pragmatism and single-minded preparation for war, the army received a new drill manual that was pruned of superfluous items. The times of military showmanship were over. Regimental and brigade exercises were also liberated from unrealistic and useless elements. The infantry regulations explicitly stated that nothing should be practiced that would be too complicated to be used against a real enemy. Tactical formations, such as the solid square, copied from the Austrian army, reflected this emphasis on simplicity and practicability. A *Normalbataillon* and a *Normalescadron* (exemplary units) served as model units for training drill instructors of individual regiments in order to ensure the uniform dissemination of the new drill to the whole army.[18]

Constraints and Opposition

Predictably, Prussian reformers soon encountered the opposition of all those interested in maintaining the *status quo*. Opposition to the reform process was aimed at a range of specific issues and based on a variety of social and professional groups: royal advisers feared losing influence to the new ministries; the provincial nobility resisted the encroachment of the central bureaucracy on their patrimonial powers as well as the abolition of tax privileges; noble officers resented the meritocratic principle in selection and promotion of officers; craftsmen opposed the abolition of the guild monopoly; serfs doubted that agricultural reforms would improve their lot; and the exempted groups were hostile to the notion of universal military service.

Prussian military and administrative élites were not simply split into reformers on the one hand and conservatives on the other hand. Instead, the camps overlapped. General Yorck, for instance, did sterling work as the father of Prussia's modern light infantry but fought social reforms tooth and claw. Many leading bureaucrats who actively assisted Stein in his social and economic reform programme viewed universal conscription with abhorrence. One of those sceptics, Baron Vincke, prophesied somewhat melodramatically that conscription would become the tomb of culture, sciences, trade, liberty and human happiness. The descent into barbarism was certain. Other high-ranking administrators shared this view. Even Stein and Hardenberg had misgivings about introducing universal military service in peacetime.

Indeed, the notion of a universal service obligation was particularly unpopular: the land-owning nobility feared the loss of labour; the traditionally exempt classes showed little taste for soldiering, in particular if they had to serve shoulder to shoulder with barely literate serfs. The *Landsturm*, an irregular force envisaged for waging guerrilla warfare against invading forces, provoked even more hostility: the higher strata of society resisted the *Landsturm*'s egalitarianism and feared it might turn its pitchforks against the propertied classes; the king was afraid that the irregulars might succumb to revolutionary agitation; bureaucrats disliked the envisaged influence of the *Landsturm*'s local defence committees on local administration; and officers were sceptical about the prospects for successful guerrilla warfare and resented the perceived waste of manpower and resources.

Differences of opinion and conviction apart, petty jealousies and self-interest also underminded the unity of reform circles. Personal hostility went so far that Scharnhorst and Gneisenau had to defend themselves against charges of attempted revolution. Scharnhorst was also undermined by treasonous intrigues of Francophile officers and officials that finally forced him to resign his positions.[19]

Internal opposition was not the only major obstacle to ambitious reforms. The reformers were also hampered by a restrictive peace treaty: the bitter fruit of total defeat. The Convention of Paris of 8 September 1808 stipulated that Prussia had to cede half her territory and population, pay an indemnity of 141 million francs, limit army strength to 42,000 men, forego a militia, open key fortresses to French garrisons and feed the occupation force. Napoleon's aim was to keep Prussia weak and teetering on the brink of total destruction, her future completely dependent on his continued toleration.[20]

The loss of territory and taxpaying subjects, added to occupation costs and the huge indemnity to be paid, ruined Prussian state finances. In 1807–8 alone, the French extracted in contributions, reparations and requisitions about 16 times the annual revenue of pre-war Prussia. The financial situation was so bleak that selling Silesia to France was seriously considered. Even more indicative of Prussian desperation was the offer to send a Prussian auxiliary corps to serve Napoleon in Spain in exchange for a reduction of contributions.[21]

Near insolvency could not fail to have a deleterious effect on military reforms since lack of cash forced the king to maintain the army at a very low level of readiness with up to half of its already small number of officers and troops on furlough. Though individual training in marksmanship and *tirailleur* (skirmisher) skills improved, the skeleton companies and battalions were often too undermanned to undergo effective unit-level training. Exercises by whole brigades, not to mention corps, were rarely feasible. The soldiers on furlough had to do with even less training. In the cavalry, most horses were given to peasants for agricultural work, with the result that the level of horsemanship was disappointing. The net effect of these financial limitations was a reduction in the effective size and training standards of the Prussian army.[22]

Not only was the training of the regular army disrupted by circumstances, if war broke out, tens of thousands of conscripts would have to be turned into soldiers within record time. Thus, the simplification of drill was a military necessity. The ability to rapidly impart a minimum of military skills was also important because the shallowness of Prussian territory would not permit much time for training before the approach of the invader. Simple drill and tactics would render the freshly mobilised conscript army battleworthy within a short time. Thus, whilst the officer corps' standard of professional training was increasing, the quality of the troops under their command was decreasing.

Whereas insolvency slowed the process of military reform, its effect on civil reforms was occasionally positive because reformers such as Stein and Hardenberg could persuade the king that political, social and economic reforms were essential to bolster the economy and thus increase revenue. Stein, for instance, calculated exactly how much money could be saved by replacing the urban bureaucracies by institutions of self-administration.[23]

Another obstacle to military reform was the occupation. The presence of French troops and the military vulnerability of Prussia to French punitive actions forced the king to generally adhere to treaty obligations. Plans of the reform commission for the establishment of a militia and the introduction of universal conscription, both important preconditions for levying a mass army, were impossible to realise under close French supervision. The unauthorised insurrection attempts of 1809, most notably Major von Schill's ill-fated adventure, did nothing to assuage French distrust, which had already led to Stein's forced dismissal as early as 1808.[24]

Not only did French pressure thin the ranks of the reformers: the apparent meekness of the king in the face of overwhelming French superiority, particularly the signing of the alliance treaty with the arch-enemy France in 1812 and the subsequent deployment of Grawert's and Yorck's auxiliary corps in support of the *Grande Armée*, prompted some officers of the wider reform circle, among them Scharnhorst and Clausewitz, to resign in disgust. A significant number of Prussian officers preferred to serve with the Russians or with the British in the Peninsula rather than be associated with the shameful French alliance. In this respect, Frederick William's efforts to hone the officer corps' integrity and sense of honour seemed to have backfired.[25]

In addition to financial penury, treaty stipulations and internal opposition, the military reformers' pursuit of military rejuvenation was hampered by the need to balance the long-term planning for offensive warfare conducted with a mass army, on the one hand, with the short-term requirement to protect Prussia with the very limited forces available at the time, on the other hand. At any time, French occupation forces could strike out from French-held fortresses or invade the largely defenceless territory from the outside.

Thus, the forces available had to be made battleworthy as quickly as possible and contingency plans for a war of survival had to be drafted. Most contingency plans called for static defence in fortified camps and fortresses, supported by guerrilla warfare. It was expected that infantry, cavalry and artillery units could be mobilised within 48 hours, whilst the trains would require 14 days. Hence, numerical weakness combined with initially insufficient logistical support made active campaigning in the field impossible at short notice. The combination of regular forces defending fortresses and fortified camps, the *Landsturm* (armed civilians led by officers and notables) waging guerrilla warfare, and population and authorities practicing passive resistance would, hopefully, buy enough time to enact conscription, train recruits and hold out until Great Britain, Austria or Russia came to Prussia's rescue. The Franco-Austrian War of 1809 seemed a good opportunity to make a bid for Prussian liberation, but the quick defeat of Austria and the king's caution prevented the implementation of these plans.

If the French invaded in Prussia's current, weak state, national and dynastic survival would be at stake. Only total resistance by the whole nation, the reformers reckoned, would be able to halt this onslaught. They were aware that the involvement of the *Landsturm* and the civilian population in general, following the Spanish example, could lead to savagery in warfare. This did not deter them. The extremely brutal Spanish guerrilla war was considered worthy of emulation. This ruthless attitude also extended to domestic enemies. Prussian subjects who failed king and country in the hour of need would see their lack of loyalty severely punished.[26]

The Outcome of the Reforms

In spite of formidable obstacles, much of Stein's and Hardenberg's reform programmes was gradually translated into law. Between 1807 and 1812, an impressive list of reform laws was the fruit of their efforts. The new laws permitted persons of any class to own any kind of property (including land), established the freedom to choose one's profession freely, broke the monopoly of the guilds, declared the abolition of serfdom, granted equal rights to Jewish citizens, distributed the tax burden in a more equal way by imposing a tax on landowners, secularised church property, granted self-administration to the towns and cities, established five central ministries headed by a prime minister (*Staatskanzler*) and promised a national representative body.[27]

Yet, the degree of real change fell far short of the aims expressed in the reform programmes. Agricultural reforms had been diluted to such an extent by the opposition of the landowning nobility and *bourgeoisie* that the serfs were turned into a rural proletariat, which was even more dependent on the lord than ever before, instead of turning into the independent and enterprising farmers envisaged by Stein. The attempt to create a dynamic and enterprising middle class, similar to that flourishing in Great Britain, was not a great success either. Whilst the higher strata of the middle class were absorbed by the nobility, the rest tried to imitate the aristocracy instead of forming a confident, innovative and commercially minded class. Economic reforms met with some success in the long run. The end of the guild monopolies opened the way for new means and ways of production, thus setting conditions for Prussian industrialisation. The right to own land as well as the availability of a rural proletariat reinforced capitalist tendencies in agriculture. Overall, the liberalisation of trade and commerce brought the economy closer towards the proto-capitalist ideas of Adam Smith.

Reforms of the central bureaucracy were partly successful. On the one hand, the establishment of ministries and the elimination of provincial privilege were largely accomplished, on the other hand, the general tax reform was partly dismantled due to the nobility's opposition to land tax. Political reform did not even come close to the reformers' ideal of a state administered by participating citizens. Although self-administration was introduced in towns, there was no equivalent in the countryside. No constitution was written nor was a national assembly established. The king would not surrender power and control.[28]

In spite of efforts to make military service acceptable to the formerly exempt classes, the reformers were aware that the educated strata of society would still be reluctant to serve in the army alongside the lower orders. Consequently, social stratification in the population was still reflected in the new organisation of the Prussian army: the division into regular army, *Landwehr*, and volunteer *Jäger*. The classes liable to canton duty would continue to be drafted into the regular army, whereas the affluent among those hitherto exempted would serve in volunteer *Jäger* detachments. Similar to the French National Guard of 1792, volunteer *Jäger* armed and equipped themselves. As an added enticement, volunteer *Jäger* would be considered candidates for non-commissioned and commissioned ranks in the regular army. The less affluent among the hitherto exempted would serve in the *Landwehr*. This tripartition was a far cry from a truly national army, but it served the purpose of gradually reconciling the formerly exempt classes with the principle of universal military service.[29]

Since the introduction of conscription or militia service was not possible under the terms of the Paris treaty, the Prussian army had to find another way of creating trained reserves over and above the authorised 42,000 troops in the short term. The *Krümper* system, originally invented for financial reasons rather than as an attempt to evade treaty restrictions, provided trained reserves: three to eight trained soldiers per company were dismissed every month and replaced by cantonists, who, in turn, were replaced by other cantonists after a month's training. In order to maintain the military skills of the dismissed cantonists, officers and non-commissioned officers were despatched into the villages to hold regular training sessions on Sundays and holidays. Since the term *Krümper* was used in a variety of ways, it is very difficult to establish how much trained manpower became available in this manner. It must also be born in mind that the reduction of the Prussian army after 1807 had released tens of thousands of regular soldiers into civilian life, trained men who could easily be recalled to the colours.[30]

The efforts of the reformers to mobilise Prussian manpower were finally put to the test with the end of Napoleon's abortive campaign in Russia. On 30 December 1812, the Convention of Tauroggen between the Prussian auxiliary corps and Russian forces prepared the way for the Prusso-Russian alliance of 26 February 1813. The first mobilisation measures, however, had already started in early

February. When Frederick William III threw in his lot with Tsar Alexander, Prussia had to win at all costs. This imperative swept away the opposition to universal service. On 9 February 1813, all exemptions were suspended for the duration of the war. All men of eligible age would have to serve in the army, *Landwehr* or volunteer units. On 17 March 1813, the *Landwehr* was officially established. Initial mobilisation was restricted to East Prussia, apart from Silesia, the only province free of French occupation. Quickly, 30,000 Landwehr were recruited to support Yorck's 20,000 regulars. The impressive mobilisation achieved in East Prussia was subsequently not replicated in full in the other Prussian provinces. Soon, the sense of desperate urgency begun to erode as French forces withdrew from Prussian territory. Still, by the end of March 1813, about 120,000 Prussians were under arms, a rapid triplication of the authorised peace-time strength. By autumn 1813, the number of Prussian troops had increased to 280,000.[31] On 21 April 1813, the *Landsturm* was established. Men in the 15–60 age range not serving in any other military organisation were liable to provide rear echelon duties or, in case of French invasion, conducting guerrilla warfare and scorched earth, aided by the rest of the civilian population. Already in July, however, fearing armed Prussian peasants more than French troops, a royal decree severely curtailed the role of the *Landsturm*, effectively killing the whole concept. Since the campaign of Spring 1813 was largely fought outside of Prussia's borders, there no longer seemed an urgent need for a guerrilla organisation in any case. The population did not seem to have much appetite for serving in the *Landsturm* either because in Silesia only 20,000 out of 32,000 liable to serve reported for duty.[32] On 3 September 1813, universal conscription for the duration of the war was introduced. Only 12 months later, with Napoleon exiled on Elba, however, a new military service law effectively re-introduced selective conscription, a retrograde step, prompted not least by the continued parlous state of Prussian state finances. However, this law also eliminated the socially based distinction between Landwehr and regular army by creating a single truly national army in which all Prussian men, irrespective of social standing, were liable to serve in principle. In this sense, the law of September 1814 qualified as a late triumph for the reformers over politically and socially motivated opposition.[33]

The massive influx of young men joining the colours in Spring 1813 would have been militarily irrelevant if they could not have been armed. Before the war, muskets had been produced at a rate of 1000 per month. This rate increased to a production of 1300 muskets and a repair rate of 1800 per month. The number of available muskets increased from 10,000 in 1807 to 75,000 by 1810. This rise in production had been achieved even though some arms factories were no longer on Prussian territory and others had been vandalised by the French.[34]

Had the reformers succeeded in instilling patriotism and dynastic loyalty? The Prussian brand of patriotism was royalist, as the reformers had hoped. The battle cry of Prussian regulars, *Landwehr* and volunteer *Jäger* was 'With God for king and country.' Prussia's intellectual elite, most famously the poets Ernst Moritz Arndt and Heinrich von Kleist, fanned the flames of pan-German nationalism. The disciples of '*Turnvater*' Jahn joined the fight with bodies steeled by physical exercise and hearts imbued with patriotism. Much of this patriotic sentiment was probably limited to the educated and affluent classes, which was reflected in the large numbers of well-to-do young men who reported for duty in the volunteer detachments. The burning desire to chase the hated French out of the country and take revenge for years of humiliation and hardship, however, was widely shared.[35]

To what extent had the reforms of the officer corps achieved their purpose? Certainly, the Prussian officer corps of 1813 was different from its counterpart of 1806. The military honour courts set up to extirpate the shame of 1806 had cashiered 17 generals, 50 colonels and lieutenant-colonels, and 141 majors, captains and lieutenants. In addition, treaty limitations resulted in the honourable dismissal of 85 generals, 584 colonels and lieutenant-colonels, and 3924 majors, captains and lieutenants. Overall, 71 per cent of generals and senior officers and 66 per cent of the more junior officers had to leave the service. The 42,000-man army could then carefully select its officer corps.

Meritocracy was not fully achieved as the regimental officers had the opportunity to select from among the graduates of the *Kriegsschulen*. Not surprisingly, preference was still given to noble candidates. Still, the reforms were not a complete failure because education, rather than birth, had become the precondition for officer rank. Noble privilege had thus been significantly eroded. Overall, the professionalisation of the officer corps had made great strides. Though the corps was still dominated by the aristocracy, it now drew on a much wider pool of talent. In 1813, even Jews reached officer rank, a remarkable development at the time. Even though mobilisation saw the reactivation of most of the dismissed junior officers of 1806/07, none of the generals, apart from Bluecher, and only few of the senior officers of that period served again. A rejuvenation of the officer corps had definitely occurred.[36]

The general staff had been reformed as intended. Whereas an elite corps of 14 fully qualified general staff officers had been envisaged, this number was significantly exceeded by 1812. This new general staff benefited from common training and education under the tutelage of Scharnhorst. Its performance on campaign was good. During 1813, the principle of shared responsibility between an army, corps or divisional commander and his general staff officer was introduced by Gneisenau. He also introduced the principle of leading by directive, later popularised as *Auftragstaktik*. The Prussian general staff became a successful model for the Prussian and later German army. Indeed, in the long run, the institution was copied by all major western armies. In Dupuy's words, '... Scharnhorst's objective had been achieved. The collective brain of the general staff had brought institutionalized military excellence to Prussia.'[37]

The operational prowess of the Prussian army of 1813 is difficult to judge as allied forces operated in mixed armies, but it appears that it performed much better on campaign than its counterpart in 1806. This time, Prussian corps, coordinated by the general staff and corps staffs, successfully concentrated for battle at Lützen, withdrew in good order in the face of a superior numbers to fight again at Bautzen, destroyed Macdonald's army at the Katzbach and Vandamme's corps at Kulm, and played their allotted role in the allied campaign plan, notably the successful concentration of field armies at Leipzig. Napoleon himself paid the Prussian troops at Lützen a compliment when he remarked that they had clearly learnt since 1806. It must be born in mind, though, that the new-born Prussian army was opposed by a hastily improvised French army which had long passed its peak.

With regards to unit and formation training, La Roche-Aymon's proposals for realistic exercises had indeed been turned into practice: mixed formations roved the brigade district, marched, bivouaced and conducted *petite guerre* exercises against other mixed formations. A number of officers could gain practical experience in independent command and all-arms combat in this way. Ironically, Napoleon inadvertently played a role in the training of the Prussian army: his insistence on Prussian participation in the invasion of Russia provided Yorck and the troops under his command with an opportunity to gain combat experience and test the recently introduced organisation and tactics. Most officers of the general staff had been assigned to the corps precisely in order to gain experience.[38] Overall, though, the small and fluctuating size of the army in 1807–12 and the absence of large number of soldiers on furlough or dismissed after a short training period, left training standards below the desired level. In 1813, the mix of veterans, superficially trained active soldiers and raw recruits posed challenges to training a mass army ready to take to the field in haste. Also, reactivated soldiers and officers had been trained according to different regulations and principles than their active counterparts, which must have caused some confusion. In spite of uneven standards of training and tactical proficiency, the Prussian army of 1813 proved capable of fighting in skirmishes and major battles; in the Großer Garten in Dresden, in the mountains of Kulm, in the villages around Leipzig and in the forests of Weissig, Königswartha, Großbeeren and Dennewitz. The indifferent quality of the French forces in 1813 provided Prussian troops with the opportunity to learn in the field.

Conclusion

Though the king clearly perceived the need for change if Prussia was ever to regain the status of a major power, he tried to retain as much of Prussia's social and political order as possible and made only those concessions he considered unavoidable. The resistance by vested interests, combined with the conservativism of the king, had slowed the civil reforms to such a degree that the driving cause for radical change, Napoleon's looming shadow, had receded before the transition had run its course. The king's willingness to promote reform stood in direct relation to the waxing and waning of the French menace. With Napoleon's demise, the transition process was stopped and even partly reversed. The case of the *Landsturm* edicts of April and July 1813 demonstrated that this adjustment could occur within months. Still, some achievements, such as central ministries, economic liberalisation, a professionalisation of the officer corps and the acceptance of the principle of universal military service, were lasting.[39]

Though the reforms fell far short of the ambitious programmes of Stein and Scharnhorst, the civil and military reforms had been successful enough to significantly aid Prussia's re-establishment as a major power. It must not be forgotten, though, that conditions for Prussia's revival were promising: the destruction of the *Grande Armée* in Russia, the subsequent alliance with Russia, then Austria and Britain as well, French war-weariness and the cumulative impact of the 'Spanish Ulcer', all had played a role in stacking the odds in Prussia's favour. It is more than doubtful that Prussia, standing on its own, could have emerged victorious in 1813. Conversely, it could be argued that the reforms strengthened Prussia sufficiently to tip the balance in favour of the Prusso-Russian alliance of Spring 1813. The stalemate achieved in the spring campaign and manifested in the armistice, in turn, was the precondition for Austria's entry into the war in autumn.

Prussian reformers succeeded in the civil and military spheres sufficiently to cement the power of the Hohenzollern dynasty and give Prussia a new lease of life. In the long run, they contributed to Prussia's rise to a dominant position in central Europe. The reforms, therefore, achieved their overall purpose.

Notes

1 On the pre-1806 reform attempts, see Bernhard R. Kroener, "Die Armeen Frankreichs und Preussens am Vorabend der Schlacht von Jena und Auerstedt" in Eckart Opitz (ed.), *Gerhard von Scharnhorst: Vom Wesen und Wirken der preussischen Heeresreform, Ein Tagungsband* (Bremen: Edition Temmen, 1998), pp. 12–30, pp. 23, 28, 44–45; Claus Telp, *The Evolution of Operational Art: 1740–1813, From Frederick the Great to Napoleon* (London and New York: Frank Cass, 2005), pp 52–56; Dierk Walter, *Preussische Heeresreformen: 1807–1870, Militaerische Innovation und der Mythos der 'Roonschen Reform'* (Muenchen: Schoeningh, 2003), pp. 245–46.

2 On Prussian performance in the Jena Campaign, see Claus Telp, "The Prussian Army in the Jena Campaign" in Alan Forrest and Peter H. Wilson (eds), *The Bee and the Eagle: Napoleonic France and the End of the Holy Roman Empire, 1806* (Basingstoke: Palgrave Macmillan, 2009), pp. 155–71.

3 Kroener, "Die Armeen Frankreichs und Preussens am Vorabend der Schlacht von Jena und Auerstedt", p. 22

4 Heinrich Friedrich Karl Freiherr vom und zum Stein, 1757–1831, Prussian minister during the reform period. Carl August von Hardenberg, 1750–1822, Prussian minister during the reform period.

5 On general reform programmes, see Memorandum, Stein, June 1807, Heinrich Friedrich Carl vom und zum Stein, E. Botzenhart, ed., *Briefwechsel* (Berlin: Heymanns, 1936), eight volumes,

Vol. II, pp. 210–31; Proklamation, Stein, 26 September 1808, Stein, *Briefwechsel*, Vol. II, pp. 530–31; Politisches Testament, Stein, 24 November 1808, Stein, *Briefwechsel*, II, pp. 583–86; Memorandum, Hardenberg, 12 September 1807, Leopold von Ranke, *Denkwürdigkeiten des Staatskanzlers Fürsten von Hardenberg* (Leipzig: Duncker, 1877), five volumes, Vol. III, p. 8.

6   Gerhard Johann David von Scharnhorst, 1755–1813, Prussian general, reformer, chief of the general staff.

      August Wilhelm Anton Neidhardt von Gneisenau, 1760–1831, Prussian officer and member of the MRK, later general, chief of the general staff.

      Karl Wilhelm Georg von Grolman, 1777–1843, Prussian officer and member of the MRK, later minister of war.

      Leopold Hermann Ludwig von Boyen, 1771–1848, Prussian officer and member of the MRK, later general and minister of war.

7   Hans David Ludwig Yorck, 1759–1830, Prussian general during reform period, later ennobled. Antoine-Charles-Etienne-Paul, Marquis de La Roche-Aymon, 1772–1849, French-born officer and reformer during reform period, later general.

8   On the military reforms in general, see Memorandum, Frederick William, July 1807, Rudolf Vaupel, (ed.*), Das preußische Heer vom Tilsiter Frieden bis zur Befreiung: 1807–1814* (Leipzig: Hirzel, 1938), pp. 8–15; Memorandum, Prince August of Prussia, 13 June 1807, Georg Heinrich Klippel, *Das Leben des Generals von Scharnhorst* (Leipzig: Brockhaus, 1869–1871), three volumes, Vol. III, pp. 764–92.

9   On the reform of military service obligations, see Memorandum, Scharnhorst, 31 August 1807, Großer Generalstab, "Die Reorganisation der preußischen Armee nach dem Tilsiter Frieden" in *Beihefte zum Militärwochenblatt* (Berlin: Mittler, 1854–1862), two volumes, Vol. I, p. 82; Klaus Hornung, *Scharnhorst: Soldat, Reformer, Staatsmann* (Muenchen: Bechtle, 1997), pp. 203–14; Telp, *The Evolution of Operational Art*, pp. 105–7; Walter, *Preussische Heeresreformen*, pp. 245–47, 262–70.

      Karl Friedrich von dem Knesebeck, 1768–1848, Prussian officer during reform period who did not take part in the reform process.

10   On the reform of military punishment, discipline, and justice, see Dorothea Schmidt (ed.), *Erinnerungen aus dem Leben des Generalfeldmarschalls Hermann von Boyen,* (Berlin: Brandenburgisches Verlagshaus, 1990), two volumes, I, pp. 244–46; Hornung, Scharnhorst, p. 182; Heinz Stübig, *Scharnhorst: Die Reform des preußischen Heeres* (Göttingen: Muster-Schmidt, 1988), pp. 79–83.

11   On plans for the militarisation of schools, see Memorandum, Gneisenau, 31 August 1807, Großer Generalstab, "Reorganisation", Vol. I, pp. 94–95; Military Reorganization Commission to Stein, November 1807, Vaupel, *Das preußische Heer*, p. 186.

12   On ideas to boost morale by rewards and punishment, see Decree, 21 April 1813, Maximilian Blumenthal, *Der preußische Landsturm von 1813* (Berlin: Schröder, 1900), p. 168, p. 176; Notes, Grolman, 1807, Vaupel, *Heer*, p. 70; Military Reorganization Commission to Frederick William, 17 April 1808, Vaupel, *Das preußische Heer*, p. 381; Memorandum, Gneisenau, August 1808, Vaupel, *Heer*, pp. 550–51; Memorandum, Gneisenau, August 1808, Vaupel, *Heer*, pp. 554–55; Memorandum, Scharnhorst, August 1808, Vaupel, *Heer*, pp. 555–56.

13   On the reform of the officer corps, see Memorandum, Military Reorganization Commission, 1808, Großer Generalstab, "Reorganisation", Vol. II, p. 496; Military Reorganization Commission to Frederick William, 25 September 1807, Vaupel, *Heer*, p. 101; Hornung, *Scharnhorst*, p. 89, pp. 186–187; Louis A von Scharfenort, *Die königlich-preußische Kriegsakademie* (Berlin: Mittler, 1910), pp. 5–19.

14 On the reform of the general staff, see Memorandum, Grolman, October 1814, E von Conrady, *Leben und Wirken des Generals der Infanterie und kommandierenden Generals des V. Armeekorps Carl von Grolman*, (Berlin: Mittler, 1894–96), three volumes, Vol. II, pp. 390; Memorandum, Major Rauch, 1808, Großer Generalstab, "Reorganisation", Vol. I, pp. 308–10, p. 316; Andreas Broicher, *Gerhard von Scharnhorst: Soldat, Reformer, Wegbereiter* (Aachen: Helios, 2005), p. 168: Trevor N. Dupuy, *A Genius for War: The German Army and General Staff, 1807–1945* (London: Macdonald and Jane's, 1997), p. 28, pp. 46–47; Peter Paret, "Napoleon and the Revolution in War" in P. Paret (ed.) *Makers of Modern Strategy* (Oxford: Clarendon, 1991), pp. 123–43, p. 136.

15 On Prussian thought regarding the conduct of operations, see Antoine La Roche-Aymon, *Über den Dienst der leichten Truppen* (Königsberg: Degen, 1808), pp. 3–5, pp. 15–21; Memorandum, Frederick William, 18 November 1806, Großer Generalstab, "Reorganisation", Vol. I, pp. 10–16; Telp, *The Evolution of Operational Art*, pp. 113–15.

16 On the reform of the train, see Memorandum, Military Reorganization Commission, 1808, Großer Generalstab, "Reorganisation", II, pp. 496–98; Martin Kiesling, *Geschichte der Organisation und Bekleidung des Trains der königlich-preussischen Armee: 1740–1888* (Berlin: Mittler, 1889), p. 14, pp. 20–27.

17 On tactical organisation and tactical doctrine, see La Roche-Aymon, *Truppen*, pp. 120–29; Prussia, *Exerzier-Reglement für die Infanterie der königlich-preußischen Armee* (Berlin: Decker, 1812); Prussia, *Exerzier-Reglement für die Kavallerie der königlich-preußischen Armee* (Berlin: Decker, 1812); Prussia, *Exerzier-Reglement für die Artillerie der königlich-preußischen Armee* (Berlin: Decker, 1812); Yorck "Instruction für sämtliche leichte Brigaden" in Werner Hahlweg, *Preußische Reformzeit und revolutionärer Krieg* (Frankfurt: Mittler, 1962), pp. 73–87.

18 On simplified drill, see Boyen, *Erinnerungen*, Vol. I, pp. 364– 65; Carl Friedrich von Blumen, Carl Friedrich von, M von Unruh (ed.), *Von Jena bis Neisse* (Leipzig: Wigand, 1904), pp. 71–73, 80; Prussia, *Infanterie 1812*, p. 69.

19 On opposition to the reform programme, see Boyen, *Erinnerungen*, Vol. I, p. 227, p. 229, p. 249, pp. 255–57, pp. 264–65, pp. 324–25, pp. 334–35; Vincke to Stein, 30 September 1808, Vaupel, *Heer*, p. 598; Marion W. Gray, *Prussia in Transition: Society and Politics under the Stein Reform Ministry of 1808*, (Philadelphia: American Philosophical Society, 1986), pp. 145–49; Thomas Nipperdey, *Deutsche Geschichte: 1800–1866* (München: Beck, 1984), p. 42, p. 49; Walter M Simon, *The Failure of the Prussian Reform Movement: 1807–1819* (New York: Cornell University Press, 1955), pp. 12–13, p. 24, p. 29, p. 32, p. 68, p. 80, p. 84; Walter, *Heeresreform*, pp. 265–67; Joseph Friedrich Theodor von Zwehl, "Der Gegensatz zwischen Yorck und Gneisenau", *Beiheft zum Militärwochenblatt*, No. 10 (1914), pp. 403–69, p. 408.

20 For the Treaty of Paris, see Treaty of Paris, 8 September 1808, M de Clercq (ed.), *Recueil des Traités de la France* (Paris: Amyot, 1864), six volumes, Vol. II, pp. 270–73.

21 On Prussia's financial problems, see Hornung, *Scharnhorst*, pp. 124–27.

22 On the impact of austerity measures on the army, see Jany, Curt, E Jany (ed.), *Geschichte der preußischen Armee: Vom 15. Jahrhundert bis 1914*, 2nd revised edition (Osnabrück: Biblio, 1967), four volumes , Vol. IV, p. 8, pp. 19–21, pp. 39–40.

23 Memorandum, Stein, June 1807, Stein, *Briefwechsel*, Vol. II, pp. 210–31.

24 At the head of his cavalry regiment, Schill had tried to start an insurrection but his outnumbered force was quickly destroyed in Stralsund. On the impact of French occupation and supervision, see Gray, *Prussia*, pp. 144–49, p. 150, p. 157; William O. Shanahan, *Prussian Military Reforms: 1786–1813* (New York: Columbia University Press, 1945), p. 158; Walter, *Heeresreform*, p. 270.

25 On the resignations of Prussian officers, see Louis Alexandre Andrault de Langeron, L G Fabry (ed.), *Mémoires de Langeron, Général d'Infanterie dans l'Armée Russe: Campagnes de 1812, 1813,*

1814 (Paris: Picard, 1902), p. 143; Gordon A Craig, *The Politics of the Prussian Army: 1640–1945* (London: Oxford University Press, 1964), pp. 54–58; Großer Generalstab, "Reorganisation", I, pp. 42–44.

26   On military contingency planning and the *Landsturm*, see; Memorandum, Gneisenau, September 1808, Vaupel, *Heer*, pp. 593–97; Scharnhorst to Frederick William, 16 July 1810, Gerhard Johann David von Scharnhorst, Lehmann (ed.), "Vier Denkschriften Scharnhorsts aus dem Jahre 1810", *Historische Zeitschrift*, Vol. LVIII (1887), pp. 55–105, pp. 86–90; Blumenthal, *Landsturm*, pp. 163–82; Hornung, *Scharnhorst*, p. 273.

27   For the texts of these laws, see Ernst Rudolf Huber (ed.), *Dokumente zur deutschen Verfassungsgeschichte*, 2nd improved edition (Stuttgart: Kohlhammer, 1961–66), three volumes, Vol. I, pp. 39–46; Fritz Stier-Somlo (ed.), *Sammlung preußischer Gesetze staats- und verwaltungsrechtlichen Inhalts*, 5th improved edition (München: Beck, 1927), pp. 1–33.

28   On the outcome of the civil reforms, see Nipperdey, *Geschichte*, pp. 36–50, pp. 67–68; Hanna Schissler, *Preußische Agrargesellschaft im Wandel: Wirtschaftliche, gesellschaftliche und politische Transformationsprozesse von 1763 bis 1847* (Göttingen: Vandenhoeck, 1978), pp. 105–10; Clive Trebilcock, *The Industrialization of the Continental Powers: 1780–1914* (London: Longman, 1981), pp. 34–35.

29   On the conditions of service in Jaeger detachments, Landwehr, and regular army, see Stübig, *Scharnhorst*, pp. 94–95

30   For the *Krümper* system, see Decree, 6 August 1808, Vaupel, *Heer*, p. 542; Shanahan, *Reforms*, pp. 13–16, p. 110, pp. 159–61; Walter, *Heeresreform*, pp. 254–55.

31   On mobilisation in Spring 1813, see Hornung, *Scharnhorst*, p. 270, p. 275; Walter, *Heeresreform*, pp. 254–55.

32   On the Landsturm in 1813–14, see Hornung, *Scharnhorst*, p. 272; Walter, *Heeresreform*, pp. 292–99.

33   On the service law of 1814, see Huber, *Verfassungsgeschichte*, Vol. I, pp 48–55; Friedrich Meinecke, *Das Leben des Generalfeldmarschalls Hermann von Boyen* (Stuttgart: Cotta, 1896–1899), two volumes, Vol. I, pp. 417–22; Walter, *Heeresreform*, pp. 300–3.

34   Jany, *Armee*, Vol. IV, p. 42.

35   On Prussian patriotism in 1813, see Hornung, *Scharnhorst*, p. 271; Matthew Levinger, *Enlightened Nationalism: The Transformation of Prussian Political Culture, 1806–1848* (New York: Oxford University Press, 2000), p. 48, p. 229, p. 233; Nipperdey, *Geschichte*, pp. 55–56.

36   On the outcome of the reforms of the officer corps, see Hornung, *Scharhorst*, p. 136; Daniel Köster, "Auswirkungen der preußischen Heeresreform auf die soziale Zusammensetzung des Offizierskorps: 1806–1848", PhD Thesis (München: 1991), p. 188, pp. 287–90; Peter Paret, *Yorck and the Era of Prussian Reform: 1807–1815* (Princeton: Princeton University Press, 1966), pp. 265–66; Walter, *Heeresreform*, pp. 559–60. Gebhard Leberecht von Bluecher, 1742–1819, Prussian general, later prince.

37   Dupuy, *Genius*, p. 44. On the performance of the general staff in 1813–14, see Broicher, *Scharnhorst*, p. 138, p. 167; Dupuy, *Genius*, p. 34, pp. 46–47; Hornung, *Scharnhorst*, p. 197; Telp, *Evolution*, pp. 130–31.

38   On the impact of exercises and Yorck's operations in 1812, see Blumen, *Jena*, p. 82; Boyen, *Erinnerungen*, Vol. I, pp. 266–67, pp. 365–66; Paret, *Yorck*, p. 166; Broicher, *Scharnhorst*, pp. 121–22.

39   For a summary of the reforms' successes and failures, see Boyen, *Erinnerungen*, Vol. I, pp. 233–34; Simon, *Reform*, pp. 4–5, p. 11.

CHAPTER 3

'Every Frenchman is permanently requisitioned for the needs of the armies'

Mobilisation in France from 1789

Dr Tim Gale

The introduction of the *levée en masse* in France in 1793 produced a significant change in how war was conducted in Europe thereafter and became a central but highly contested concept in the idea of citizenship in France and elsewhere.[1] Prior to this measure being taken by the revolutionary government, limited conscription had occurred in France, but the mobilising of all able-bodied men by the state was unprecedented. It created an entirely different relationship between the armed forces and the people of the country, as well as enabling the creation of larger armies than had been possible previously that crucially could be rapidly refurnished with men in the event of heavy casualties. The revolutionary government of France promoted the idea that, with the abolition of the monarchy and the enfranchisement of adult men, defence of the nation was no longer the business just of the state but of its citizens as well. By widening the pool of available men so extensively, armies could be larger, but almost inevitably, the quality of troops declined due to the difficulties of training such large numbers of men, which in turn forced changes in tactics to play to the strengths and avoid the weaknesses of enthusiastic levied troops with limited training. By 1914, the idea of the citizen army was so entrenched in the French psyche that a country with less than 20 million adult men was able to mobilise over eight million men into its armed forces. This chapter will examine how France mobilised its army from the *ancien régime* of the Bourbons to just prior to World War II and how the concept of the nation in arms generated a constant tension between the idea and the reality.

The armies of France in the 18th century were armies of the monarch and war was a matter for the king, not his subjects. It followed that subjects of the crown would not expect to be involved in military affairs and the populace viewed the military with some suspicion. In particular, the widely held view was that military service was to be avoided at all costs; a view reinforced by the fact that, given sufficient funds, it was always possible to purchase a substitute for one's military obligations. This meant that the burdens of the existing limited conscription fell largely on the peasantry who were unable to buy their way out of the draft, unlike the middle classes. Only in the aristocracy was there the idea of an obligation to serve in the military and that was primarily because a career as an officer was the only option for the many sons of aristocrats who would not inherit their father's property. Thus, for the most part, with the exception of technical arms such as the artillery and engineering, officers had to be from the nobility. For example, in the French army in 1789, only 10 per cent of the officer corps of 10,000 were commoners.[2]

The ordinary soldiers of the Bourbon armies were long-service professionals who enlisted for six-year periods, although there were various ruses adopted by the authorities to encourage enlistment, including some monetary inducements. By contrast, the militia was subject to conscription but it was only expected to serve in France and not to fight against professional troops except in an emergency. As the tactics of the time required well-trained troops, there was a strong incentive for the authorities to retain soldiers for as long as possible. This was a problem as 18th-century armies could expect to lose approximately 20 per cent of their strength during wartime per year to disease and desertion, which meant that deserters were, in general, welcomed back to the army without punishment.[3] Indeed, considerable effort was made to attract deserters from foreign armies into the French army. However, it is worth noting that while enlistment was voluntary, it could be extended by the army without agreement from the recruit; for example, some men who enlisted in 1758 were not released from service until 1766.[4] The idea that subjects should desire to serve in the army for patriotic reasons simply did not exist in France during this period.

Despite the fact that the Seven Years War (1756–63) was truly a global war in scope, Louis XV actually mobilised fewer men for the French armies than Louis XIV had at the beginning of the century. Despite Louis XIV having a smaller population base to draw upon, between 1701 and 1713 he raised nearly 500,000 men.[5] Nonetheless, the French army of the Seven Years War required 38,000 replacements a year just to maintain its much smaller strength of approximately 270,000 men.[6] By comparison, 100,000 men served in the militia between 1756–58 and these men were sometimes used to bring the regular army up to strength, such as in 1760 when 13,000 militiamen were assigned to the army to make up losses.[7] France actually mobilised fewer men than many other European countries over the 18th century prior to the revolution; the French military took approximately one adult man in 11, whereas the German armies took nearly one man in four.[8] However, most of the difficulties encountered by the Bourbons in raising large armies were the result of an inefficient bureaucracy and a constant lack of funds. By the time of the revolution,

France was not a county that had a tradition of mobilising a large part of its adult population, particularly compared to many of its competitors in Europe.

The revolutionary government inherited an army that was inefficient, relatively small and a constant reminder in its structure of the previous regime. With the aristocracy so entrenched in the officer corps, the government was faced with an institution that was led by men largely out of sympathy with the new regime. This antipathy was demonstrated by the fact that by 1791 over 60 per cent of the officer class had left the country.[9] In an attempt to give the revolution an armed force with no doubts about its loyalty, the Paris authorities raised the National Guard in July 1789, which was both paid better than the army and organised differently in legions rather than battalions. From the point of view of officers and NCOs, a better inducement was the prospect of significantly quicker promotion based on talent rather than seniority.

The first step taken on mass conscription by the revolutionary government was the *loi Jourdan* of 1789. This introduced male conscription, covering all unmarried men but with exceptions for priests, civil servants and students, as well as the physically unfit. As had been the case previously in France, men were called to the colours via a ballot to fill the required quotas.[10] This system worked no better than Louis XV's system had and only 131,000 men out of the initial 400,000 called up arrived to serve with their units.[11]

On 11 July 1792, the National Assembly reacted to the Prussian-Austria alliance against France by declaring that 'the country was in danger' (*la Patrie est en danger*) and that it could only be saved by all citizens working together. This was the first step towards the *levée en masse* because it introduced the idea that the defence of the country was the responsibility of all its citizens, not just the government. The War of the First Coalition (1792–97), as the revolution's first conflict with the monarchs of Europe became known, had begun with a stunning victory by French forces at the battle of Valmy (20 September 1792), although this was really due to the technical superiority of the French artillery rather than any revolutionary spirit motivating the army. This was followed by numerous French military successes which covered up the increasing inefficiency of the French military and allowed the revolutionary government to overestimate its military strength. However, by the middle of 1793, the military situation had deteriorated sharply, as exemplified by the heavy French defeat at Neerwinden on 18 March 1793, which resulted in French forces having to evacuate Belgium in a hurry and large numbers of men deserting. By March 1793, France was at war with Prussia, Austria, the United Provinces (current-day Netherlands), Britain and Spain. To add to the government's troubles, a large-scale insurrection broke out in the Vendée region in response to a February decree aimed at raising 300,000 men across France. Thus, by mid-1793, France was in the midst of civil war in the Vendée and was at war with five great powers in Europe. Unsurprisingly, there were not enough men in the armed forces to deal effectively with such a plethora of problems and there were increasing calls to introduce an emergency form of conscription, particularly after the fall of Mainz in July 1793.

Leading members of the National Convention (primarily Bertrand Barère and Lazare Carnot) drafted a decree on conscription that was duly enacted on 23 August 1793. This historic document is worth quoting in detail, from its first forthright paragraph (with ten clauses omitted as they contain technical details relating to how the mobilisation would be enacted):

1. From this moment, until the enemies have been driven from the territory of the Republic, the French people are in permanent requisition for service in the armies. The young men shall go to battle; the married men shall forge arms and transport supplies; women shall make tents, clothes and shall serve in the hospitals; children shall turn old linen into lint, older men will take themselves to public places to encourage the warriors, while preaching the hatred of kings and the unity of the Republic.

2. National buildings will be converted into barracks, public places into armament workshops; cellar floors will be washed in lye to extract saltpetre [an essential element of gunpowder] from them.

3. Fire-arms will be turned over exclusively to those who march against the enemy; service in the interior shall be carried out with hunting pieces and edged weapons.

4. Horses are called for to complete the cavalry units, draught horses, other than those used in agriculture, will haul artillery and supplies.

5. The Committee of Public Safety is charged with taking all necessary measures to establish without delay an extraordinary manufacture of all types of arms, in accordance with the state and energy of the French people. It is authorized, in consequence, to constitute all establishments, manufactories, workshops, and factories deemed necessary for the execution of such works, as well as the requisition for such purpose, throughout the entire extent of the Republic, the artists and workmen who may contribute to their success...
   [...]

7. No one may obtain a substitute for service to which he is summoned. Public functionaries will remain at their posts.

8. The levy shall be general. Unmarried citizens or childless widowers, from eighteen to twenty-five years, shall go first; they shall meet, without delay, at the chief town of their districts, where they shall practice manual exercise daily, while awaiting the hour of departure.
   [...]

11. The battalion organized in each district shall be united under a banner bearing the inscription: *The French people risen against tyrants.*...[12]

As can be seen, the decree introduced several ideas that would change warfare in Europe and resonate through its history for the next 200 years. In particular, the decree stated that France in its entirety was now at war against its various enemies; each citizen (including the young and old who had traditionally been exempted from work for the military), horse, firearm and factory could now be potentially requisitioned by the armed forces to defend the country. In article 11, an attack on France was no longer characterised as an attack on the current regime but as an attack against the French people. Article 7 abolished substitution for military service and made such service a personal obligation for each male citizen.

The exact number of men mobilised subsequent to the decree is impossible to determine but it was approximately 750,000 men. The large numbers of men called up changed the character of the French army significantly as the new recruits could not be trained or treated like those of the 18th century. The mechanical drill of the 18th-century infantry could not be replicated in the time available to train men from the *levée en masse* and, therefore, tactics had to be simplified. However, soldiers were now fighting for their country, rather than money, and thus, the endemic desertion of the previous regime's army was not a major problem initially. This meant that infantry could be trusted to forage without going missing, which in turn enabled much larger armies to be fielded than hitherto had been the case because they could now live off the land to a degree that was impossible previously. With larger armies came the opportunity for a different organisation of armed forces, eventually leading to Napoleon's corps system of large independent commands. Napoleon also realised that citizen soldiers would need encouragement as well as discipline if they were to be effective. He introduced numerous military awards for the rank and file, promising them that there was 'a marshal's baton in every soldier's backpack'.[13]

The army was already highly politicised by 1793 because the revolutionary government was determined from the start to have an army that reflected its political ideals. *Demi-brigades* of infantry were created by coupling one existing line battalion to two volunteer battalions, with the latter expected to keep the former in ideological line. *Commissaires aux armées* were recruited from ardent Jacobins (hard-line revolutionaries) and introduced to keep a close eye on the army, particularly the officers. The government gave the *commissaires* extensive powers to intervene in military affairs, including the authority to suspend or arrest even the highest ranking officers; in 1793 and 1794 over 80 generals were executed for perceived failure. By 1793, there was little of the pre-revolutionary army left with 95 per cent of the troops having joined up since 1789.[14]

The following year was one of considerable success with French victories against both the Austrians and Spanish at Fleurus and Black Mountain respectively. 1795 and 1796 saw further successful campaigns in the Netherlands and Italy, the latter led by the rising star of the French army, Napoleon Bonaparte. By 1797, all but Britain were out of the war with France, the latter gaining the Austrian Netherlands as part of the Treaty of Campo Formio.

As enthusiasm for the both the war and the revolution itself had waned, the problem of desertion had returned and the 750,000 men raised by the *levée en masse* in 1793 had been reduced by desertion to 381,909 men by 1797.[15] Although France was no longer at war, the issue of manpower was still important enough to receive the attention of the government. Previous mass conscription measures such as the levée had been intended as temporary reactions to specific threats. The idea of a permanent obligation for personal military service during peacetime was introduced in the *loi Jourdan* of 5 September 1798. This set the template for all future French mass conscription by classing all Frenchmen into age classes from 20 years old to 25; those reaching 25 without being called up would be then permanently released except in times of national emergency.[16]

After his *coup d'état* in November 1799, Napoleon would alter the character of war far more significantly than the revolutionary governments that had preceded him. Leading Napoleonic scholar Charles Esdaile characterises the change thus:

> What then marks out the Napoleonic Wars from what had gone before? Head of the list must come the idea that, just as the Seven Years War made conflict in Europe a global affair, so the struggle that began in 1803 was the first one waged by nations-in-arms.[17]

Napoleon was a firm believer in the merits of conscription and said that 'conscription forms armies of citizens, voluntary enlistment forms armies of vagabonds and criminals'.[18] Although he would use the *loi Jourdan* as the basis for his regime's approach to conscription, in his initial campaigns Napoleon would have little need of mass armies. The early campaigns of Napoleon's rule, up to 1801, would see only 30,000 men conscripted every year, significantly less than under the revolutionary government from 1796–99. By 1805, over half the men and nearly all the officers and NCOs, some 250,000 men, of the French army had been serving since before 1800, and thus, they had voluntarily extended their service.[19] This would result in what one historian has called 'Napoleon's improbable synthesis' of an imperial army with a very real meritocratic ethos, which resulted in good cohesion and morale.[20]

However, as the Napoleonic wars increased in size and intensity, conscription became vital in the struggle to keep the large Napoleonic armies fully manned and rose to an average yearly call-up of 127,000 between 1809 and 1812.[21] The battle of Austerlitz in 1805 had been fought by Napoleon with just over 70,000 men.[22] By comparison, the force Napoleon took over the Saxon border in October 1806 at the beginning of his Jena campaign against the Prussians was 180,000 strong, and he raised over 600,000 men in 1812 for the campaign against Russia, albeit a number that also included non-French troops.[23] The army formed for the invasion of Russia, *La Grande Armée de la Russie*, was so large that 80,000 men had to be conscripted for the defence of France because so much of the regular army was moving east.[24] Thus, the search to supply the required manpower became a source of serious friction with the populace and an increasing burden on the imperial bureaucracy.

Enforcement of conscription had hitherto been left at a local level, largely unsupervised by the *departments* or Paris. Conscription was gradually moved under central control and standardised from 1804 to 1811, with prefects being sent to check on the mayors and councils that enacted the conscription laws. As the demand for men increased, the imperial bureaucracy would encounter difficulties with one of the most contentious aspects of the conscription laws, namely exemptions from military service; a problem that would continue into the Great War itself.

The revolutionary levies had contained exemptions from service for a variety of reasons; for example, married men were exempt as were those with health issues, as well as various blanket exemptions for skilled tradesmen, such as bakers and notaries. During Napoleon's reign, further exemptions were introduced and the list of exempted artisans was extended. While the *loi Jourdan* had abolished the ability to buy oneself out of military service by purchasing a replacement, this was quickly abandoned, allowing the middle classes to avoid conscription, although as the demands on manpower increased, so did the price of avoidance. Between 1806 and 1810, 25,000 thousand replacements were purchased out of a total of 556,000 men levied for service.[25] However, for the majority of Frenchmen, purchasing a replacement was financially impossible and other methods of avoidance were resorted to. One such method was to become a *Reformé*; someone with a medical certificate exempting them from military service through unfitness. The criteria for unfitness was wide enough to make many believe that a minor mutilation, such as the removal of a finger, was worth undertaking to avoid serving in the army and there were widespread examples of this practice. In addition, a lucrative trade in false medical certificates occurred across the country. Increasing numbers of imperial bureaucrats, usually accompanied by military officers, were sent throughout France to ensure conscription was being implemented effectively, although it was accepted that certain regions such as the ever-rebellious Vendée would always deliver fewer draftees than their allotted number. Conscription evasion became so serious that mobile military columns, manned by the *gendarmerie* and the regular army, would occupy entire areas and search for deserters; during 1811, such units caught 100,000 deserters and draft evaders. Indeed, the situation in the last years of the Empire was so dire that the authorities began to use collective punishments against communities with a high rate of desertion or conscription avoidance.[26]

By 1815, the perception had become that conscription was a heavy price for the French population to pay, but this was primarily due to the unprecedented numbers involved rather than the actual minimal dislocation of society that occurred. While the French armies of the Napoleonic era were huge compared to the armies that had preceded them, the burden of conscription on the French people was not as high as this might suggest, with 2,500,00 men called to Napoleon's recruitment centres and only 1,500,000 of these actually conscripted. Even during a period of great danger, such as 1813–14, the number of those who actually saw service never exceeded 41 per cent of those called up.[27] Thus, the proportion of the population mobilised for the army in the Napoleonic Wars was comparatively modest compared to the proportion of the male French population mobilised in the Great War as will be discussed below.

The fall of Napoleon in 1815 saw the return of a rather hesitant monarchy to France, which was grudgingly accepted by its subjects. Not confident of the loyalty of the army that he inherited, Louis XVIII (monarch from 1815 to 1824) tried to turn the clock back by reintroducing aristocratic requirements for officers and to detach the army from the populace. The first measure was strongly resisted, but the population was more than content to be uninvolved in military matters after nearly two decades of war.

The officers' school in Paris was reopened once Louis XVIII was crowned and required candidates to demonstrate four generations of nobility on their father's side, as had been the case prior to the revolution. This provoked vehement objections from the Chamber of Deputies, the French second chamber, who argued that this was clearly in breach of the constitutional arrangements that had been an essential part of the restitution of the monarchy, which guaranteed wide access to the army and civil service.[28] As the monarchy was still establishing its legitimacy, there was no question of allowing such an issue to become a dangerous fault line between it and the chamber and the nobility requirements for aspiring officers were quickly dropped. Those of noble birth continued to be disproportionately represented in the army's officers from the Restoration to the Franco-Prussian War, with 8 per cent of the officer corps coming from the nobility during this period, but their domination over the army was now over.[29] It is notable that this attempt by the king and his advisors to return command of the army to the nobility was a failure; a strong indication that the changes initiated during the revolutionary period had broken irrevocably with the past.

In relation to detaching the army from the people, this was rather more successful and there was little or no resistance to the return of a relatively small professional army. This suited the populace, as they were no longer under the shadow of conscription, and the authorities because they could recruit soldiers that could be relied on to enforce law and order when necessary, without the worry that they might side with anti-government forces. As Louis XVIII's immediate successors (the Bourbon Charles X and Louis-Philippe of the house of Orleans) had no interest in military adventures, a small army presented them with no difficulties.

The situation changed when the monarchy was overthrown in the revolution of 1848 and the Second Republic was formed. Louis-Napoleon Bonaparte, who was first President of the republic and then, through a *coup d'état*, Emperor of the Second Empire (1851), had to balance his desire for military glory with the knowledge that a large army raised from the general population might present a political threat to his regime. Initially, the small professional army seemed more than adequate for

Napoleon III's military needs with reasonable success during the Crimean War followed by considerable success against the Austrian army in Italy (1859). However, the disastrous intervention in Mexico by Napoleon III (1862–66) provoked some doubts about what a small army could achieve, particularly as with commitments in the Far East and Algeria, as well as in Europe, the French army had been clearly overstretched in its attempts to pacify the Mexican opposition. The Prussian defeat of Austria in 1866 rang further alarm bells because Prussia had mobilised an army nearly twice the size of the French one from a population with two million fewer men. As Prussia under Bismarck was squaring up to France, this was very worrying because the Prussian army had no commitments outside Europe and the entire force could be committed to a European campaign, whereas by contrast, the French army had nearly 100,000 men permanently stationed in Algeria. By this point in his rule, Napoleon III had lost sufficient authority that he was unable to force through his desire to conscript a large-scale army along Prussian lines; an idea that was instantly rejected by both civilian and military leaders. Despite the rejection of his conscription plans, Napoleon III was able to form a large reserve for the army, the *Garde Mobile*, which could, in theory, produce nearly 400,000 men but they had very little training, if any, by the time of the Franco-Prussian War. The imperial army's poor performance in that war, despite having a number of technological advantages over the Germans, was largely the result of inept leadership at most levels, perhaps epitomised by the surrender of the intact French army at Sedan on 2 September 1870. A Government of National Defence was declared in Paris two days later and the war continued until the remnants of the French army had been defeated and an armistice declared on 5 February 1871. A revolution occurred in Paris in January 1871 that took two months to suppress, with great brutality, by the French authorities.

France's Third Republic was born from the defeat of 1870 and its military policy thereafter was a reflection of the fact that the country was almost evenly divided between the left and the right. The bitterness in French politics that resulted from the suppression of the Paris Commune would take decades to dissipate; for example, it took until 1889 for the government of France to be conducted from its capital of Paris. So disputatious was the idea of the republic itself that it was 1875 before a series of constitutional laws were agreed and these were far more conservative in nature than the radical republicans had argued for.[30] After an initial period, when there was a real chance of the monarchists prevailing, both conservative and radical republicans rallied to cement the idea that France was naturally a republic, and by the end of the 19th century, the argument between right and left was about how the republic should be run rather than about its very legitimacy. The return of conscription in 1871 had been widely accepted as an appropriate response to an existential threat to the country, but there was no reason to believe that resistance to peacetime conscription would diminish. However, conscription was returned to the political agenda of the Third Republic by politicians keen to use the army to reinforce the republican state's legitimacy with many calling for the army to be the school of the state. It, therefore, followed that there would have to be a re-imposition of obligatory military service through mass conscription, justified as part of the new social and political order.

The *loi Cissey* of 27 July 1872 introduced five years of personal military service to men aged 20 to 40, but this was reduced to two years' service in the *loi Freycinet* of 15 July 1889. There was continuous agitation from the army high command to increase the length of service because two years was not enough time to adequately instruct troops and three years' service was reintroduced with the *loi Barthou* of 7 August 1913.[31]

By the latter date, the French army's universal male conscription was organised as follows. Every year, men in their 21st year, that year's class, would enter into three years of active service with the Active Army. Upon finishing their initial three years, men would enter the active Army Reserve (men 24 to 34 years old) and then the Territorial Army (men 35 to 41 years old), followed by the Territorial Army Reserve (men 42 to 48 years old). Each tier of army service required less time under the colours; for example, the Territorial Army trained for only nine days a year and the Territorial Army Reserve only for one day. The state could also call on the Colonial Army; consisting entirely of long-service professionals, it was tasked with defending the colonies and was originally controlled by the navy but had been transferred to the War Ministry and the army in 1905. A corps-sized group of three colonial divisions came under the jurisdiction of the War Ministry; the divisions based in Paris and various French ports.

The French colonial empire would also be called on to supply men for the French army. The largest overseas territory, Algeria, was technically part of France rather than a colony. It supplied the army with XIX Corps, consisting of four divisions, one of which garrisoned Tunisia. As it was politically unacceptable to garrison non-white troops in France, only four battalions of *Zouaves* (raised from white Algerian settlers) from XIX Corps were serving in France in 1914. In principal, conscription had been introduced in Algeria in 1912, but it was patchily enforced until the war began with most of the North African regiments being manned by volunteers. However, by December 1915, 64,000 men had been conscripted into the French army from Algeria, and by the end of the war, a total of 158,533 Algerians would have served in combat units in the French army.[32] Tunisia also supplied conscripted troops to XIX Corps and Morocco provided 20,000 men in 1914–15. While Tunisia continued to supply significant numbers of troops, eventually contributing 54,000 men to the French army during the course of the war, the political and military situation in Morocco was so precarious that conscription was all but impossible and only 37,000 Moroccan troops were in the army by November 1918.[33] By the Armistice, the French army had 83 Algerian-Tunisian battalions and 12 Moroccan battalions in service.

The question of raising troops from the West African colonies was highly contentious in France prior to the war, with many arguing that this was necessary to balance the manpower deficit with Germany. One such was Charles Mangin, a well-known colonial soldier, who promoted the idea of raising large numbers of men in West Africa (known generically as Senegalese, a term which also includes recruits from French Equatorial Africa – AEF) via his polemic *La Force Noire*.[34] His ideas were met with considerable doubt, mainly the result of the widely held racial stereotypes of the time, but the losses incurred in 1914 undermined opposition to Senegalese recruitment. William Merlaud-Ponty, Governor-General of French West Africa (AOF), raised 34,000 West Africans for France during 1914–15, but after his death in mid-1915, recruitment in the AOF to all intents and purposes stopped for a year. In the second half of 1916, 50,000 men were recruited after a parliamentary army commission reopened interest in troops from AOF but, once again, recruiting impetus was quickly lost and then ceased. By 1918, French manpower requirements were in near crisis and the French premier, Georges Clemenceau, sent a highly successful recruiting mission to West Africa. This resulted in a total of 77,000 men being recruited, of whom 63,000 came from West Africa, with the rest being recruited in French Equatorial Africa. In total, West Africa supplied 181,500 soldiers of whom 134,000 served on the Western Front and Algeria, with the rest campaigning in Cameroon and Morocco.[35]

Other colonies also contributed to French manpower. Although there were only three million people in Madagascar, its Governor-General, Lieutenant-Colonel Garbit, managed to send 41,000 troops and 5000 workers to France between 1914 and 1917. Unfortunately, Garbit was transferred to France in 1918 and recruitment that year fell to only 1000 men.[36] French Indo-China offered men in 1914, but at that point in the war, it did not seem necessary and the offer was refused. However, as the war of materiels developed, the Saigon arsenal sent munitions workers and Vietnamese volunteers were increasingly employed in specialist roles, particularly as drivers, there being 5000 of these in France by 1918. By the end of the war, there were 50,000 Vietnamese in France, including 17 infantry battalions at the front. To illustrate how far afield the French authorities were prepared to go to acquire manpower, a *Bataillon Mixte du Pacifique* was raised in New Caledonia in the South Pacific for the Western Front from the indigenous Canaque people. Two companies of men were added to the battalion from Tahiti and it was shipped to France in mid-1916 to act as a pioneer unit. However, due to the manpower difficulties in 1918, it was retrained as a combat battalion and fought with French X Army, receiving an army citation for its part in operations in October 1918.[37]

Although the colonies provided significant amounts of manpower to the French army, as the war progressed there was increased resistance to conscription outside of France and a number of rebellions broke out in the French Empire, often primarily motivated by opposition to conscription. The most egregious of these occurred in West Africa, in an area now encompassing parts of Mali and Burkina Faso, when a dozen villages rose up against the colonial authorities in November 1915 and refused to supply men for the French armed forces. The revolt, known as the Volta-Bani War, rapidly spread, eventually covering an area with nearly 900,000 inhabitants, and was only fully suppressed by September 1916.[38]

By 1914, France had 39,601,464 inhabitants and a further 40 million in the colonies, of whom seven million were in Algeria and Tunisia.[39] Upon mobilisation, the French army had 884,000 troops stationed in France, Morocco, Algeria and Tunisia. With the troops guarding the colonies, there were approximately 950,000 men under arms.[40] After mobilisation, this number rose to 3,800,000 men, of which 2,700,000 were destined for the army or the defence of fortified places. From 1–15 August 1914, 1,800,000 reservists and 1,100,000 territorial reservists would arrive at the regimental depots.[41] Of the former, nearly 200,000 were destined for the existing regiments, with a further 500,000 used to form the reserve regiments.[42] Thus, there were roughly 1,700,000 effectives almost immediately placed under the command of General Joseph Joffre, the *général commandant en chef*.[43] General Maxime Weygand wrote after the war that 'the mobilisation and concentration was executed with a remarkable order and precision'.[44] By 21 September 1914, there were 35,399 officers and 1,562,709 men in the French army on the Western Front and this had risen to 44,172 officers and 1,863,739 by November of that year.[45]

The reaction to the declaration of war had been mixed within France, with some jubilation but more often quiet resignation reigned. However, there was a very real sense of the nation pulling together in August 1914, throwing aside, for the moment, the deep political divisions that had wracked the country in the previous decades. President Raymond Poincaré called on the Chamber of Deputies for a *union sacrée* on 4 August, in effect a government of national unity; a political consensus that lasted until November 1917. Corporal Louis Barthas, a barrel maker from the Languedoc region, could hardly believe how quickly people's differences were cast aside as war was declared and wrote in his notebook that:'The first effect of the war was the accomplishment of a miracle; peace, concord, reconciliation among people who hated each other.'[46]

The French authorities had expected that up to 13 per cent of those called up would try and avoid service but less than 2 per cent evaded the initial mobilisation.[47] Indeed, enthusiasm for mobilisation was such that it caused a number of problems of its own; too many doctors and pharmacists flocked to the colours in certain areas, which resulted in an excess of them in the military and a deficit in the civilian population.[48] Significant numbers of men arrived at their depots before equipment was available to them, leaving them to drill without uniforms or arms. In fact, men arrived at their depots so quickly that efforts to count them were rapidly abandoned by the authorities. The confusion was not helped by the lack of junior officers and NCOs. The heated political discourse over the army in the decades prior to the outbreak of war had severely impacted on the number of these officers in the army by making it, for many, an unattractive career. This deficit meant that many divisions would be mobilised without their full establishment of junior officers, the 5th Infantry Division, for example, had 96 lieutenants and 2nd lieutenants available rather than the regulation 172.[49]

Thus, during the initial weeks of the war, there was not an issue for Joffre and GQG (French GHQ) with the quantity of men mobilised, other than getting the maximum number of them to the front in order to have a decisive and immediate result in what was expected to be a short war.[50] As mobilisation in the Franco-Prussian War was seen as having been poorly handled, the French army was determined that a subsequent mobilisation would be carefully planned. The railways had been organised under military supervision before the war in order to be able to handle the large amount of traffic that would be required upon mobilisation. Before the war, four bureau of the French general staff was tasked with ensuring the French rail network would be ready for war, and on 1 August 1914, all the railways in France came under the control of the War Minister.[51] Over the course of the first four days of mobilisation (2–5 August), over 10,000 trains were utilised across the entire French rail network, transporting over one million men, 400,000 horses and 80,000 motor vehicles. On the northern network alone, just over 1000 trains transported 439,135 men, 117,601 horses and over 4000 tonnes of materiel.[52] Even moving the Algerian troops through France and the Alpine Division (based in the south of the country) required nearly 250 train loads.[53]

However, as casualties mounted in the initial fighting on the frontiers, further measures to mobilise more men were felt necessary. Although most of the Territorial Army Reserve was not initially called up, due to the belief that they were not suitable for combat duties, the class of 1914 was mobilized, despite not being due to join the colours until October, with the class of 1915 being called up in December 1914.[54] By the end of 1914, the French army had lost over 500,000 men. These were either killed, captured or evacuated from the front.[55] During September 1914 alone, casualties were 4179 officers killed, wounded or missing and 210,075 men killed, wounded or missing.[56] Despite these losses, there were 2,300,000 men at the front by January 1915, largely the result of stripping men from the civil service, the railways and industry. In addition, the reserve of the Territorial Army began to be incorporated into the active army and a decree was issued in September 1914 that required all men aged under 43 who had not been called up to be re-examined to ascertain if they were fit for service.[57]

There was one general misconception held that would cause considerable confusion in the immediate response to the heavy casualties of 1914. The assumption was that the number of wounded who could be returned to the army would be similar to previous wars, namely 50 per cent of those wounded would be permanently lost from the three or four wounded for each man killed. Thus, for every 100 men killed, the French army was expecting to have up to 200 men so seriously wounded that they would never be fit for military duties, an assumption that was expected to apply to the German army as well. In reality, there were only 60 wounded men per 100 killed that would be permanently lost to the army.[58] As can be imagined, this misconception led to a grave overestimation of German casualties on the Eastern Front, which mislead the French into believing that 'time will work for us' in terms of numbers and the concurrent belief that this meant a short war was inevitable.[59]

By mid-1915, it was clear that these beliefs were incorrect and a new search for men was required. In 1915, a re-examination of the age exemptions (for those over 43) and of those working for the *service auxiliaire* allowed approximately 700,000 men to join the army as reinforcements and left only 250,000 men with the *service auxiliaire*.[60] The *service auxiliaire* was for those men declared unfit for military service who were then sent to serve in the offices, depots and medical services of the army. Those unfit for service were known as *les réformés* and they were divided into two categories; those whose unfitness occurred due to or during army service and those who did not. There were other exemptions for those men working in essential non-military services, such as the railways and the telegraphic and postal services, known as *affectés spéciaux*. A decree of 9 September 1914 had required all *réformés* and other exemptions to go before a commission that would decide if they were exempt from service or should go into the *services auxiliaire*.

The year 1915 would see the three main issues affecting French military manpower become clear as the nature of the war became clearer, i.e. that it was a war of materiels as much as of men. The drain on French manpower would come from: military casualties (both from combat and for other reasons, such as the Spanish Flu in 1918), the needs of industry (so the country could fight) and the necessity to maintain France's agricultural sector (so the country could be fed).

In relation to casualties, these had been unprecedented. The enormous casualties of 1914 were compounded in the French offensives in the spring and autumn of 1915, with that year seeing 348,850 men killed. Those two years would see the highest casualties. In 1916, the year of the battles of Verdun and the Somme, 252,300 men were killed, and in 1917, the year of the disastrous Nivelle Offensive, there were 163,700 men killed.[61] Thus, for example, in 1916, the army needed to find an average of 21,020 men per month to replace those killed. Additionally, the wounded needed to be taken into account, with an expectation that there would be three or four of these for each man killed.

A prodigious effort was made during the war to recuperate wounded men and return them to the front. By 1918, the French military medical system was highly efficient; from March to November of that year, more than two million wounded, gassed or sick men were transported for treatment by the 4000 ambulances of the French army.[62] Another 900,000 were transported by railway on 200 hospital trains, which had places for 60,000 wounded men and a further 30,000 lightly wounded men.[63] Of those evacuated from the front, only 10 per cent would not ultimately return to the army; the majority of those treated in the army zone would return within approximately a month, while those evacuated to the interior would return in an average of five months.[64] From August 1917 to November 1918, French army doctors undertook 29,553 surgical operations and in 1918 carried out 162,576 X-ray procedures; the latter an increase of over 50 per cent compared with 1917.[65] The increase in French medical efficiency can be demonstrated by that fact that for those wounded men treated in the interior, the mortality rate in 1914–1915 was 2.25 per cent which by 1918 had fallen to 0.94 per cent.[66]

During 1915, the French army reorganised itself in reaction to the growing difficulties with manpower; a process that would continue for the rest of the war. The infantry company was reduced in 1915 (to 200 officers and men), 1916 (to 194 officers and men) and 1918 (to 175 officers and men), and in mid-1916, the infantry battalions lost one of their four companies. Despite these measures, the army had to disband 71 active infantry battalions and a further 180 territorial battalions during the course of 1917. As well as reorganising its formations, the French army looked to technological solutions to mitigate its manpower losses and undertook massive armament programmes under successive commanders-in-chief. In addition to massive orders for artillery pieces and shells, common to all the combatants on the Western Front, the French army made extensive development and investment in aircraft and tanks. General Philippe Pétain, for example, on taking command of the French army in May 1917 almost immediately ordered 2870 aircraft and 2500 tanks. By the end of the war, France was the most motorised army and had the most tanks, nearly 3500, of any country in the world.

However, industrial production on such a mass scale put pressure on the very pool of manpower that the army needed. The war of materiels on the Western Front required skilled men in factories to make it function, men the army was compelled to give up, no matter what pressures there were on personnel. The initial call-up had not exempted skilled industrial workers and the factories that would provide munitions, guns and small arms were initially denuded of their staff. For example, the Renault factories that would eventually produce large numbers of tanks and aircraft engines, as well as other war materiel, had nearly 5000 workers employed in January 1914, but by October, this had fallen to 1539. A rapid return of skilled men from the front brought the numbers back to a pre-war level by January 1915, and the Renault factories would by the end of the war employ over 22,500 workers.[67] Despite returning a significant number of men from the front in 1915, the pressure on French industry to keep up with the increasing materiel demands of the army created an unceasing tension between the needs of the front and those of the home front. Artillery pieces and shells were needed in enormous numbers. For example, between 17 and 22 October 1917, VI Army's artillery fired just over 1.5 million shells at the German positions prior to the battle of Malmaison, including over 200,000 gas shells. The high-powered long range 155mm guns (155 GPF) used nearly 9000 shells, with giant 280mm mortars firing over 3000 shells during this period.

The demand for armaments prompted an ongoing reconsideration of the position of skilled workers, usually to the detriment of the army. For example, in August 1915, the *loi Dalbiez* was passed, which lost the army nearly 300,000 men who were returned to the factories.[68] In 1916, due to the increase in industrial production, another 250,000 men had to be returned to industry. The colonies also supported the war effort by supplying large numbers of workers for French factories and the rear area. Nearly 100,000 men came into France from Algeria and Tunisia with the other colonies sending a similar number in total. With the 37,000 men hired from China, nearly a quarter of a million Frenchmen were released to the army by these foreign workers. From mid-1915, women were drafted in to fill those industrial roles that they were able to; for example, in the Renault factory in Paris only 3 per cent of employees were women in 1914 but this had risen to over 30 per cent by 1918.[69] However, women did not have many of the required skills and men simply had to be released to the industrial sector; in 1918, there were half a million military-aged men working in industry and other critical war sectors such as the railways.

In addition, there were other areas where men simply could not be replaced, such as agriculture. Significant numbers of men had to be returned to their agricultural work to keep the agrarian economy going, and there were also considerable numbers of men given individual permission to attend to their small-holdings at various times in the farming year. These men remained theoretically open to recall to service in emergency but, of course, their military efficiency would have been degraded while away from the army. By January 1917, French agriculture was in a particularly parlous state and over 60,000 men had to be returned immediately to the agricultural sector, with the condition that they would be recalled for the April offensives. Between 1 April 1917 and 1 March 1918, 210,000 military men had to be permanently returned by the army to the agriculture sector, with a further 135,000 temporally ceded by the army to the sector.[70]

By harnessing both new technology in the shape of tanks and aircraft and developing doctrine that put an onus on minimising battle casualties, GQG and successive commanders-in-chief were able to manage the competing demands on manpower from within and outside of the army with some skill. There were some alarming moments for Pétain and GQG in early 1918 when it appeared there was a real danger of running out of military-aged men if the war went on into 1919, having mobilised such a great part of the male population. Fortunately, the coming of the Americans in great numbers in 1918 provided a reprieve, as did the arrival of significant numbers of tanks and aircraft on the front. These factors enabled the French army to conduct a series of successful offensives from mid-1918 that were carefully managed to ensure the minimum number of casualties. Nonetheless, casualties in the open warfare of 1918 were high, but despite this, there were only 54,000 fewer men in the French army in November 1918 than in March, demonstrating the success of GQG in handling its manpower in that year.[71]

By the time of the Armistice, the French army had 2,562,000 men on the Western Front, 41,000 men in Italy, 191,000 men in Serbia, Bulgaria and Romania, 6000 men in Asiatic Turkey, as well as garrisons in Morocco and the other colonies.[72] The final number of French casualties in the Great War was 674,700 men killed in action, 250,000 men who died of their injuries, 225,300 men missing who were presumed dead, with a further 175,000 who died from various illnesses, most notably from the flu epidemic of 1918 (although the highest number of deaths from this would occur after the war), giving a total of 1,325,000 dead from all causes.[73] France suffered greater per head of population casualties than any other country in the war, with the exception of Serbia, but this does not really convey the impact the war had on France. Casualties over the course of the war had fallen most heavily on those classes active at the time of mobilisation and the reserve classes that had been incorporated at the beginning of the campaign. In the class of 1914, 29.2 per cent of those mobilised were killed and the classes of 1911, 1912, 1913 and 1915 were similarly hit. Later classes mobilised were not as significantly denuded, unsurprisingly as they were fighting for a shorter period, but only the classes of 1918 and 1919 avoided very serious losses (8 per cent and 1.5 per cent killed of those mobilised respectively).[74] Thus, nearly one third of French men mobilised in the 19 to 24 age group in 1914 had been killed in the war. Along with the killed, there were also very large numbers of wounded men that were permanently invalided and would require state support; 90,000 soldiers had had surgical amputations by the end of 1919, with 50,000 of these receiving prosthetics. By 1 April 1920, there were nearly 200,000 Frenchmen receiving permanent invalid pensions, with a slightly larger number on temporary pensions, and both numbers would rise significantly in the following five years.[75]

Unsurprisingly, these casualties had a severe impact on French population growth between the world wars, particularly in relation to Germany, which to the French army seemed to indicate that mass conscription was not going to be the answer to the potential German threat. Military service was reduced over the years and by 1928 conscripts had to serve only one year before moving into the reserve formations. This was raised to two years' service in the active army in 1935 but there was no increase after this. The French military authorities' conception of the next war was that it would be protracted and thus require a national mobilisation on the scale of the Great War. The French army could not hope to equal the number of men in the German army and, therefore, other solutions needed to be found to address the numerical imbalance. This led to French national defence being based around destroying the German army in the fortresses of the Maginot Line and to other technology such as tanks and aircraft.[76] One mistake from the Great War that was not repeated was in relation to the non-white North African formations; in 1939, there were four North African divisions and several Moroccan regiments based in France itself, providing a strong professional core for homeland defence.

Although the mobilisation in 1939 did not go as smoothly as that of 1914, much of this can be attributed to the different technological environment, particularly in relation to air power and mechanisation. However, 5,000,000 men were eventually mobilized, and by 1940, the French army had 103 divisions on the north-eastern front in France. One mistake from 1914 that was repeated in 1939 was that too many skilled industrial workers were called up and had to be rapidly returned to their factories. However, the mobilisation itself was efficient enough and the collapse of the French armed forces in 1940 was due to their sclerotic command systems and being operationally out thought by the German army. The armistice with the Germans of June 1940 restricted the French state, now the Vichy regime, to an army of 100,000 men, although there were significantly more troops left in place defending French colonial possessions. As the Vichy regime gave very limited military support to the German army, there was no attempt to pursue conscription within France before the Allied invasions of 1944 and end of the regime.

After the end of World War II, France returned to a system of universal male conscription but continued to rely for the most part on the colonial army to guard the colonies, and it was an entirely professional force that fought the Indo-China War. Conscripts were used extensively in the Algerian War (1 November 1954–19 March 1962); a factor that increased the war's unpopularity in France and hastened its end. The time served under the colours was gradually reduced over a number of years until conscription was finally abolished in 2001. However, the spirit of the nation in arms is still potent in France's psyche and there were calls for return of conscription after the serious terrorist attacks in 2015. These calls were more about fostering a spirit of national commitment in the young, harking back to the Third Republic's idea of the army as the school of the republic, than about any military necessity. This is just one illustration of the fact that the appeal for the nation to rise up as one first made in 1793 remains strongly embodied in the very idea of the state and its relationship with its citizens in France today.

Notes

1   For other countries' experience, see Daniel Moran and Arthur Waldron (eds), *The People in Arms – Military Myth and National Mobilization Since the French Revolution* (Cambridge: CUP, 2006).
2   Hew Strachan, *European Armies and the Conduct of War* (London: Routledge, 1983), p. 38.
3   Lee Kennett, *The French Armies in the Seven Year's War* (Durham: Duke University Press, 1967), p. 76.
4   *Ibid.*, p. 83.
5   Charles Esdaile, *Napoleon's Wars – An International History 1803–1815* (London: Penguin, 2007), p. 7.
6   Kennet, *French Armies*, p. 77.
7   Kennet, *French Armies*, p. 80.

8   Kennet, *French Armies*, p. 78.
9   Strachan, *Armies*, p. 38.
10 Esdaile, *Napoleon's Wars*, pp. 118–19.
11 Esdaile, *Napoleon's Wars*, p. 120.
12 Aulard, F-A, *Recueil des Actes du Comité de Salut Public avec la Correspondance Officielle des Représentants en Mission et le Registre du Conseil Exécutif Provisoire* (Paris: Imprimerie Nationale, 1893), Vol. 6, 15 Août 1793–21, Septembre 1793, pp. 72–76. Clauses 6, 9, 10 and 12 to 18 omitted. Author's translation.
13 Rafe Blaufarb, *The French Army 1750–1820 Careers, Talent, Merit* (Manchester: MUP, 2002), p. 2.
14 Strachan, *Armies*, p. 40.
15 Strachan, *Armies*, p. 39.
16 Harold D. Blanton, 'Conscription in France during the era of Napoleon' in Donald Stoker, Frederick C. Schneid and Harold D. Blanton (eds), *Conscription in the Napoleonic Era – A Revolution in Military Affairs?* (London: Cass, 2009), pp. 6–23, pp. 9–10.
17 Esdaile, *Napoleon's Wars*, p. 9.
18 Esdaile, *Napoleon's Wars*, p. 131.
19 Frederick Schneid, 'Napoleonic Conscription and the Militarisation of Europe?' in Donald Stoker, Frederick C. Schneid and Harold D. Blanton (eds), *Conscription in the Napoleonic Era – A Revolution in Military Affairs?* (London: Cass, 2009), pp. 188–206, in particular p. 192.
20 Blaufarb, *French Army*, p. 164.
21 Blanton, *Conscription*, pp. 19–20.
22 David Chandler, *The Campaigns of Napoleon* (London: Weidenfeld & Nicolson, 1966), p. 421.
23 Chandler, *Campaigns*, p. 468.
24 Chandler, *Campaigns*, p. 754.
25 Blanton, *Conscription*, p. 16.
26 Blanton, *Conscription*, p. 17 and p. 18.
27 Blanton, *Conscription*, pp. 19–20.
28 Blaufarb, *French Army*, p. 194.
29 Blaufarb, *French Army*, p. 195.
30 Alan Forrest, *The Legacy of the French Revolutionary Wars – The Nation-in-Arms in French Republican Memory* (Cambridge: CUP, 2009), pp. 133–34.
31 Douglas Porch, *The March to the Marne – The French Army 1871–1914* (Cambridge: CUP, 1981), Chapter 10.
32 Mangin, Charles, *Comment finit la Guerre* (Paris: Plon, 1920), p. 255.
33 Mangin, *Comment finit la Guerre*, p. 256.
34 Charles Mangin, *La Force Noir* (Paris: Hachette, 1910).
35 Mangin, *Comment finit la Guerre*, p. 257.
36 *Ibid.*, p. 258.
37 SHD – 26N875-24, *Historique du Bataillon Mixte du Pacifique 1916–1919.*
38 Patrick Royer, "La guerre coloniale du Bani-Volta, 1915–1916" in *Autrepart* (2003), pp. 35–51.
39 General Palat, *La Grande Guerre sur le Front Occidental*, Vol. 1 (Paris: Le Chapelot, 1917), p. 211.
40 Anonymous, "L'Effort Militaire", p. 14.
41 *Ibid.*
42 Anonymous, "L'Effort Militaire", p. 15.
43 *Ibid.*
44 *Les Armées françaises dans la grande guerre* (Paris: 1937), Tome XI, p. v. French official history. All volumes referred to as AFGG hereafter.
45 AFGG I/4 (1934), Appendix 3, p. 553.

46 Louis Barthas (translated by Edward M. Strauss), *Poilu – The World War One Notebooks of Corporal Louis Barthas* (New Haven: YUP, 2014), p. 2.

47 Hew Strachan, *The First World War – Volume 1: To Arms* (Oxford: OUP, 2001), p. 155.

48 General Palat, *La Grande Guerre sur le Front Occidental*, Vol. 2 (Paris: Le Chapelot, 1917), p. 21.

49 Leonard Smith, *Between Mutiny and Obedience: The Case of the French 5th Infantry Division during World War 1* (Princeton: PUP, 1994), p. 38.

50 Pierre Boutroux, "Nos Effectifs – (Aout 1914 – Mars 1918)" in *La Revue de Paris* (15 August 1919), pp. 818–43, p. 819.

51 Colonel Le Hénaf and Capitaine Henri Bornecque, *Les Chemins de Fer Francaise et la Guerre* (Paris: Librairie Chapelot, 1922), p. 17.

52 *Ibid.*, p. 29.

53 *Ibid.*

54 Boutroux, "Nos Effectifs", p. 819 (Footnote 2), p. 820.

55 *Ibid.*, p. 823.

56 AFGG I/4, Appendix 4, p. 554.

57 Mangin, *Comment finit la Guerre*, p. 243.

58 Boutroux, "Nos Effectifs", pp. 821–22.

59 Mangin, *Comment finit la Guerre*, p. 245.

60 *Ibid.*, p. 243.

61 Anonymous, "L'Effort Militaire", p. 32.

62 Médecin Inspecteur Général Toubert, "Influence des modifications de l'armement ou de la tactique sur l'organisation du Service de Santé en guerre" in *Revue Militaire Francaise* (July 1935), pp. 311–22, p. 321.

63 *Ibid.*

64 *Ibid.*

65 Médecin Inspecteur Général Toubert, "Les Pertes subies par les Armées françaises pendant la guerre 1914–1918" in *La Revue d'Infanterie* (1921), pp. 305–9, p. 307.

66 Toubert, "Les Pertes", pp. 307–8.

67 Gilbert Hatry, *Renault, Usine de Guerre 1914–1918* (Paris: Editions Lafourcade 1978), p. 83.

68 Boutroux, "Nos Effectifs", p. 824.

69 Hatry, *Renualt,* p. 85.

70 Boutroux, "Nos Effectifs", p. 833.

71 Mangin, *Comment finit la Guerre*, p. 252.

72 Lt Col. Larcher, "Données statistiques concernant la Guerre 1914–1918" in *Revue Militaire Francaise*, (January and March 1933), pp. 190–204, pp. 291–303, p. 292.

73 Anonymous, "L'Effort Militaire", p. 31.

74 Anonymous, "L'Effort Militaire", p. 33.

75 Toubert, "Les Pertes", p. 308.

76 Eugenia C. Kiesling, *Arming Against Hitler – France and the Limits of Military Planning* (Lawrence: UPK, 1996).

CHAPTER 4

From Defeat to Rebirth

The Enlargement of the German Army in the Interwar Period (1918–39)

Dr Matthias Strohn

On 28 June 1919, the German delegation signed the Treaty of Versailles and World War I officially came to an end. The terms that the Germans had to agree to were harsh: Territorial losses and the acceptance of war guilt enraged the German population. In military terms, the treaty degraded Germany to a third-rank power, not only inferior to the strong Entente powers such as Britain or France but also to potentially hostile neighbours such as Poland and Czechoslovakia. The general staff was abolished, as were the military academies and schools. The army's armaments were limited, and it was not allowed to sustain modern weaponry, including tanks, aircraft or gas. Conscription was abolished and the army was restricted to 100,000 men of long-serving volunteers. Officers had to serve for a minimum of 25 years, while the other ranks had to enlist for at least 12 years; this was to prevent the creation of a reserve that the Germans might be able to use in the future. In the military context of Europe at the time, the consequences were grave: Germany did no longer have an army but merely a para-military defence force, and this force was by no means able to stop an invasion of Germany by potential enemies, let alone take the offensive and invade other countries. And yet, this small, badly equipped and under-funded army became the nucleus for one of the most impressive military machines that the world has ever seen. Only 20 years after the Treaty of Versailles, the *Wehrmacht* marched to war conquering most of Europe, before finally suffering one of the most drastic and comprehensive defeats ever witnessed. How could such a small military force as the *Reichswehr*[1] be grown into a fighting machine of approximately 4.7 men within a few years? How had the army prepared for such an enlargement and what were the political parameters within which the army operated? What difficulties were encountered and how were these – if at all – overcome? These are the underlying question that this chapter will answer.

The general view in Germany in the interwar period was that this time was just a temporary period of weakness and that, at some point in the future, a new war would have to be fought that would reverse the outcome of World War I. In particular, the loss of territory in the east and the existence of a Polish state on former German territory was a thorn in the national German flesh. Regaining these territories was, therefore, part of the national agenda of the Weimar Republic and the Third Reich. And yet, the first step to a reborn, mighty German military machine was the realisation that Germany had actually been beaten in World War I and that the army had to adapt to the new political and military realities of the Weimar Republic. This might sound trivial today, but it was an important matter in the immediate aftermath of the war. The idea that Germany had been stabbed in the back by socialists, Jews and other groups working against the established monarchical order of Wilhelmine Germany could not really be upheld by leading military personnel who knew the military reality of the autumn of 1918. Nevertheless, the immense impact that the German surrender would have was not clear to everybody. The period between the end of hostilities in November 1918 and 7 May 1919, the day when the terms of the Treaty of Versailles were handed to the Germans, was a time of self-delusion among civilians and military personnel. Had the army not achieved all its war aims? Germany had not been invaded by an enemy and the country still existed as one united Reich. It seemed that the war had ended in some sort of geo-political stalemate rather than a real German defeat. Victor Klemperer, a scholar whose published diaries have become famous in Germany, noted that in Munich there had been hardly any animosity between the Bavarian population and the occupying French forces between the end of hostilities and May 1919. Klemperer wrote in his diary that 'They [the French] were neither full of hatred nor big-headed, just content and pleased by the way they have been received by the local population. And this was understandable, because there were no hostile looks, just sympathetic ones.'[2] Of course, internal German political issues also played a role here. The catholic Bavaria claimed, as Klemperer put it, that 'that war had been the fault of the Prussian Empire. The empire did not exist anymore. Bavaria was free and why should the newly created free state not exist in close comradeship with the French Republic?'[3] When the terms of the treaty were handed to the Germans on 7 May 1919 it caused an outcry in the country. In several meetings, high-ranking officers even argued for a new call to arms. Among them was General Walther Reinhardt, the first *Chef der Heeresleitung* (commander-in-chief of the army) and the most senior German officer. They knew that the result could only be a *finis Germaniae*, but they were willing to accept this in order to uphold German national honour, which would form the nucleus for a rebirth of a mighty Germany.[4] This self-delusion did not stop after the signing of the Treaty of Versailles. Even Generaloberst Hans von Seeckt, *Chef der Heeresleitung* between 1920 and 1926, seemed to have struggled with the new realities. Seeckt had fought World War I predominately on the Eastern Front and in the Near

East, and his view of a future war was thus influenced by these theatres of war. He supported a small professional army over a mass army based on conscription. Yet, in January 1921, Seeckt wrote a memorandum entitled *Grundlegende Gedanken für den Wiederaufbau unserer Wehrmacht* (Basic Thoughts for the Reconstruction of our Army) in which he elaborated on a possible enlargement of the army. He had outlined a plan for an 'organic', long-term enlargement of the field army to a strength of 63 divisions. Together with auxiliary forces and replacement units, this army would comprise 2.8m soldiers.[5]

Naturally, in the context of the time, this was an illusionary figure, and yet, it took another event two years later to really show everybody how defenceless Germany had become and that it was no longer the master of its own fate. On 10 January 1923, French and Belgian forces occupied the Ruhr area, Germany's industrial heartland. The official reason was that Germany had fallen behind with the payment of reparations that had been agreed to in the Treaty of Versailles.[6] The German federal government under Chancellor Dr Wilhelm Cuno called for passive resistance, which developed into a general strike, and stopped supplying the French and Belgians with any goods.[7] After nine months, Germany eventually succumbed to the pressure; facing political problems, economic collapse and the threat of civil war, Germany called off passive resistance. In August 1924, a conference was held in London that had to decide on the Dawes Plan, which had been developed in order to bring clarity into the matter of reparation. At the conference, the Germans demanded that the hostile troops be withdrawn from the Ruhr. The new French prime minister, Edouard Herriot, gave in to international pressure and agreed to the withdrawal. This practically ended the Ruhr crisis, although it was agreed that the French would be allowed to stay for another year owing to internal French political pressure on the prime minister. Accordingly, the French started withdrawing their troops from the Ruhr area on 14 July 1925. It was this event and the inability of the German military to stop an invasion of German territory that opened peoples' eyes. Hans von Seeckt expressed this view in an article, published in the *Militärwochenblatt*, the leading military journal at the time, on 15 January 1923. He stated that:

> The Frenchman has occupied the Ruhr area. The Lithuanians have occupied the Memel area. Instinctively, the hand goes to the place where the sword used to be. It only grabs air: we are unarmed. Today, one cannot conduct a war with flails and hayforks....[8]

In a letter written on 16 February 1923, Seeckt stated that he saw the futility of military action and that Germany would not engage in active fighting. The *Reichswehr* leadership had to acknowledge that the army was not fit to face the French army – or any invasion force for that matter – in battle. The *Heereswaffenamt*, which was in charge of the acquisition of equipment and materiel for the army, stated on 8 May 1923 that 'our current stock of ammunition of the *Reichswehr* and illegally kept ammunition is so small that we are currently absolutely unable to go to war'.[9] At the end of May, the *Heereswaffenamt* distributed a report on the available ammunition. Only 47 million rounds of infantry ammunition were stockpiled, approximately half of what the Treaty of Versailles allowed. Moreover, there were only 107 rounds of ammunition available for every piece of artillery, and the artillery was very weak anyway. In accordance with the treaty, the German army only had 84 guns of the medium 10.5cm calibre. Summing up the situation, one author, using the pseudonym Lucius Cincinnatus, wrote in the *Militärwochenblatt* that:

> ...the French could march into Germany wherever they wanted to. Taking our military powerlessness into consideration, it would be half madness to engage them with force of arms.... As hard as this realistic truth may sound to the friend of the fatherland, it has to be uttered, since one can hear the strangest opinions about the German possibilities of defence even from otherwise responsible people.[10]

As a result of the events, the *Truppenamt*, the disguised German general staff, prepared two studies that dealt with possible German reactions and an enlargement of the army to meet the French forces.[11] These studies carried the code names *Sommerarbeit* (Summer Work) and *Winterarbeit* (Winter Work), respectively. *Winterarbeit* dealt with the creation of a *Notheer* (emergency army) on the basis of the available manpower, weapons and materiel. The question of manpower was of secondary importance because, at this time, enough trained men with combat experience from World War I were still available. In the years to come, the question of trained manpower would become one of the most burning questions for the army in the light of a possible rearmament. In 1923, however, the discussion centred more around the issue of available weapons and materiel. In *Winterarbeit*, it was envisaged that units and formations would be set up successively in the different military districts, as long as weapons and materiel were available. The *Truppenamt* reckoned that the army might then comprise 18 infantry divisions and three cavalry divisions, which would be supported and reinforced by weak reserves and the border guards. In these plans, the field army would have a strength of about 450,000 men. The *Truppenamt* came to the conclusion that this army would not be in a position to conduct a 'serious war (*ernsthafter Krieg*)', not least because it would not be able to sustain a force of 21 divisions and replenish lost and destroyed materiel. As a consequence, the *Truppenamt* concluded that this army would only be able to 'solve easy tasks, limited in time and space' and that it would not be able to achieve victory over a determined and strong enemy.

The second study, *Sommerarbeit*, focused on the mobilisation of a large army that would be able to withstand a strong and well-equipped enemy. The army reckoned that a force of 35 infantry divisions and three cavalry divisions, supported by auxiliary forces such as border guards, was needed for this task. Again, the main problem was not the mobilisation of manpower but the question of materiel. This problem was increased by the demand that the units and formations had to be raised in the military districts simultaneously. A more gradual process would allow the enemy to defeat the army while it was still being increased and reinforced. Only if the strong army could be formed under these prerequisites, the *Truppenamt* was confident that the forces 'stood a good chance against a strong enemy' in a defensive war.

The problem was that such a build-up was impossible. On 1 June 1923, the operations' branch of the *Truppenamt* wrote a statement on the chances for *Sommerarbeit*.[12] Not enough weapons were available to equip the army, even if illegally kept stocks were taken into consideration. Putting the industry on a war footing would take time and this luxury would not be given by a determined enemy who could simply march into Germany or, as was still the case in the summer of 1923, actually occupied the industrial heartland of Germany. Manpower problems were now also expected. It was reckoned that 1m soldiers were needed to meet the manpower demands of the army. This figure included the field army, replacements and auxiliary forces. During the mobilisation phase and the first four weeks of the campaign, the army would have to rely on volunteers; only after this period would drafted soldiers be available to be sent to the units. Time for a thorough training would not be available and the army would have to rely mainly on veterans from World War I. Calculating the number of reserves, the study showed that, at first glance, a large enough manpower pool was available until 1927. However, the *Truppenamt* concluded that the previous training and experience of the reserves would not be enough to cope with the increased demands of modern war. As a consequence, the *Truppenamt* concluded that, with the means at hand, *Sommerarbeit* could not be carried out and Germany was practically defenceless.

The plans for *Sommerarbeit* were regarded as unachievable; they belonged in the realms of utopia, so the establishment of the *Winterarbeit* emergency army became the primary aim of the army's internal planning. However, it soon became apparent that even this army of 21 divisions could not be built-up and sustained by the *Reichswehr* and German industry. On 19 May 1927, the *Truppenamt* ordered the offices of the *Reichswehr* ministry to take stock on all matters of mobilisation. The *Heereswaffenamt* worked out a programme for the build-up of the so-called *A-Heer* (*Aufstellungsheer* or 'build-up army') of 21 divisions, as outlined in the *Winterarbeit* of 1923.[13] The aim was to build-up supplies of the most important goods for a period of five months. The *Reichswehr* had already increased its orders from industry from 35 million Reichsmark in 1924 to 50 million in 1927, but it soon became apparent that this was not enough to meet the demands for an army of 21 divisions.[14] Therefore, the *Truppenamt* reduced the number of divisions of the *A-Heer* in February 1928 from 21 to 16 divisions, and the calculations for the necessary supply was now based on the assumption of an even smaller army of 15 divisions.[15] This concept of a 16-division army (*Notstandsheer* or 'emergency army') remained in place until 1930, when the new rearmament programme saw a return to an army of 21 divisions.[16]

The army also realised that it had to ally itself more closely with its political masters than had been done hitherto. Seeckt had adopted a strict isolationist approach and had tried to keep the army away from politics and the political masters as far as possible. He feared that a politicisation of the army would bring internal unrest and he also believed that unreliable politicians, such as the Social Democrats, could not be trusted with military secrets. He was convinced that sooner or later information would be leaked to the Entente about the army's illegal practices of stockpiling ammunition, running paramilitary training courses and other measures implemented to alleviate some of the pressures placed on the army by the restrictions of the Treaty of Versailles. The most prominent of these actions was the increased military cooperation with the Soviet Union. In 1925, the *Reichswehr* opened a secret air-force training school at Lipetsk, in which 240 airmen and also ground crew were trained between 1925 and 1933. In 1926, the *Reichswehr* signed a treaty resulting in the establishment of the tank school at Kama and in 1928 it opened a gas warfare school at Tomka. The army was not able to keep these engagements secret for long and, finally, it was pushed into opening up to its civilian masters on these matters. On 5 December 1926, the *Vorwärts*, the Social Democrats' newspaper, printed an article stating that the *Reichswehr* had established close links with the Soviet Red Army,[17] and on 6 December 1926, the Social Democratic Party (SPD) faction in the Reichstag handed over materiel to the defence minister, Oto Gessler, which supported these allegations. As a consequence, Gessler and the senior army leadership briefed representatives of the government parties and members of the Social Democrats' faction of the Reichstag on the existence of paramilitary organisations and the cooperation with the Soviet Union. Chancellor Wilhelm Marx and Foreign Minister Gustav Stresemann made clear that further disclosure of the *Reichswehr*'s plans and actions would result in major international dispute and asked the audience not to mention these again publicly, because they undermined the effort of the army to prepare for a future rearmament.

The cooperation of the audience showed that the fears of Seeckt had been exaggerated and, over the years, it had become apparent that the army needed the government's support if its plans for enlargement were to be successful. A pure military solution proposed by military men would not be acceptable or workable within the political framework of the Weimar Republic. Only a close cooperation between the military and the civilian leadership could ensure that Germany could prepare for a future rearmament. Accordingly, the army slowly left Seeckt's isolationist course and tried to connect with the civilian leadership of the Reich. Already in 1922, the *Truppenamt* had drawn up plans to establish a defence council (*Reichsverteidigungsrat*), which would coordinate the military and civilian aspects of home defence.[18] Seeckt's scepticism meant that nothing came of these proposals, but the idea was revived by General Wilhelm Heye, Seeckt's successor as *Chef der Heeresleitung*. Between November 1926 and February 1927, Heye repeatedly suggested the formation of a defence council to the cabinet but was met with reservations from the civilian side, who feared that they might be used by the military for their purposes. However, eventually, the mood changed and on 14 October 1932, General Kurt von Schleicher, the new *Reichswehr* minister, issued the 'regulations for the preparation of the Reich defence',[19] which meant the factual establishment of a Reich defence council. It met only once after Hitler's assumption of power in January 1933. The meeting was chaired by the *Reichswehr* minister instead of the chancellor and brought together the heads of the army and the navy with the ministries of foreign and interior affairs, finance, economy and the newly created ministry of propaganda under Goebbels and the air ministry under Göring. The only session of the council enabled the constitution of a working committee of all the ministries of the Reich (*Arbeitsauschuß der Referenten für die Reichsverteidigung*, from 11 March 1935 onwards called *Reichsverteidigungsausschuß*). It was here where the important work was done. Moreover, owing to the amorphous structure of the Nazi state, many decisions were taken in direct consultations between the involved ministries. From a military point of view, the committee strengthened the position of the armed forces in relation to the civilian ministries. Up to this point, the civilian authorities had only had to support the *Reichswehr* in its efforts to prepare Germany for a future war; now these authorities were officially obliged to assist in any possible way. However, this positive outlook changed on 4 September 1938, when the *Reichsverteidigungsrat* was reorganised. The heads of the three services of the armed forces remained in the council, but it was no longer chaired by the supreme soldier of the armed forces but by Hermann Göring. This move showed once more what had become apparent by this time: Despite the official rhetoric that the Nazi state was based on the two pillars of the Nazi party and the armed forces, the party did not tolerate any competition when it came to the ruling of the state. To continue the strengthening of the civilian grip on the armed forces, the council, now renamed *Ministerrat für die Reichsverteidigung* (Ministerial Council for the Reich's Defence), decreed that in times of war the administration of the military districts would be passed from the military commanders to the local party leaders (Gauleiter). This was a clear break from the practice of World War I, when the deputy commanding general had held the military and civilian powers of the military district in his hands.

The theoretical preparation for an increase of the army went hand in glove with the conceptual development of the German army to prepare intellectually for a new war. On 1 December 1919, Seeckt, as head of the *Truppenamt*, launched a programme to analyse the German army's experiences during World War I. In a directive issued to all major *Reichswehr* departments, he sketched out a programme to form 57 army committees that would deal with questions of tactics, doctrine and equipment.[20] Every department of the Reichswehr ministry had to contribute to this programme. Responsibility for collecting and evaluating the work of the committees was given to the training office (*Ausbildungsabteilung*) T4 of the army. Its members could recommend changes to the subjects of the committees and suggest the appointment of additional experts. As a result, the training office would initiate a further 29 studies on subjects which had not been covered by Seeckt's directive of 1 December 1919.[21] Including the serving and former officers working on the questions of aerial warfare, over 500 of the most experienced German officers were involved in the evaluation of the experiences of World War I. Much of the source material dealing with the creation of manuals for the *Reichswehr* has been lost, but the tactical studies still available from the ground forces show a clear link between the committees' work and the new regulations and manuals that were issued from 1921 onwards. The most important regulation issued under Seeckt was *Heeresdienstvorschrift 487 Führung und Gefecht der verbundenen Waffen* (F.u.G.), published in two parts in 1921 and 1923, respectively. This regulation did not restrict itself to the current state of the army. It was clear that the new doctrine was intended to be the foundation for an enlarged army and it did not concentrate on the small *Reichswehr* and its inadequate training possibilities and equipment. In the introduction to the F.u.G., Seeckt made clear that the regulation was based on the army of a 'modern, military great power' and not on the army of 100,000 men as prescribed by the Treaty of Versailles.[22] He was convinced that 'Only if we can keep alive the memory of the fighting means, which have been taken away from us (aircraft, heavy artillery, tanks, etc.), will we find ways and means to resist an enemy, even if we do not have them at our disposal.' The special character of the F.u.G., i.e. the concentration on principles rather than detailed elaboration on every aspect of warfare, and the general orientation towards a modern, strong army rather than towards the weak *Reichswehr*, meant that the regulation would still be relevant in the event of Germany regaining its military sovereignty. The same approach can be found in the regulations which superseded the F.u.G, the *Heeresdienstvorschrift 300. Truppenführung* (Unit Command). It was issued in two parts in 1933 and 1934, respectively, and remained in service until 1945. It has been called 'the most influential doctrinal manual ever written' and 'it also represents one of the most thoughtful examinations of the conduct of operations and leadership ever written'.[23] The manual was intended to provide a formula to serve as a basis for the training and education of the German army and the preparation of the entire army for any type of future conflict. Both the F.u.G. and the *Truppenführung* stressed the importance of the conceptual component of fighting power, in particular for an army that could expect to be numerically weaker than the enemy. The explanation for the tactical and also operational successes of the German *Wehrmacht* in World War II can be found in these regulations.

On 3 February 1933, only a few days after his appointment to chancellor, Hitler revealed his political aims to some selected members of the *Reichswehr*. In his elaborations, Hitler made clear that war was unavoidable in the long run, because he aimed at 'the conquest of living space in the east and its ruthless germanisation (Germanisierung)'.[24] Despite the disclosure of Hitler's intentions, actual military planning did not change instantly because the *Reichswehr* was not yet in a state to fulfil the *Führer's* demands. As a first step towards full rearmament, the decision was taken in December 1933 to enlarge the peace-time army to 300,000 men organised in 21 divisions; a figure that had been mentioned by the *Reichswehr* since the 1920s.[25] In the case of war, this new army would be able to mobilise 33 field divisions and 30 reserve divisions. The date for the announcement was not a coincidence. On 2 February 1932, the Conference for the Reduction and Limitation of Armaments had started in Geneva. Germany made the point that it was practically defenceless and surrounded by countries with strong militaries and it demanded full equality for its armed forces. In reality, this demand equated to a call for German rearmament, because the other nations were unwilling to reduce their military forces. The French, in particular, rejected the German claim, but by the middle of April 1932, the negotiations had reached a point that represented a modification of the Treaty of Versailles, which in principle, although not in its scope, contained all elements that the *Reichswehr* envisaged for a strengthening of Germany's military power: introducing more graduated periods of service, supplementing the standing army with a militia and equipping the army with modern weaponry. This should guarantee equality in a system which gave security to all nations. Eventually, the worsening political situation in Germany and Hitler's assumption of power on 30 January 1933 prevented a continuation of the talks and the conference failed. Germany withdrew from the conference in October 1933. Despite the eventual failure, it was obvious that the Treaty of Versailles was dead and that Germany would be able to rearm.

The following events have to be seen in this light and in the understanding that the international community as a whole would not object to German actions that undermined the Treaty of Versailles. Thus, on 16 March 1936, conscription was reintroduced and the strength of the peace-time army was to be increased to 36 divisions. Already a few days earlier, on 7 March 1936, the Rhineland had been remilitarised. This was of considerable importance for the future military planning of the *Wehrmacht* because additional resources had become available, especially the manpower pool for the envisaged increases of the armed forces. Also, the remilitarisation of the Rhineland meant that the Ruhr area, with its factories vital for the German war effort, was less endangered than it had been hitherto. The view that this development had improved Germany's military situation was shared by foreign powers. The British army had argued on 27 July 1935 that 'Once Germany has reoccupied and fortified the Rhineland, it is doubtful whether France, with her wasting man-power, would risk a land invasion of Germany. The French air threat to the Ruhr would be balanced by the German air threat to Paris and the French industrial regions.'[26]

With the extension of the duration of military service to two years, the *Wehrmacht* was able to increase its strength to 520,000 men by the end of 1936.[27] The *Wehrmacht* now comprised 36 infantry and three tank divisions, which were, however, not at full strength. A conflict became apparent in the military leadership: Ludwig Beck, the chief of the general staff, had argued for a gradual enlargement of the army. Only if enough personnel and materiel for new units was available should these be formed. This would ensure a gradual growth and one which would not reduce the overall quality of the army. The problem was that this approach would take time, one thing that Hitler was not willing to tolerate. So, Hitler and parts of the organisation office of the *Truppenamt* argued for cadre units that would be filled up whenever possible. On paper, this would produce a strong army more quickly. The result was that while the nominal strength of an infantry division was 14,300, the real average strength was in the region of 10,000, and, accordingly, the army was considerably smaller than it appeared in the official order of battle. Despite these insufficiencies, Hitler demanded in 1936 that the rearmament should be accelerated. Accordingly, the *Oberkommando des Heeres* (supreme command of the army, or *OKH*, the re-named *Truppenamt*) reckoned with a peace-time army of 830,000 men from October 1936 onwards.[28] Even more significant was the planned increase of the wartime army. While this force had comprised 54 divisions in the 1935 plans, it was now anticipated that the army would increase to 102 divisions with over 4.6m men of which 2,421,000 would serve in the field army. This intention presented the *Wehrmacht* with a number of significant problems. Interestingly, these issues were mentioned in the *OKH*'s plans, but solutions to them could not be found. For instance, the *OKH* was aware of the fact that the increased enlargement would create an actual deficit of 72,600 officers. To alleviate this problem, 'extraordinary measures' had to be taken, but nobody knew what these might be and it was, therefore, stated that this 'question is currently being dealt with' by the *OKH*. Between October 1933 and October 1935, the officer corps had already increased from 3800 officers to 6533 – an increase of 72 per cent. Even this increase – modest to the envisaged large increase in the October 1936 plans – had been achievable only by bringing into the officer corps individuals and groups formerly outside the corps. Thus, all officers of local defence units had been incorporated into the *Reichswehr* on active duty as members of the so-called supplementary officer corps after March 1935. This group, comprising 3073 officers, consisted mainly of older age groups. In the summer of 1935, 1200 police officers were also transferred to active service in the army and 400 experienced non-commissioned officers had been promoted to officers in the summer of 1934.[29] In December 1933, Ludwig Beck had considered 7 per cent of the total personnel strength as the final aim for officers. In 1936, this number stood at a bare 1.3 per cent, and internal calculations and predictions concluded that the shortfall would only be eliminated in 1950.[30] Using some interesting mathematical explanation, the 7 per cent benchmark was dropped when the illusionary figures became known.

Similarly, it was obvious that the materiel demands of the enlarged *Wehrmacht* could not be met in the near future.[31] For instance, it was anticipated that the

Wehrmacht on the whole would be lacking 40,000 lorries. Initially, it was suggested that these could be requisitioned from the civilian world, but it soon became obvious to the *OKH* that this would bring economic life in Germany to a standstill. For the tanks, the *OKH* anticipated that only the Mark I and II tanks would be available in sufficient numbers. For the better armed and armoured Mark III and IV tanks, the *OKH* expected deficits of 35 per cent and 80 per cent, respectively. These difficulties did not go unnoticed by foreign authorities. On 30 November 1938, the British Military Attaché in Berlin, Colonel Mason MacFarlane, reported that the *Wehrmacht* was facing severe difficulties.[32] The main problem, as he saw it, was the rapid expansion of the German army, which did not leave enough time to train officers and NCOs sufficiently. 'The army,' Mason MacFarlane stated, 'has continually been asked to run before it should, in theory, have been able to walk.' However, the military attaché was convinced that the German army would overcome these difficulties. '…the German army will be passing through its last period of real difficulty, during which war would take it at a very considerable disadvantage, in the winter of 1939–40.' After that winter, the army would have reached its full strength. From that period onwards, the size of the wartime army would depend on the rate of armament production rather than on the level of training of new recruits.

The problems were aggravated by the fact that the army now stood in competition to the navy and the newly established air force. For instance, the navy increased its manpower from 15,000 men of all ranks in 1933 to 78,892 by the outbreak of the war, a fivefold increase in barely seven years. In particular, the naval build-up also meant that the army was now competing more and more for raw materiels and resources. Building a fleet is costly and ships need steel – a finite resource that would now not be available for army equipment. The annual expenditure in ship construction rose from 49.6 million Reichsmark in 1932 to 603.1 million in 1937.[33] A fierce inter-services struggle for raw materiels was the result. On 15 April 1939, a memorandum written in preparation for a report by the commander-in-chief of the army to Hitler shows how the army high command viewed the situation:

> The present situation resulting from the shortage of bar steel is similar in certain respects to that before the First World War. At that time the creation of the three army corps, which were not available in the first year of the war to bring about a quick decision, was not possible, because parliament refused the necessary funds. Today the army is being denied the necessary quantities of bar steel to equip itself with modern offensive weapons. The consequences could be similar to those of 1914.[34]

These difficulties did not stop Hitler from pursuing his political aims. On 5 November 1937, Hitler gave a talk to the commanders-in-chief of the three services and leading politicians in the Reich chancellery.[35] Although the meeting was originally designed to resolve the quarrels over the distribution of raw materiel among the different services, Hitler soon launched into a monologue lasting over two hours on Germany's necessity to expand its territory by use of force within the following few years. He argued that time was not on Germany's side and that it would be imperative to act by 1943–45 at the latest. The relative strength of the German army would decrease from that time onwards, since other states would increasingly enlarge their forces. Declining birth rates, not least as a result of the losses of World War I, and the ageing of the Nazi 'movement' and its leaders were added points to underline what he described as his 'unalterable determination to solve the German problem of space by 1943–45 at the latest'. Hitler said it would become necessary to strike sooner if France became enveloped by internal conflict or if it had to fight a war against another power, making it impossible to engage in military action against Germany. In either case, the time would also be ripe to attack Czechoslovakia. Moreover, Hitler saw the distinct possibility that Britain and France could go to war with Italy over matters in Spain. In this case, Hitler was determined to attack Czechoslovakia and Austria immediately – even in 1938 when rearmament was still in full swing. This action would secure the eastern flank for possible future operations in the west and would enable the Germans to make use of the armament production in Czechoslovakia. Although Hitler talked for two hours, he did not convince his audience, and he was obviously under no illusion about the negative responses.[36] What worried the generals was not the use of force itself, but its premature application. In May 1937, Beck had refused an order to draw up plans for executing *Fall Otto* (Case Otto), the German plan for an invasion of Austria, on the grounds that such a move might cause a world war before Germany was ready for such a conflict. He finally resigned in August 1938 because he believed that Germany was still not ready for a major European war that would, in his view, follow the annexation of Czechoslovakia he had been ordered to prepare by Hitler.

When World War II started on 1 September 1939, the *Wehrmacht* was, by the judgement of its military and political masters, not ready and the rearmament of Germany had not been fully achieved. Owing to the rapid expansion, the army, navy and air force were all lacking in materiel and equipment. From a pure personnel perspective, the army was prepared: On 1 September 1939, the field army comprised 2,758,000 men, which was more than the envisaged strength of 2,421,000. Instead of 44 divisions, the active army now stood at 35 infantry, three mountain, six armoured and four light divisions, as well as four motorised infantry divisions and one cavalry brigade. In total, the army mobilised 103 formations for war. However, the army was really a one-shot weapon without structural depth: The infantry divisions in the field army were divided into four different categories. In peacetime, the 35 divisions of the first category had 78 per cent active-duty personnel with only very few reservists. In contrast, the mobilised 16 divisions of the second category had only 6 per cent active-duty personnel, but 83 per cent of their reservists had had at least nine months' training. The 20 divisions of the third category were composed mainly of reservists from the supplementary reserve units of the army and of men who had previously served in the militia – some of them had received their military training during World War I. The 14 divisions of the last category contained 21 per cent of *Wehrmacht* reservists who had recently received their military training, but the bulk were reservists from supplementary reserve units with rudimentary or outdated military training.[37] In order to produce an army that looked impressive on paper, the number of divisions had been increased; breadth was seen as more important than depth with regards to men and materiel. As a consequence, not even the divisions of the first category were at full strength when the war broke out and the tank divisions had to make do primarily with under-armed and under-armoured Mark I and II tanks, which were easier, cheaper and faster to produce than the Mark III or IV. Within the organisational structure, reserves in equipment were hardly available and, right from the beginning of the war, the army had to fight hard in order to keep its units at full combat strength and with the necessary amount of materiel.

The stunning victories of the *Wehrmacht* in the first half of World War II were achieved despite this and were based mainly on the conceptual preparation of the long-serving professional soldiers and officers of the *Reichswehr*. The Treaty of Versailles had intended to prevent the Germans from creating reserves by mandating that the soldiers in the *Reichswehr* had to be long-serving volunteers. They tried to avoid the same mistake that the French had made after the defeat of Prussia in 1806, when the Prussians were able to create a reserve by calling up soldiers for short periods of time before releasing them again so that new recruits could be trained. By avoiding this, the victorious powers of World War I made it possible for the Germans to create what became known as a *Führerheer* or army of leaders: The long periods of service meant that all soldiers of the small *Reichswehr* could be trained and educated intensively. The aim was that every soldier should be able to fulfil the role and duties of a soldier at least two ranks above him.

Compared to their enemies, the German soldiers did not have superiority in men and, especially, materiel, but they understood better how to use what was available to them. Maybe this is the most important lesson of the German rearmament in the interwar period: At least as important as materiel and equipment, perhaps even more important, is the conceptual preparation for war. To say it with Virgil: *Mens agitat molem* – The mind moves the matter. It is perhaps no wonder that this phrase is still the motto of the German armed forces staff college today.

Notes

1   Officially, the Reichswehr was comprised of the Reichsheer (army) of 100,000 men and the Reichsmarine (navy) of 15,000 men. In German terminology, and in line with the traditional view of Germany as a land power, the term Reichswehr was often used for the army. In March 1935, the armed forces were re-named the *Wehrmacht*. This chapter will concentrate on the army as Germany's main military arm.

2   Victor Klemperer, *Man möchte immer weinen und lachen in einem. Revolutionstagebuch 1919* (Berlin, 2015), pp. 31–32.

3   *Ibid.*

4 For the crucial meeting see William Mulligan, *The Creation of the Modern German Army. General Walther Reinhardt and the Weimar Republic, 1914–1930* (Oxford, 2005), p. 101.

5 Bundesarchiv-Militärarchiv (BA-MA), Seeckt papers, N 247/139, folio 4–5.

6 For the Ruhr occupation, see Conan Fischer, *The Ruhr Crisis, 1923–1924* (Oxford, 2003).

7 Auswärtiges Amt (ed.), *Aktenstücke über den französisch-belgischen Einmarsch in das Ruhrgebiet* (Berlin, 1923), p. 26.

8 Hans von Seeckt, "Germania sub pondere crescit" in *Militärwochenblatt* (1922–23), Vol. 107, No. 24.

9 BA-MA RH 8/v. 904, p. 7.

10 Lucius Cincinnatus, "Militärisches zur Besetzung des Ruhrgebietes und des Kehler Brückenkopfes" in *Militärwochenblatt* (1922–23), Vol. 107, No. 26.

11 For both studies see *Vortragsnotizen für die Besprechung mit den Chefs der Wehrkreiskommandos am 14. Mai 1923*, BA-MA RH 8/v. 911.

12 *Die personelle Mobilmachungsvorbereitung im Rahmen eines Rüstungsprogramms*, RH 12 – 1/25, folio 41–46.

13 *Die Entwicklung der Dienststelle für Wehrwirtschaft im Waffenamt 1924–1933*, BA-MA RH 8/v. 1516, folio 501–502.

14 For the figures see Ernst Willi Hansen, *Reichswehr und Industrie. Rüstungswirtschaftliche Zusammenarbeit und wirtschaftliche Mobilmachungsvorbereitungen 1923–1932* (Boppard, 1978), p. 119.

15 See *Truppenamt. betr. Rüstungsprogramm*, 2 February 1928, BA-MA RH 8/v. 892.

16 Michael Geyer, "Das zweite Rüstungsprogramm, 1930–1934" in *Militärgeschichtliche Mitteilungen*, Vol. 17 (1975), pp. 125–72.

17 "Sowjetgranaten für Reichswehrgeschütze" in *Vorwärts*, 5 December 1926.

18 For a general overview of the development of the defence council, see Jun Nakata, *Der Grenz- und Landesschutz in der Weimarer Republik 1918–1933. Die geheime Aufrüstung und die deutsche Gesellschaft* (Freiburg 2002), pp. 339–41; Jürgen Förster, *Die Wehrmacht im NS-Staat. Eine strukturgeschichtliche Analyse* (Munich, 2007), pp. 19–34; and Rudolf Absolon, *Die Wehrmacht im Dritten Reich*, five volumes, Vol. IV, *5. Februar 1938 bis 31. August 1939* (Boppard am Rhein, 1979), pp. 1–5.

19 Michael Geyer, *Aufrüstung oder Sicherheit: Die Reichswehr in der Krise der Machtpolitik, 1924–1936*, (Wiesbaden 1980), p. 388

20 BA-MA RH 2/2275, folio 33–37. On this matter, see James Corum, *The Roots of Blitzkrieg. Hans von Seeckt and German Military Reform* (Lawrence, 1992), pp. 37–38.

21 Corum, *The Roots of Blitzkrieg*, p. 38.

22 *H.Dv 487. Führung und Gefecht der verbundenen Waffen (F.u.G.)*, Berlin 1921, p. 3.

23 Williamson Murray, "Leading the Troops: A German Manual of 1933" in *Marine Corps Gazette* (September 1999), p. 95.

24 See the notes of Generalleutnant Liebmann, in BA-MA MSG 1/1688.

25 Wilhelm Deist, "The Rearmament of the Wehrmacht" in Militärgeschichtliches Forschungsamt (eds), *Germany and the Second World War* (nine volumes), Vol. I, *The Build-up of German Aggression* (Oxford, 1990), pp. 373–537, here pp. 399–401.

26 TNA WO 190/344, Notes on probable military results of a war between Germany and the anti-German bloc (France, Russia, Italy, Czechoslovakia), folio 2.

27 For the enlargement during this period see Herbert Schottelius and Gustav-Adolf Caspar, "Die Organisation des Heeres 1933–1939" in Militärgeschichtliches Forschungsamt (eds), *Handbuch zur deutschen Militärgeschichte* (six volumes), Vol. IV, *Wehrmacht und Nationalsozialismus 1933–1945* (Munich, 1983), pp. 299–307.

28 BA-MA RH 15/70, folio 189–202.
29 For the numbers, see Deist, p. 427.
30 Deist, p. 439.
31 For a thorough discussion of the rearmament problems, see Deist, pp. 373–540; and Bernhard Kroener, "Der starke Mann im Heimatkriegsgebiet" in *Generaloberst Friedrich Fromm. Eine Biographie* (Paderborn, 2005), pp. 225–582.
32 TNA CAB 21/949, folio 157–160.
33 Deist, p. 457.
34 Deist, p. 454.
35 *Trial of the Major War Criminals before the International Military Tribunal* (Nuremberg 1947–49), Vol. XXV, pp. 402–13. The report of this meeting has become known as the 'Hoßbach Protocol'.
36 Friedrich Hoßbach, *Zwischen Wehrmacht und Hitler 1934–1938* (Wolfenbüttel, 1949), p. 219.
37 For the figures, see Deist, p. 455.

CHAPTER 5

Marking Time

The Expansion of the British Army (1914–16)

Colonel Martin Todd

In 1914 the BEF suffered a shattering defeat. The army survived, but it did so by effectively reverting to the idea of limited liability on the continent of Europe – at least until 1916. It had no option, for the General Staff had embraced a continental strategy without creating a continental army. This was true organizationally, and doctrinally, but above all in terms of recruitment. Britain had no alternative from the autumn of 1914 than to mark time, for it now had to create a mass army which its strategy demanded of it.[1]

The expansion of the British Army during World War I saw the number of soldiers in full-time service expand from just below 250,000 in 1914 to a peak of over 3.9 million men in March 1918, with a total throughput of 5.7 million men throughout the war.[2] For Britain, this represented an unprecedented commitment for a nation whose strategic culture had been characterized by maritime primacy, limited land commitment and voluntary enlistment. The creation of this mass citizen army was more remarkable because it was a task for which the British state and people were largely unprepared. As a consequence, it was built upon thin foundations, without a blueprint to guide its construction and, for the first 17 months, it was sustained entirely by volunteers, reflecting that for the British the war was a limited commitment. For all these impressive achievements, it was also a chaotic and improvised process, widely enabled from the outset by private and civic enterprise, which compensated for lack of central direction and administrative capacity. From 1915 onwards, the government belatedly realized the necessity of assuming increasingly direct control of the levers of power to achieve a national war effort that wrought significant and enduring changes in political, administrative, social and economic systems.

While the impact of expansion on the British Army was profound, it was also in some senses temporary. 'Paradoxically, from the perspective of the 1920s it seemed that the wartime creation of a "nation in arms" changed society more than it had changed the army,[3] which – notwithstanding the technical and tactical innovations that it had assimilated – quickly reverted to its pre-war ethos and roles. This was, in part, because much of the expansion was achieved by creating new structures so that the regular army remained largely distinct from the mass of 'territorial' and 'service' units that represented the bulk of the expanded force. For the political and military establishments, the war represented a strategic aberration that was not to be repeated. Hence, while the regulars went back (with some relief) to imperial policing, the territorials reverted to a neglected home-defence role and the surviving volunteers and conscripts went back to a society and an economy that were changed forever. Nevertheless, the expansion of the Army from 1914 to 1916 and the sustainment of that structure until 1918, is the most important example in British history of its small professional army being expanded rapidly in time of national crisis.

The Need for Expansion

The reasons why such rapid and massive expansion of the Army was necessary in 1914 lay in part in Britain's long-term political and strategic cultures and in the short-term decision making that turned this established rationale on its head.

Since its inception as a standing regular force in 1660, the 'establishment' of the British Army (i.e. the officially sanctioned structure of the force) was actively suppressed by parliaments ever alert to the costs and political dangers of maintaining a sizeable standing army at home; Cromwell's recourse to martial rule cast a long political shadow. When the Army was expanded, it was in response to increased military commitments overseas and seldom to counter threats to the British mainland. Behind the wooden walls of the Royal Navy, home security was vested largely in the militia, which reassuringly were under the control of local political elites. Indeed, the militia enjoyed primacy for recruiting and its personnel were debarred from transferring to the Regular Army until 1807. Thus, while the Army expanded with each period of conflict, in the absence of a requirement for a large standing army at home, it contracted in peace, tempered only by the demands of garrisoning an expanding empire. This latter requirement necessitated a professional army, which, being expensive to maintain, also had to be as small as possible. This approach entailed obvious risk against the ability to respond quickly to contingent emergencies, but as generally these manifested themselves overseas, there was time and discretion to take a gradual and *ad hoc* approach to expansion.

The series of major wars between 1793 and 1815 saw the size of Britain's land forces increase dramatically, but the war effort so depleted the national exchequer that the coming of peace was greeted by savage retrenchment. The Regular Army was severely depleted and almost wholly consumed by its colonial commitments. This imbalance was neither sustainable nor effective in maintaining a force available for contingent needs, as was amply demonstrated by failings in the Crimean War, which provoked widespread unease at the Army's inadequacies. Coupled with a growing threat from imperial France, this created an impetus for change that ultimately bore fruit in the Cardwell-Childers reforms of 1870–81.

Edward Cardwell's tenure as secretary of state for war (1868–74) has been described as 'the making of our modern Army'.[4] In structural terms alone, Cardwell reduced overseas commitments; balanced the home and overseas establishments; created a framework that grouped 'paired' regular battalions, local militia and volunteer forces within county districts; and established a reserve of 80,000 ex-regulars. Despite staunch military opposition, in 1881, Cardwell's successor, Hugh Childers, consolidated this design by forming large county regiments in each district, each comprising two regular and two militia battalions. However, while the symmetrical balance assured the supply of trained manpower to overseas garrisons, the reformers had still not addressed the ability of the Army to respond to overseas crises of any scale or duration, fragilities that were once again cruelly exposed in the Second Anglo-Boer War (1899–1902).

Despite its ultimately successful conclusion, the Boer War burst a bubble of imperial hubris, exposing the inefficiency and inadequacy of the Army in virtually every facet of its capability and function. It gave, in Kipling's phrase, 'no end of a lesson'[5] and internal and external inquiries were convened to assess failings in its command, staff, doctrine, training, equipment, logistics, manpower and organisation. As Kipling had hoped, it did the Army no end of good; the conclusions of these inquiries set the agenda for a decade of far-reaching reforms that would transform the nation's land forces, both regular and reserve. In structural terms, these reforms centred on those implemented by Richard Haldane as the Secretary of State for War from 1906 to 1912. These finally addressed the challenge of equipping the nation with a properly constituted expeditionary force. This would be generated from home-based regular units augmented by individual reservists and a new category of high-readiness 'Special Reserve' units that would provide resilience and non-front-line functions to the deployable force. In providing the basis of a well-balanced and well-trained force, Haldane had enhanced the capacity of the Army to respond in a timely and effective manner to unforeseen crisis but only on a limited scale. What he had not fully achieved was to equip the nation with the means to generate a mass army able to fight a major continental war. Based on his design, the British Expeditionary Force (BEF) that sailed for France in August 1914 might well have been 'incomparably the best trained, best organized and best equipped British Army that ever went forth to war' as the official history claimed, but as it also admitted, 'it was almost negligible in comparison with the Continental armies even of the smaller States'.[6] As Edward Spiers has noted, this was because 'the size of that force did not relate to a strategy …; it simply reflected the exigencies of peacetime'.[7] A decade of reform had produced a masterpiece in miniature, but it had done little to

Table 5.1 Comparative deployed strength of the principal armies on the Western Front in August 1914

Nation	Manpower	Divisions
BEF[8]	130,000	6
French army	1,300,000	54
German army	1,360,000	77
Belgian field army	117,000	7

address the disparity in scale between the British Army and its principal continental counterparts, as shown in Table 5.1.

In fact, just four infantry divisions and a cavalry division had been deployed by the time of the battle of Mons on 23 August 1914: a force of a little over 100,000 men that was directly opposed by a German force of three times that number. The official history might have been right about the BEF's essential quality, but there would have been some justice to the Kaiser's alleged dismissal of it as a 'contemptibly small army'.[9] Despite the national mythologizing of Mons, Le Cateau and the retreat to the Marne, in reality the BEF was defeated and left hanging on until it could be meaningfully augmented by newly constituted forces at the scale required to be significant in a continental war.

That the BEF did manage to hang on was due to that degree of strategic depth that Haldane had managed to establish, albeit vested in a body designated ostensibly for home defence – the Territorial Force. Haldane's subsequent claims in his post-war memoirs that his reforms were precisely calculated for the exact circumstances that arose in 1914 have been rejected by Edward Spiers, who concluded that 'Economy and not Europe had been the *sine qua non* of Haldane's army reform.'[10] Nevertheless, Haldane had aspired to a regional auxiliary force that would embody Britain as 'a nation in arms': a mass citizen army in waiting to defend the nation's interests at home or overseas.[11] The trouble was that this vision was at variance with both political and public opinion. Even those in the National Service League, led by Lord Roberts, who advocated compulsory national service, had little time for a force founded upon partially elected local associations. Both political and military establishments abhorred the notion and hence political expedience obliged Haldane to reduce the scale and independence of his territorial force. Even then its potential was further undermined by an indifferent public (it was never fully recruited) and a disdainful military. Both factors militated significantly against its ability to meet the much-expanded military requirements of the nation in the autumn of 1914.

The irony is that just at the time that much of Britain's military and political establishment were renewing their aversion to a large standing army, elements of the same establishments were espousing a 'Continental commitment' that would necessitate just such an instrument. By the end of the 19th century, Britain's lack of alignment with other major powers (especially in view of growing German might that threatened both the balance of power in Europe and Britain's global interests) left it isolated in a way that was more dangerous than splendid. Hence, over the opening years of the new century, Britain established a succession of bilateral ties with Japan, France and Russia, although only the former constituted a formal military alliance. However, the military implications of these international commitments were masked by what David French has labelled a 'strategy of business as usual'.[12] This assumed that, in the event of war, Britain's contribution would be met principally by the Royal Navy blockading Germany and cutting off its international trade. In this scenario, the role of the British Army could be limited to a small expeditionary force that might help to tip the balance of forces sufficiently to ensure that Germany would not defeat France as it had in 1870. This balancing act would buy time for Russia to mobilise its overwhelming mass to defeat Germany militarily, while the blockade crushed her economically. Informed by this strategic logic, the Haldane reforms appeared to deliver exactly what was required: a well-equipped, well-trained and well-balanced expeditionary force of minimal scale. However, this strategy was unrealistic. For a start, it assumed that Britain's strategic partners would be willing and able to shoulder the burdens of fighting on land. It also ignored the risks that war would be prolonged and that, once committed, a token land force might not meet the demands of either coalition partners or military necessity.[13]

Realisation of the shortcomings of this strategic calculation and the consequent poverty of the nation's military resources dawned suddenly on the outbreak of war in 1914, principally through the agency of Lord Kitchener as the newly appointed Secretary of State for War. Elements within the General Staff had for some time recognised the inadequate scale of the planned expeditionary force in the context of a European war, but these voices went unheeded outside military circles. This had not prevented the same General Staff from making plans for its employment as an extension of the French Army's left wing, perversely founded upon the converse argument that a force of six divisions would have a decisive effect. These plans had even gained some official approval, if not the absolute endorsement that some claimed, by the Committee for Imperial Defence in August 1911.[14] Later that year, Lord Kitchener voiced his belief to Lord Esher that a European war would be more protracted and more expensive than assumed, being decided only by 'the last million' that Britain could throw into the scales.[15] In August 1914, having been called upon to fill the void as Secretary of State at the War Office, Kitchener was suddenly in a position to realise this vision. Accordingly, with a reduced BEF already committed to embark for France and with mobilisation of existing military forces in train, Kitchener sought first cabinet and then parliamentary approval for what he later described as the raising of 'a new army sufficiently large to count in a European war.'[16] This step, more than any other, committed Britain to a path that would see it carry an increasing military burden on the mainland of Europe in a manner that was entirely contrary to its pre-war strategy and the principles of 'business as usual'.

On assuming office on 5 August 1914, Kitchener immediately highlighted the disparity between the scale and likely duration of the challenge that confronted the nation and the military means at his disposal. On that day, the first meeting of the War Council heard a frank assessment by Douglas Haig, commander of I Corps, that the war would last several years and that a mass army would be required to fight it. 'I mentioned one million men as the number to aim at immediately' Haig related in his diary, before 'remarking that this was the strength originally proposed for the Territorial Force by Lord Haldane.'[17] From this point, Kitchener took a very personal lead, exploiting his renown and the cabinet's dependence on his professional military judgement to force first the cabinet and then parliament to accede to the rapid expansion of the Army. Kitchener recognised that the idea of mobilising a mass army while at war countered conventional wisdom, but he was convinced that by the time Britain's new mass citizen army was trained, the continental armies would be exhausted, thus allowing Britain to dictate terms to its friends and foes alike.

So, empowered by a polity stunned into acquiescence by the shock of sudden war, Kitchener set about exploiting his popular standing by making a direct and personal 'call to arms' to the British people, which was extended by stages throughout the autumn of 1914. These appeals initiated a surge in recruiting that saw nearly 300,000 men enlist by the end of August and a further 462,000 in September.[18] Kitchener intended that most of these men would serve in what was termed a 'new expeditionary force', initially comprising four armies of six divisions each, which would be prepared for decisive intervention during 1916, when the German and French forces would be exhausted. However, despite the initial abundance of volunteers, what soon became known simply as the 'New Armies' were not the only elements of the force competing for manpower. The Regular Army was desperate to make good its grievous early losses and the Territorial Force was gradually coming up to strength and creating second line units for home service. While the relative scale of this 'rush to the colours' and the extent to which it reflected popular enthusiasm for the war have all been qualified in recent decades,[19] the impressive fact was that total British military strength doubled within two months to over 1.5 million men. This sudden influx placed immediate and unprecedented demands upon the Army's capacity to administer, equip and train a force of such scale, which, as its stood, was wholly inadequate and conceptions about how these shortfalls should be addressed differed starkly.

The Sequence of Expansion

In August 1914, the legacy of a decade of reform and strategic realignment was a total military establishment of some 800,000, of which two thirds were various categories of reserves. If this represented the theoretical military might of the nation, then the reality was somewhat less impressive. For a start, neither Haldane's vision of

Table 5.2 Establishment and strength of the principal components of British land forces on 1 August 1914[20]

Force	Establishment	Strength	Difference
Regular Army	256,798	247,432	−9366 (-3.5%)
Army Reserve	145,000	145,347	+347 (+0.2%)
Special Reserve	80,120	63,933	−16,187 (-20.2%)
Territorial Force (including its reserves)	316,094	270,859	−45,235 (-14.3%)
Total	798,012	727,521	−70,523 (-8.8%)

'a nation in arms', nor the perceived threat of growing German military might, had filled its ranks, with the result that (as shown in Table 5.2) its principal components were undermanned, as will be explored more fully later.

While these shortages were not that severe in percentage terms, they exacerbated an inherent lack of resilience in the Regular Army; the effects of which were focused in the 'Home Army' that would furnish an expeditionary force. The 85 (of 157) infantry battalions and 60 (of 114)[21] field gun batteries that were assigned to overseas formations and garrisons were also the best manned and best trained. Hence, the expeditionary force would be at a disadvantage in both quantitative and qualitative terms because as one analysis concludes: 'The largest and most effective part of the British army … was to be found in India, not in the United Kingdom.'[22]

From this limited baseline, Britain commenced the process of expanding its land forces to an unprecedented level, aided initially by vigorous voluntary enlistment. By the end of 1914, the numbers of men under arms had more than doubled again to 1.69 million and by July 1916 it was 3.18 million. Thereafter, it continued to grow to a peak of 3.89 million in March 1918, only dipping then on the technicality that on 1 April 1918 the personnel of the Royal Flying Corps became part of the newly established Royal Air Force.[23]

Despite the impressive scale of these figures, the expanded Army was far from monolithic. In the words of John Keegan, 'Britain, between 1914 and 1918, put four armies into the field in succession'.[24] In this sense, the term 'army' denotes a broad cadre of manpower; the sequence of which ran: The Regular Army (augmented by its reserves); the Territorial Force; the 'New Armies' of volunteers; and, finally, the conscripted class of 1916–18. In the broadest terms, this succession of forces provided the means by which Britain's military effort on land was sustained throughout the war. Importantly, Britain was also able to call upon the Indian Army and the forces raised by the dominions and colonies of the empire, which are not discussed here. Except in their inception, none of these entities was ever pure, but the units that carried their stamp represented the basic building blocks from which each field force was constructed. By the end of the war, the nominally 'British' Army was an amalgam of them all.

For the War Office and the rest of the military administrative structure, each of these four 'armies' presented very different challenges. It took far more than human resources to build a military unit, let alone whole armies. Enlisted men had to be fed, accommodated, administered, equipped, trained and led if they were to be fused into effective fighting units. If this point was not entirely lost on the War Office in 1914, it represented a scale and breadth of challenge for which it was wholly unprepared and, therefore, unequal. Its immediate priorities were to oversee and resource the mobilisation of the BEF and, thereafter, to release regular units from garrison duties so that they could be committed to the war effort.

The Regular Army

In theory, the home component of the Regular Army represented a well-trained professional force; the cream of which would generate an elite expeditionary force comprising six infantry divisions and a cavalry division, supported by a full suite of supporting arms and services. In a mobilisation process that was rehearsed annually, units would be brought up to the 'war establishment' (roughly 25 per cent above its 'peace establishment') by absorbing their reserves and proceeding to their designated point of embarkation. In reality, the demand for additional manpower was increased significantly by shortfalls in recruiting and the unavailability of soldiers under the age of 19; in training or otherwise unfit for operational duties. Indeed, as routine priority for trained manpower was accorded to overseas units, these fragilities tended to be focused in the home units that furnished the BEF.

A typical example was 1st Battalion, The Queen's Own Royal West Kent Regiment, stationed in Dublin, which in 1914 was a 'home' posting. When the battalion was warned to mobilise late on 4 August, exactly 200 of its strength of 672 of all ranks were unable to deploy (most of whom were underage) leaving a core of 472 – less than half of its war establishment of 1000 all ranks. Fortunately, by 7 August nearly 600 reservists had reported to the regiment's depot in Maidstone and were being equipped and given hasty refreshment training prior to reinforcing the 1st Battalion; the 2nd Battalion in India was, for now, a second priority. Before embarking, the battalion was obliged to detach three officers and 15 non-commissioned officers to form the basis of a sixth 'general service' battalion that would form part of the first New Army.[25] This was typical of most home-based infantry battalions and the same was true for other arms. One analysis of the BEF in August 1914 shows that reservists constituted between 55 per cent and 62 per cent of the infantry divisions, 27 per cent of the cavalry division and between 50 per cent and 63 per cent of the divisional artillery.[26] These stark facts challenge the perception, largely created by the official history, that the initial BEF was a uniformly professional and well-trained force, unlike its continental counterparts.

The Regular Army had two sources of immediate augmentation in generating the BEF. The first and larger of these was the Army Reserve, comprising ex-regular soldiers who remained liable for recall to their original units under the terms of their original enlistment. In 1914, they numbered some 145,000, more than sufficient to meet the requirements of a full-scale expeditionary force establishment of 160,000, although inevitably a number were unavailable or unfit for deployment. More importantly, those that did deploy were generally lacking in both training and fitness, deficiencies that there was not time to address within the scope of immediate deployment. These were serious issues that certainly affected the BEF's performance at Mons, Le Cateau and the long retreat to the Marne. By October 1914, all useable manpower in the army reserve had been absorbed in ensuring that deployed units reached and retained something like their war establishment. However, this effort had so depleted the resource that few reservists were available to lend their relative experience to the units of the New Armies.

The second element of the reserve component that augmented the Regular Army was the Special Reserve; a product of the Haldane reforms and their most immediately useful one. Created to replace the militia, the Special Reserve was organised into units held at high readiness, each with designated roles in supporting the expeditionary force. Some of these were auxiliary roles, such as artillery ammunition supply and specialist engineers, for which there was inadequate provision within the affordable regular force structure, it being reasoned that in these roles their relative lack of training and experience was a manageable risk. Within county infantry regiments, Special Reserve battalions were numbered behind the regular battalions and ahead of the territorials. Their purpose was to provide formed drafts of reinforcements or replacements to the regular battalions, while offering a structure that could be itself augmented to expand the force in case of a larger or more enduring commitment. Central to all these roles was a commitment to serve overseas at short notice, which was encouraged by regular rates of pay for time served and bonuses for meeting training and readiness criteria. However, in August 1914, the overall strength of the Special Reserve was 20 per cent below its establishment of just over 80,000. Even thus depleted, Special Reserve battalions quickly assumed key home-defence tasks (for example, the 3rd Special Reserve Battalion of the Royal West Kents was tasked to guard military installations across Kent[27]) while also acting as training units to supply drafts to deployed battalions; rarely did they deploy on active service in their own right. In these ways, by October 1914 all deployable Special Reserve manpower had been mobilised, which John Keegan has suggested 'purists may rightly claim' constituted a distinct fifth army in its own right.[28]

Thus, the first phase of the expansion of the British Army in World War I saw the generation of the Regular Army into deployable formations, first as the initial BEF and, thereafter, as reinforcements to it as far-flung garrisons were relieved by territorial units. Initially, just four infantry divisions and the cavalry division were despatched to France on the basis that until the Territorial Force was properly embodied two regular infantry divisions were required to guard against German raids on the east coast. Founded upon a rehearsed plan and unconstrained, as yet, by materiel insufficiencies, mobilization and deployment of the BEF proceeded with considerable efficiency and in remarkable secrecy. Hence, by 20 August, and unknown to the Germans, a force of just 100,000 men was concentrated around Maubeuge, lying on the western flank of French armies numbering some 1.3 million and directly alongside General Charles Lanrezac's Fifth Army, which numbered 300,000. It lay also directly in the path of Generaloberst Alexander von Kluck's First Army, which itself comprised 300,000 men. A fifth infantry division would arrive just in time for the first engagement at Mons on 23 August, and a sixth in early September. By November 1914, a total of eight infantry divisions and three cavalry divisions had been despatched to the continent, bringing the total numbers that had deployed to nearly 230,000.[29] However, by this stage, the regular core of the BEF had been eviscerated by over 95,000 casualties (of which 18,000 were dead), requiring the urgent despatch of drafts of replacements from Special Reserve units and the hope that the war would be short had been exploded.[30] These stark facts further exposed the inadequacy of Britain's land forces in the context of a major war and the prescience of Kitchener's call to arms in early August became more apparent. By March 1915, three more infantry divisions, constituted from units relived from garrison duties by territorial units, had been deployed, and in August 1915, a separate guards division was created in France. This gave a total of 15 regular divisions, which were maintained, at least nominally, as such until the end of the war. However, by 1915, the capacity of the regular force had been all but exhausted and it only survived by 'reverting to the idea of a limited liability on the continent of Europe – at least until 1916.'[31] There is some irony in the fact that this survival was due to a force that many in the Regular Army had dismissed with disdain – the Territorial Force.

The Territorial Force

On paper, the territorials represented the largest single military force available to the nation in 1914, comprising 14 infantry divisions and 14 cavalry brigades, all complete with supporting arms and ancillary services. To many, it also appeared to offer the most logical and effective means for expanding the Army; this role had been central to Haldane's vision for it. However, for several reasons, real and perceived, this capacity and utility was not fully realised. First, as a force designated for home defence, just 7 per cent of its manpower had volunteered for overseas service, although this figure rose dramatically when war was declared on 4 August. Second, its strength was 45,000 men below its establishment, meaning that generating units at deployable strength took time and resource, especially as it was soon competing for manpower with the New Armies. Third, it was short of equipment and most of that which it held was out of date. Making good these deficiencies in men and materiel against the competing claims of the regular army and the New Armies was a challenging process, not assisted by the War Office's refusal to prioritise its requirements over those of the New Armies.

More pernicious were the persistent questions raised over the fighting quality of territorial units. While these questions had foundations in poor attendance and inadequate performance at annual training camps (themselves in part functions of deficits in manpower and equipment), it also reflected a deeper disdain for part-time soldiering on the part of the military establishment. It was an attitude personified by Lord Kitchener, who famously dismissed it as a 'town clerk's army', and his personal control of the war effort at the outset had significant implications for the territorials.[32] His antipathy may have originated in the shortcomings of auxiliary forces in the Boer War, but it also betrayed the War Office's distrust of the independence that the 93 county associations enjoyed. Whatever its cause, this prejudice, reinforced by the fact that the County Associations were already struggling to mobilise their existing forces, explains why Kitchener discounted the Territorial Force and its supporting structure as the means by which to expand the Army.[33]

Despite this official distrust, the territorials were soon engaged in the war effort. In the case of the Royal West Kents, on the declaration of war, the 4th and 5th Territorial Battalions were already formed *en route* to Salisbury Plain for annual training, alongside many other such units. They were quickly returned to the regimental depot to start preparations for enduring commitments in India.[34] The immediate imperative to release regular units in imperial garrisons to serve in France and Belgium, meant that in September the first territorial division was embarked for Egypt, with others soon following to India, Gibraltar, Aden, Malta and Cyprus. However, persistent concerns over military effectiveness initially limited deployments to the continent and especially into front-line roles, but the mounting scale of the BEF's losses and the intensification of German pressure around Ypres meant that 33 territorial units (principally infantry battalions and yeomanry regiments) had joined the BEF by the end of 1914. By April 1915, such concerns were moot as the truly regular BEF had ceased to exist and five full territorial divisions had been deployed to the Western Front. These divisions formed the core of the offensive at Loos, suffering the same grievous losses as their regular counterparts, which they did again at Suvla Bay in August during the Gallipoli campaign.

Meanwhile, the structure of the Territorial Force itself expanded steadily. From August 1914, county associations were authorised to raise second-line units to replace those that had volunteered for overseas service, so providing a source of trained drafts for deployed (or first-line) units. From September, these new units were formed into 14 second-line divisions, which maintained the structure of the home army, although seven of these divisions would themselves deploy overseas in 1916 and 1917, with their places at home taken by newly raised third-line units. However, recruiting remained problematic for the territorials throughout the first two years of the war, largely due to the greater attraction of the New Armies, so providing trained drafts was always challenging, especially when heavy casualties were sustained in major offensives. Inevitably, this led to drafts being diverted from the better-recruited home units to deployed units of different regiments. This trend, while pragmatic, was contrary to the legally established principle of territorial integrity and became increasingly random, which provoked significant ill feeling within a system founded upon local identity. However, friction could also arise between first- and second-line units of the same cap badge. Ian Beckett has cited the example of the Buckinghamshire Regiment, a wholly territorial unit, within which enduring antipathy arose between its first- and second-line battalions based upon the sizeable contingent of original first-line soldiers who opted for home service in 1914, even though most volunteered subsequently to deploy with the second-line battalion in 1915.[35]

It is without doubt that the Territorial Force made a very timely contribution to the British war effort at home and abroad, but it was also impressive in terms of its scale. Despite being overshadowed by the New Armies, the territorials raised 34 divisions and a total of 692 battalions over the course of the war, of which 25 divisions and 318 battalions deployed overseas. Despite these very considerable achievements and their impact from 1915 onwards, the territorials could never quite throw off their reputation of being part-time (and, therefore, second-rate) soldiers. This disdain, however ill deserved, persisted throughout the war, despite the dilution of pure territorial identities, and remained towards the newly styled Territorial Army well into the 1930s.

By drawing on the military structures existing in 1914, albeit expanded and brought into full-time service, the Army generated 49 combat-arm divisions out of the total of 85 that it generated throughout the war. This represented, in purely structural terms, an expansion of deployable capacity of some 600 per cent, which accounted for 57 per cent of the total land force generated by Britain in the whole war. These facts challenge the common perception that the expansion of the British Army in World War I was achieved principally through the raising of what were known colloquially as Kitchener's Armies, but more formally as the New Armies.[36]

The New Armies

While Haig's diagnosis of the strategic situation in August 1914 mirrored that of Kitchener, the immediate connection that he had made to the War Cabinet between an expanded army and the Territorial Force did not. Kitchener was accustomed to trust his own judgement and his instinct was that the expansion of the Army must be under the central control of the War Office and not assigned to the Territorial Force, despite the invocations of Haig, Haldane and others that it should. The concept was to raise local volunteer battalions for 'general service' as temporary accretions to the Regular Army. The social bonds of the parish, workplace and sports club would help fuse citizens into naturally cohesive military units. Thus, were born the 'pals battalions' that so characterised and shaped the impact of the war on British society.

Kitchener's preference for central control did not mean that the existing military command structure was any more prepared than the county associations for the task of creating a mass of new formations from scratch. Several senior figures in the War Office left to join the BEF, leaving in their place subordinates who lacked the presence or confidence to challenge Kitchener's dominance. Furthermore, the General Staff and the staffs supporting the Adjutant General (AG), Quartermaster General and Master General of the Ordnance (respectively, responsible for manning and recruiting, materiel, and arms and munitions), were scaled to supervise an army of a quarter of a million not one of several millions. The same lack of staff capacity and experience was felt in the regional commands upon which the task of constituting new divisions fell, with implications for the levels of support they could afford new formations and units. Fortunately, much of this deficit in official capacity was taken up by civic, corporate and individual enterprise, as town councils, major employers and other bodies took it upon themselves to provide the framework, facilities and financial resources required to create fresh units. This was entirely consistent with the concept of establishing formations and units forged upon local identities, but it belied the principle of central control that characterised Kitchener's approach to expansion.

In all, five New Armies were raised between August 1914 and April 1915, comprising a total of 30 divisions. The first three were established in the first two months of the war, each composed of divisions raised by the Scottish, Irish, Northern, Eastern, Western and Southern Commands; the London and Aldershot Commands were exempt. A fourth New Army was established in December 1914 and a fifth gradually established up to April 1915. Each division mirrored those of the Regular Army, comprising 13 infantry battalions (divided into three brigades of four battalions and a battalion for general duties), supported by artillery, engineers and signals units. Each 'service' battalion was numbered in order of its creation taking precedence after the territorial battalions of the same regiment. Officially, they were part of the Regular Army but stark distinction was drawn between regular and service units, and especially their officers.

The early existence of these nascent formations, and the citizen soldiers who filled their ranks, was bedevilled by inadequacies in the Army's capacity to house, feed, pay, equip and train them. While these frictions applied in various degrees across the expanded force, they were most keenly felt in the New Armies, which had no more administrative provision than had been left for them in the depots vacated by deployed regular units. Thus, despite the ingenuity of their civil sponsors, the winter of 1914–15 proved especially miserable, with many under canvas or billeted on local households. Unsurprisingly, this disorder provoked widespread discontent that soon attracted parliamentary attention, which at least helped speed remedial action by the War Office. Despite these issues, units and formations steadily took shape, and by May 1915, the first three divisions of the First New Army were declared ready to deploy on operational service, followed in stages by the rest of the divisions. By June 1916, all divisions had been committed to operations, if not into action.

Although termed 'armies', the New Armies did not fight as such, with their component divisions being embedded within established corps and armies to enable their continued training and gradual introduction to combat. Thus, the divisions of the first two New Armies, sent overseas from May 1915, were split between the Western Front and Gallipoli. Like the territorial divisions, these early New Army divisions were blooded at Loos, but it was on the Somme nearly a year later that the BEF sought to exploit the great mass of volunteers that the nation had generated in 1914 to strategic effect.

The New Armies were central to the expansion of the British Army: 557 battalions were raised of which 404 deployed overseas, representing over one-third of the total force. Culturally, they have become even more significant, coming to symbolise in the public mind the British Army of World War I.

The Conscripted Army

By 1916, the principal steps of expansion had been taken, but it continued to grow steadily until March 1918. In terms of combat formations, it peaked at 85 divisions (from a pre-war total of 21), although this structure was constantly being reshaped, either to meet new operational demands or simply to reflect the large numbers of casualties suffered in every major operation, especially on the Western Front. However, it grew also in terms of the arms that operated the range of new weapons of war. This saw the dramatic expansion of the Royal Flying Corps, Royal Artillery, Royal Engineers and all the support services that sustained the fighting divisions, and the establishment of the Machine Gun Corps in October 1915, which itself spawned the Tank Corps in July 1917. Over the course of the war, the Royal Artillery expanded from c.93,000 to over 548,000 (73 per cent of whom were regular servicemen), while the Royal Engineers grew from c.11,500 to 237,000, again with the majority being regulars. The Royal Flying Corps, Machine Gun Corps and Tank Corps were all fully regular organisations, although the vast majority of new personnel were engaged only for the duration of the war. Meanwhile, by 1918, the scale of the Royal Flying Corps and, more importantly, the scope and significance of its operations had so expanded that its 144,000 personnel formed the basis of the world's first independent air force.[37]

Accordingly, primary focus switched from expansion to maintaining formations and units at combat effective strength. This was achieved by deploying conscripted manpower to fill gaps in the existing structure rather than being embodied into distinct units and formations as had the preceding cadres of manpower. Nevertheless, the manpower losses sustained in 1917 and early 1918 necessitated 12 divisions to be comprehensively reconstituted at the expense of five home service divisions that were broken up, a process that was reflected on an even greater scale at unit level.

An inevitable result of this constant churn was to blur distinctions between the formal designations of regular, territorial and volunteer elements. Initially, newly arrived divisions had been consciously intermingled with more experienced divisions so as to 'bring them on' but their founding identities had remained intact. However, these were rapidly eroded as conscripted manpower flushed through their ranks, directed more by operational need than regional or any other affiliation. As will be examined later, by the end of the war such designations were of little significance, although the prejudices attached to them tended to linger on.

Enabling the Expanded Force

The progressive structural expansion of the Army from 1914 charted above was both shaped and enabled by the comprehensive transformation in the nation's approach to waging war. In essence, this entailed the progressive militarisation of the nation, including its political, economic and social structures in order to sustain the means to fight a war of unprecedented and wholly unanticipated scale and intensity. This transformation may best be understood in terms of several distinct but interrelated transitions as the nation slowly adapted the ends towards which the war was prosecuted, the means applied to conduct it and the ways in which they were applied.

The first transition, and the one that drove all others, was in the strategic ends for which the war was prosecuted. Since 1746, Britain had been able to fight her wars at distance (and often by proxy), enabling her to limit her exposure to the direct effects of warfare and, consequently, to limit the means that it had to expend in its prosecution. These instincts towards limited liability remained in August 1914, when the cabinet did not feel itself to be irrevocably committed to war and retained discretion as to how it should intervene if it did commit. This may have been a war entered into by choice, but the political and military decisions taken that summer effectively committed the nation to a principal role in a continental war that would quickly demand far more than the limited approach to which the nation was accustomed. However, it took months for the government to realise the implications of its decisions and far longer to establish the centralised control of its resources demanded by the war as it progressed. In the meantime, Britain's war effort was 'chaotic because it believed it could fight the war successfully by waging less than total war'.[38] As a result, it lacked central coordination and became fixated upon recruiting a large army, for which there were insufficient arms, ammunition, clothing, equipment, accommodation and training capacity, and for which the military's doctrine and leadership were wholly inadequate.

The second transition, therefore, was in the approach to manpower as a key resource. In terms of governance, the War Office 'lost control at an early stage and, after September 1914, the real work of raising the New Armies was very largely performed by the Parliamentary Recruiting Committee and civilian bodies up and down the country'.[39] However, they could not prevent the slow demise of the voluntary principle as popular support waned and the necessity of managing the supply of manpower and skills across the whole war effort became more apparent. However, at the outset, the success of the initial call to arms was so spectacular that it suggested a much-expanded force could be recruited and sustained without recourse to compulsion. This early momentum proved something of a false dawn, with numbers falling away sharply from October 1914. Mounting casualty lists played their part in this drop-off, but it is also clear that the overt patriotic fervour that drove enlistment was far from universal. While before the war military service had held little attraction for those with the skills to prosper in civilian life, in wartime it was among these better educated and more prosperous elements that patriotic sentiment carried more weight. Those employed in the professions, finance and entertainment were the most likely to volunteer (c.40 per cent by 1916), while employees in transport, industry and agriculture proved less so (c.28 per cent), perhaps influenced by the initial opposition of the Labour movement to the war.[40] This may help explain the particular appeal of the pals battalions, which claimed to offer a higher form of soldiering, although in reality these quickly became melting pots of all backgrounds.[41] In this light, the impressive numbers enlisting up to October 1914 may be seen to represent the bulk of a somewhat limited section of the population most inclined to volunteer and once this was committed numbers fell away accordingly.

This trend also had unintended consequences for industry by suddenly depriving firms of mangers and skilled workers, just at the time when their expertise was required to help ramp up production to meet escalating demands for war materiel. By May 1915, this impact was clear to Lloyd George, who, as the new Minister of Munitions, informed the House of Commons that 'the time has come when there must be discrimination, so that recruiting should not interfere with the output of munitions of war'.[42] Accordingly, he was quick to apply measures to recall 50,000 recruits with key skills back into the civilian workforce and to establish a list of 'starred' occupations from which individuals were prevented from enlisting. Even so, the New Armies were still replete with skilled workers, whose contribution to the war effort would have been greater on the factory floor than it was on the front line.

As the inclination to enlist dwindled and the needs of industry entered the equation, the War Office was obliged to be steadily less stringent in its requirements in order to maximise the flow of recruits. The age limit for enlistment was gradually increased from 30 to 40, while the height requirements were steadily decreased to 5 feet 2 inches by July 1915, with 'bantam' battalions being established for those below that. In fact, the general physical condition of recruits had been a major concern from the outset, with large numbers of potential recruits having to be turned away on medical grounds, which reflected concerns over the physical condition of British recruits (especially those from urban backgrounds) during the Boer War. Furthermore, hastily conducted enlistment medicals often overlooked conditions that subsequently necessitated medical discharge, thereby wasting much effort. In this way, and a myriad of others, a small but significant proportion of those enlisting never made it to the front line.

Despite such adjustments and increasing efforts to reinvigorate recruitment without recourse to compulsion, the supply of new recruits during 1915 fell consistently short of that required to replace losses to existing units and to maintain the expanded structure. The last gasp of the voluntary system was a scheme implemented by Lord Derby (as Director General of Recruiting), which required all fit and eligible men to attest in public their willingness to enlist. However, by 11 December 1915, 38 per cent of the 318,553 identified as fit and eligible had refused to enlist, an outcome that presaged parliamentary acceptance of conscription the following month. Under the terms of successive Military Service Acts, between January 1916 and November 1918, just over 2.5 million men were enlisted; a figure just 37,000 greater than that generated through voluntary recruitment in the first 17 months of the war.[43] More importantly, this suspension of the voluntary principle represented the British government, for the first time in its history, managing the nation's human capacity as a strategic resource.

As manpower resources were steadily managed to better effect, so too the industrial capacity of the nation and the empire had to be adapted to meet the demands of unlimited warfare. Britain's lack of preparedness for a prolonged major war was most marked in terms of its ability to arm, equip and sustain an expanded military force. Despite the relatively limited range of materiel demanded, the stocks held to sustain an expeditionary force were wholly inadequate for the actual rates of consumption required by the intensity and duration of the war. Despite initial faith that the private sector would quickly satisfy any excess demand, it was soon clear that there was a lack of suitably adapted industrial capacity to meet the shortfall. Meanwhile, the mobilisation of the Territorial Force and the creation of the New Armies created parallel demands for equipment of all types. Hence, supply problems, in terms of quantity and quality, dogged the BEF, expeditionary forces on other fronts and formation training in the UK until 1916. Lloyd George and Sir John French, as commander of the BEF, were united in blaming Kitchener and the War Office for materiel shortages, but the real issue was the absence of pre-war planning to provide for the demands of an expanded military force in wartime. These demands were not adequately met until the government assumed greater control of the economy and the industrial workforce.

'Nowhere was the inadequacy of pre-war calculation more evident than in the sphere of munitions.'[44] Before the war, the supply of arms and ammunition was largely dependent upon the government administered Royal Ordnance factories, with only a limited number of external contracts being let to private suppliers on an irregular basis. As this situation did not incentivise private suppliers to retain specialist production lines, most diversified into other products. Other capacity was committed to the production of naval ammunition, which the Admiralty was keen to maintain, despite the lesser demand for it. Hence, alternative suppliers had to be found and approved quickly, which not only placed a considerable demand upon the tiny ordnance staff in the War Office but caused serious problems with production quality that had implications on the battlefield.

At the same time, operations on the Western Front were demonstrating the inadequacy of the British Army's pre-war inventory. From the first encounters, the BEF's lack of heavy guns saw its artillery consistently outranged by their German counterparts and the establishment of extensive trench systems made this asymmetry more severe. The last factor was exacerbated by the fact that the Royal Artillery, anticipating engagement of troops in the open, had preferred shrapnel to high-explosive (HE) shells. As the war progressed, the Allies, forced onto the offensive to drive the Germans out of France, found that the key to successful assaults lay in the weight of preliminary bombardment. In this, shrapnel could clear wire, but HE was essential to destroy trenches and dugouts. Consequently, munitions producers, while increasing production at an ever-faster rate, also had to meet to demands for new designs and natures of ammunition. Their response was arguably relatively impressive, but the issue came to a head in the 'shell crisis' of spring 1915 when Sir John French appeared to blame the failure of the British attacks at Neuve Chapelle and Aubers Ridge on a shortage of HE shells, which he attributed to War Office incompetence. While this is widely seen as an excuse manufactured to divert attention from French's own failings, the resulting scandal gave a political pretext for the new coalition government to wrest control of munitions from the War Office by creating a dedicated department under Lloyd George. This was the first step in adopting 'a total war economy' for which 'Lloyd George had become the leading exponent',[45] and which he would apply fully when he became prime minister in November 1916.

Similar shortages existed for most items of personal equipment such as uniforms, boots and webbing, although in this area private enterprise was much readier to meet additional demand, at least while supplies of raw materials lasted. Here too, the haphazard and uncontrolled character of the expansion had unfortunate effects by distorting priorities. With the War Office swamped by the demands of mobilising the BEF, the task of equipping other forces was delegated out to whoever took up the challenge. Thus, public-spirited magnates and corporations, often armed only with promises of reimbursement from the War Office, went directly to industry to secure uniforms and other basic requirements for their new units. Where British suppliers were unable to deliver, those overseas, especially in the United States, were swift to respond to this burgeoning new market. Consequently, the pressure for such routine items was both less urgent and more easily satisfied than that for arms and ammunition.

Another commodity in which the support provided to the expanded army was initially deficient was accommodation. The pre-war Army was well represented across the home nations, which provided a basic framework of infrastructure that could support at least limited expansion. Accordingly, in the six regional commands designated to raise New Armies, the first recruits were accommodated in the lines of deployed units. However, it soon became clear that neither commands, nor their facilities, were prepared for, or had capacity to meet, the scale of expansion directed by the War Office and to which so many had responded so quickly. Hasty contracts were put in place for wooden hutments for designated divisional concentration areas, but few of these had these been built by the onset of winter. The reality for most recruits was being crammed into drill halls, depots, tented camps or large premises provided by local authorities or businesses. Their tales of privation and shortages in food and equipment probably played some part in reducing inflow from its initial peek, but as with clothing and accoutrements, this deficit was at least relatively easy to address once the necessary skills and resources had been applied.

The final transition that characterised the overall transformation of the British war effort to create and sustain a mass citizen army was within the military instrument itself. While ultimately it proved temporary, the impact of expansion had profound effects on everything the Army did, from the War Office down to the training of individual recruits. If pre-war policy had left it ill-matched to the scale of the war it was fighting, then soon operational experience was adding to the challenge by highlighting deficits in its doctrine, leadership, structures, equipment and logistics. None of these could be put right quickly, especially while simultaneously growing a new mass force from scratch and fighting enemies that were themselves constantly adapting their approach. Consequently, from 1914 until 1917 at the earliest, the British Army was playing catch-up, not only in terms of scale but also in materiel and, ultimately, in fighting performance. It gained parity, and even some dominance, only as other powers exhausted their resources, due in no small part, to the significant military contributions of the principal dominions. Nevertheless, it did realise something like Kitchener's ambition in 1911 that it should prove a decisive force at the end of the war.

The Army was hampered in its transition to a large-scale force by its pre-war structure and culture. Notwithstanding the gradual professionalisation of military thinking in the previous decades and the recent programme of extensive reforms that had been in part a by-product of it, the British Army remained essentially a conservative institution that struggled to conceive of itself beyond its habitual model of a small professional force accustomed to small-scale expeditionary warfare against largely non-professional opponents. This self-conception was reflected in its doctrine, which had recently been encapsulated for the first time in the Field Service

Regulations (FSR) issued in 1909 and updated in 1912. This at least gave a detailed and authoritative basis for training reservists and new recruits: the activation order for the first New Army included a comprehensive training progression from individual to formation training. However, its principles had been tailored to a professional force that could call upon 'sound military knowledge, built up by study and practice until it has become instinct.'[46] It did not offer clear and easily assimilated direction to a mass of citizen volunteers under inexperienced leaders, who would have been better served by a set of simple drills. Instead, it prescribed delegated responsibility and initiative: 'the method of obtaining the objective should be left to the utmost possible to the recipient. It is usually dangerous to prescribe to a subordinate at a distance anything he should be better able to decide on the spot.'[47] Such a delegated approach was a pragmatic response to the inability of superior commanders to command in detail over large distances, but it presupposed that subordinates had sufficient experience to exercise independent tactical judgement. Likewise, the FSR placed great emphasis on marksmanship, but a lack of skilled instruction, limited range availability and a shortage of weapons and ammunition for training, soon meant that the rate and accuracy of the BEF's musketry quickly fell away as individual replacements and new formations arrived at the front. Perhaps most importantly, the published doctrine was quickly left behind by the rapid tactical evolution that took place on the Western Front. FSR had been written in the light of lessons from the war in South Africa and those gleaned indirectly from the Russo-Japanese War; it did not reflect the demands of fighting against a modern, massed opponent armed with the weapons of the industrial age. Nor, initially, were the numerous lessons learned painfully by the BEF in the opening months of the war rapidly relayed to those formation training at home.

Just as problematic was an inability to think (and, therefore, function) at higher than divisional level. In 1914, there was no doctrine for anything above divisional level and the only corps that was permanently established with its own staff was that at Aldershot. The division was the highest level of command for which there were doctrine, permanent structures (including headquarters staff) and training (for staff or formations). Consequently, most of the higher headquarters that commanded the BEF had to be improvised on mobilisation, and rapid expansion created a mass of additional new formations further commanded and staffed by officers with no experience of operating at the level suddenly required of them. As the force grew, so the problem intensified, with officers often promoted to higher echelons of command based on necessity rather than proven capacity. Far from remedying this by establishing training for senior commanders and staff, the Staff College was given over to running short courses for junior officers. New talent was grown from within, but this took time and too often a dearth of experienced formation commanders meant that there was pressure to retain those with demonstrably poor records. One example was Lieutenant General Sir Aylmer Hunter-Weston, who after brave and competent command of a brigade in 1914, was promoted to command a division and then a corps at Gallipoli and, thereafter, on the Somme. Despite clear evidence that his formations consistently suffered dreadful casualties for negligible gains, he retained command of his corps until the end of the war. Of course, there were contrary examples of brilliance rewarded, but it is arguable that the British Army's struggle to adapt mentally to fighting at such a scale continued until the Armistice.

At a lower level, Haldane had sought to address a recognised lack of junior officers to lead even the extant regular and territorial contingents. However, his establishment of Officer Training Corps at public schools and universities had done little to remedy this deficit and the dramatic expansion merely made the situation worse. The same was true even more so of non-commissioned officers. This lack of trained leaders affected all elements of the army, but it was in the training of the New Armies that its impact was most severe. British society was not militarised in the same way that those in Germany and France had been and military experience was a rarity; hence, new units seldom had more than a handful of officers at any level with meaningful military experience. In many cases, responsibility for training units had to be vested in those long-retired, so-called 'dug-outs', whose currency in military affairs often pre-dated the Boer War. However, it must be noted that similar observations were made about the poor quality and inexperience of both French and German reserve officers in 1914, which has been held to explain the appalling casualties on both sides in the opening phases of the war. Hastily arranged short courses were established, but as these could only cover the basics, despite the zeal of those under training, they did not deliver officers ready to exercise independent tactical judgement required on a dispersed battlefield. At a lower level, battalions either selected the most promising candidates as non-commissioned officers or allowed men to elect their own junior leaders, either way they simply learned on the job. In due course, some of the shortfall was taken up by officers and non-commissioned officers invalided or rested from the front, but for the most part, the New Armies trained under leaders who lacked relevant military experience to a doctrine that increasingly failed to reflect the reality of combat. Despite these unpropitious beginnings, those raw young officers and non-commissioned officers of the territorials and New Armies who survived grew rapidly in experience and produced their own share of outstanding leaders.

Finally, it is worth making some reference to the qualitative differences (or those that were perceived) between the regular, territorial and New Army cadres. At the outset, the all-regular BEF was evidently an elite force, but the scale of early casualties meant that the quality of regular formations soon fell away. Conversely, both territorials and volunteers started from a very low base of military experience, but increasing combat experience made them steadily more reliable. The post-war Kirke Report noted that they were less resilient than regulars and best employed in static positions rather than mobile operations, but it also acknowledged that their higher intelligence often enabled them to learn tactical lessons more quickly.[48] The catastrophe of the first day of the Battle of the Somme seemed to bear out Haig's fear that the committal of the New Armies was premature, but there was no clear evidence that regular formations enjoyed much greater success. Indeed, one of the few British successes that day was enjoyed by XIII Corps, comprising two New Army divisions (18th Eastern and 30th Division), which was alone in securing all its objectives. These divisions were entirely typical of their kind, except perhaps in that the 18th was commanded by Major General Ivor Maxse, whose acknowledged expertise as a trainer saw him become Inspector General of Training in 1918.

By 1918, through growing experience and the blurring brought about by increasing cross-posting of officers and men, 'there was little to differentiate Territorial, Regular or New Army units'.[49] Jonathan Boff cites the example of 46th (North Midland) Division, which played a critical role in the breaking of the Hindenburg Line in September 1918. This was a Territorial Force division that had a poor record at Loos and the Somme but flourished late in the war under the dynamic leadership of Major General G. F. Boyd. On 29 September 1918, it brilliantly improvised a crossing of the St Quentin Canal and pushed deep into the German defences, enabling the 32nd Division to exploit onwards. This action illustrated how far this division and the British Army had come, and that 'by this stage, it was not just elite formations that the Germans had to fear.'[50]

Gary Sheffield has described how the 'much-maligned' British Army of World War I 'underwent a bloody learning curve and emerged as a formidable force' reflecting the severe and multiple challenges that it faced and the ultimate success that it gained in 1918.[51] However, this interpretation has been qualified, citing the evidence of its poor operational performance for much of the war and its very severe casualties throughout it. Peter Hart has noted that 'the learning curve theory is not a mantra that can deflect all criticism' but acknowledged that one did exist and that 'the British Army slowly ascended it, though occasional, heart-stopping "big-dipper" moments still occurred right to the very end of the war'.[52] Recent work has refocused attention on the extent of operational learning,[53] but the debate continues over how quickly and effectively the British Army learned lessons from its first experience of warfare on an industrial scale.

Conclusions

There is, perhaps, much credit due to a nation that, from a standing start and while fighting a war of global span, managed, for the first time in its history, to create, train and sustain a mass citizen army. Nevertheless, the first year of Britain's engagement in World War I saw a string of near disasters. Having pursued a strategy founded on naval power and limited land involvement, the government had committed the nation to a war in which its naval strength could not be brought readily to bear, while finding its land force caught up in a conflict of a scale and character for which it was wholly unfit. Thus, when its elite, but undersized, professional force was obliterated within a few months, the Army struggled for four years to build the capacity and competence that would make a strategic difference. By 1918, it had done so; a year that Jonathan Boff has described as 'the most successful year in the history of the British Army', although he was careful to include in this accolade the 'forces from the dominions and colonies of the empire'.[54] This ultimate success should not mask the inadequacy of the initial response, which owed much to a lack of strategic clarity and foresight in pre-war planning.

Nevertheless, Haldane's reforms of the auxiliary forces, while lacking the scale demanded in 1914, provided a degree of organisational depth to the professional force, yielding a supply of sufficiently trained forces that enabled Britain to stay in the war, albeit at the expense of imposing a greater burden on her unfortunate allies. While the mobilisation of manpower and economic capacity from Britain and her empire took time, ultimately it would deliver and sustain a potent fighting force that was strategically influential in the final years of the conflict, much as Kitchener had intended. By this final phase of the war, the British Army was what Haldane had originally envisioned; a manifestation of a 'nation in arms', able to call upon the capacity, expertise and resolve of the whole population. Had the political and military foresight existed before the war to provide the contingency plans, administrative framework and necessary resources to enable such an expanded force, then Britain would not have had to mark time for so long and the point at which it could deploy a strategically significant and militarily capable force in the Allied cause would undoubtedly have been advanced significantly. If it is fruitless to speculate as to what strategic impact this might have had, as is explored in the following chapter, the experience of expanding the army in World War I was instrumental in shaping the way that Britain and its army went to war in 1939.

Notes

1   Hew Strachan, "The British Army, its General Staff and the Continental Commitment 1904–14" in David French and Brian Holden Reid (eds), *The British General Staff: Reform and Innovation, 1890–1939* (London: Cass, 2002), p. 94.

2   War Office, *Statistics of the Military Effort of the British Empire in the Great War 1914–1920* (London: HMSO, 1922), pp. 29–36. These figures exclude the military contributions of the dominions and colonies, which have been excluded from this analysis to focus on the purely British experience. However, this does not detract from the fact that militarily and industrially they were both integral and vital to the overall British war effort.

3   Keith Jeffrey, "The Post-War Army" in Ian Beckett and Keith Simpson (eds), *A Nation in Arms: A Social Study of the British Army in the First World War* (Manchester: Manchester University Press, 1985), p. 231.

4   David Ascoli, *A Companion to The British Army: 1660–1983* (London: Harrap, 1983), p. 42.

5   Rudyard Kipling, "The Lesson" first published in *The Times*, 29 July 1901 and then in *The Five Nations* (London: Methuen, 1919).

6   Brigadier Sir James E. Edmonds (ed.), *History of the Great War: Military Operations, France and Belgium, 1914*, Vol. I: Mons, the Retreat to the Seine, the Marne and the Aisne, August–October 1914 (London: Macmillan, 1928), pp. 10–11.

7   Edward Spiers, *Haldane: An Army Reformer* (Edinburgh: Edinburgh University Press, 1980), p. 192.

8   The figures for the BEF reflect the five infantry divisions (1st, 2nd, 3rd, 4th and 5th) and one cavalry division that formed the BEF from 23–31 August 1914; the 6th Division arrived in France between 8–9 September.

9   This infamous comment is probably apocryphal, but in regards to the relative scale of the BEF it would have been justifiable.

10   R. B. Haldane, *Before the War* (London: Cassell, 1921), quoted by Spiers, *Haldane*, p. 22 and p. 73.

11   R. B. Haldane, 'Second *Memorandum on Army Reform*', 1 February 1906, Haig MSS, National Library of Scotland (NLS), paragraph 2, Vol. 32a.

12   David French, *British Economic and Strategic Planning 1905–1915* (London: Allen & Unwin, 1982), p. 1 and pp. 22–37.

13   *Ibid.*, p. 1.

14   The evolution of these plans and their reception by the CID is dealt with in detail by John Gooch, *The Plans of War: The General Staff and British Military Strategy c.1900–1916* (London: Routledge & Keegan Paul, 1982), pp. 278–95.

15   Viscount Esher, "Lord K" in *National Review*, July 1916, p. 698, quoted in Peter Simkins, *Kitchener's Army: The Raising of the New Armies, 1914–16* (Manchester: Manchester University Press, 1982), p. 38.

16   Speech to MPs on 2 June 1916 quoted in Simkins, *Kitchener's Army*, pp. 39–40.

17   Haig War Diary for 5 August 1914, in Gary Sheffield and John Bourne (eds), *Douglas Haig: War Diaries and letters 1914–1918* (London: Weidenfeld & Nicolson, 2005), p. 54.

18   War Office, *Statistics of the Great War*, p. 364.

19   See Ian Beckett, "The Nation in Arms 1914–18" in Ian Beckett and Keith Simpson (eds), *A Nation in Arms: A Social Study of the British Army in the First World War* (Manchester: 1985), pp. 7–10.

20   War Office, Statistics of the Great War, p. 30.

21   Figures taken from Bruce Gudmundsson, 'The Expansion of the British Army During World War I' in Matthias Strohn (ed.), *World War I Companion* (Oxford: Osprey, 2013), p. 51.

22   Tim Bowman and Mark Connelly, *The Edwardian Army: Recruiting, Training and Deploying the British Army, 1902–1914* (Oxford: Oxford University Press, 2012), p. 216.

23   War Office, *Statistics of the Great War*, pp. 228–31.

24   John Keegan, Foreword in Beckett and Simpson, *A Nation in Arms*, pp. viii–x.

25   C. T. Atkinson, *The Queen's Royal West Kent Regiment 1914–1918* (London: Simkin, Marshall, Hamilton & Kent, 1924), pp. 2–5.

26   Bruce Gudmundsson, *The British Expeditionary Force 1914–15* (Oxford: Osprey, 2014), p. 19.

27   Atkinson, *Royal West Kent Regiment 1914–18*, p. 4 and pp. 64–67.

28   Keegan, in Beckett and Simpson (eds), *A Nation in Arms*, p. x.

29   War Office, *Statistics of the Great War*, p. 64.

30   War Office, *Statistics of the Great War*, p. 253.

31   Strachan, "The Continental Commitment 1904–14", in French and Holden Reid (eds), *The British General Staff*, p. 94.

32   Viscount Grey, *Twenty-Five Years*, 1892–1916 (London: Hodder & Stoughton, 1925), Vol. II, p. 68.

33   For a fuller examination see Simkins, *Kitchener's Army*, pp. 40–42.

34   Atkinson, *Royal West Kent Regiment 1914–18*, p. 4 and pp. 68–72.

35   Ian Beckett, "The Territorial Force" in Beckett and Simpson, *A Nation in Arms*, p. 150.

36   Hence, the First New Army was known as 'K1', the Second as 'K2' and so on.

37 War Office, *Statistics of the Great War*, pp. 162–235.
38 David French, *British Economic and Strategic Planning*, p. 173.
39 Simkins, *Kitchener's Army*, p. 323.
40 Based on official figures quoted by Jay Winter in 'Britain's Lost Generation of the First World War' in *Population Studies*, Vol. 31, No. 3 (1977), p. 454.
41 See Ian Beckett in Beckett and Simpson (eds), *A Nation in Arms*, pp. 7–9.
42 HMSO, Hansard Parliamentary Debates, 5th Series, Column 1014, 4 May 1915.
43 War Office, *Statistics of the Great War*, p. 364.
44 Simkins, *Kitchener's Army*, p. 278.
45 French, *British Economic and Strategic Planning*, p. 149.
46 War Office, 'Field Service Regulations, Vol. I, Operations' (London: HMSO, 1914), p. 14.
47 *Ibid.*, p. 27.
48 War Office, "Report of the Committee on the Lessons of the Great War" dated October 1932, Public Records Office, WO 32/3116, pp. 35–36.
49 Ian Beckett, "The Territorial Force" in *A Nation in Arms*, p. 144.
50 Jonathan Boff, "The British Army in 1918" in Matthias Strohn (ed.), *1918: Winning the War, Losing the War* (Oxford: Osprey, 2018), pp. 121–6.
51 Gary Sheffield, *Forgotten Victory: The First World War – Myths and Realities* (London: Headline, 2001), p. xi.
52 Peter Hart, *The Somme* (London: Weidenfeld & Nicolson, 2005), pp. 11–12 and p. 533.
53 See Aimée Fox, *Learning to Fight: Military Innovation and Change in the British Army 1914–1918* (Cambridge: Cambridge University Press, 2017).
54 Boff, 'The British Army in 1918' in Strohn (ed.), *1918*, p. 97. Also, Sheffield, *Forgotten Victory*, p. xi.

CHAPTER 6

Never Again?

The Role of the Territorial Army in Military Plans for Expansion (1919–39)

Dr Alexander Jones

> While armies are organized and trained for mass warfare, as in our own case, it is only logical that a dominant factor in estimating their capacity for success must be their existing size or, failing that, their power of expansion.
>
> J. R. KENNEDY, *THIS, OUR ARMY* (LONDON, 1935), P. 177

Military reconstitution in an era of total war was not a task any nation undertook lightly. The effective expansion of force structures and infrastructure to fight a war at scale necessitates a far broader approach than an army alone can provide. Expansion requires the full embrace of all elements of mobilisation, whether physical, conceptual or moral, in order to exploit the nation's resources to best effect. Only this level of commitment can generate the scale of forces necessary to fight a war of national importance.

Nevertheless, there are key enabling factors that only a military can deliver. In this regard, the availability and efficiency of a viable military reserve structure remains an essential component. This is as relevant now as it has been in the past. The 2017 Army Reserve (AR) Sub-Strategy specifically lists one of the AR's four strategic tasks as the provision of a framework for military reconstitution. As it states: 'In anticipation of a general or prolonged conflict or an enduring commitment, the Reserve would be a foundation for the recruiting, training and preparation of a greatly increased Army drawing on the wider resources of the nation.'[1] This acknowledges the Army Reserve's formal role as the sole basis for the reconstitution of any large-scale, wartime British army.

Although it is true that the reserve's wider reinforcement liability is now far broader, in essence these responsibilities are the same as those undertaken by the Territorial Army (TA) between the two world wars. Indeed, the sub-strategy specifically mentions the example of the key role played by the TA as the framework for expansion in 1939. The existence of the territorial structure certainly enabled Britain to embark on an ambitious wartime enlargement programme, aimed at raising a target figure of 55 divisions. Yet achieving this capacity was not without difficulty, and working out how to convert a small, underfunded voluntary force into a wartime national army posed some major problems for the War Office.

Historically, Britain has no grand tradition of fielding large, conscript-based armies. In line with a traditional antipathy towards militarism and a large standing force, the nation had always taken a rather improvised approach to military expansion, which had more often than not led to a great deal of inefficiency and a general waste of money, effort and lives.[2] Although Britain has a deep association with the citizen soldier through its 'amateur military tradition,' this was more commonly linked to liberal concepts of voluntarism and the defence of hearth and home during the 19th and 20th centuries.[3] This approach may have accorded with the broad views of British society (although the popularity of the National Service movement before 1914 shows this was certainly contested), but the inevitable corollary was that the army lacked an adequate and reliable structure for expansion. By continuing to rely on a voluntary system of recruitment, Britain could not benefit from one key advantage of conscription: the option to recall discharged conscripts for further service in an emergency.

The experience of 1914–18 was a crucial turning point, as it demonstrated in clear and graphic terms the dangers Britain ran in failing to plan for the contingency of conducting an attritional struggle against a modern enemy. Through improvisation and by accepting the need (eventually) for compulsion, the army did manage to implement an impressive expansion programme, growing from an effective strength of 247,432 in August 1914 to nearly 3.8 million by the 1918 Armistice, before shrinking again to 217,986 by November 1922.[4] However, this had not been an easy process, and some senior military figures even regarded World War I as an aberration, unlikely to be repeated.[5] In such circumstances, it would be understandable if the army had simply ignored the demands of warfighting at scale. Indeed, it was long assumed that the interwar army wasted little time in reverting to 'serious soldiering' within the Empire, concerning itself only with garrison duties and the occasional imperial expedition.[6]

Yet, in reality, this was not the case. Instead, the interwar army followed a clear guiding principle that never lost sight of the potential need to fight another 'national war'. Its doctrine embraced the combined arms' lessons of 1914–18, and its training policy remained geared towards the demands of fighting a modern, peer enemy.[7] The general staff understood that the problems of expansion had to be engaged with as a necessity rather than a choice. Indeed, as the Kirke Committee on the Lessons of the Great War emphasised, 'one of the most important lessons to be learnt should be how we are to expand our small army for the purposes of war'.[8]

However, unlike some other continental militaries, as a colonial power, it was inevitable that Britain had to focus most of its peacetime resources on the demands of small wars, imperial policing and the provision of military aid to the civil power. Lacking the luxury of a sustained period of genuine peace in which to reflect, the army was never in a position to prepare exclusively for high-intensity continental warfare.[9] Its broad responsibilities also meant that it needed to be capable of managing its expansion across a wide spectrum of commitments. As a result, it had to develop an organisational structure that could provide for a relatively limited augmentation of existing resources at one end, through to a mass framework upon which to mobilise the nation's manpower at the other.

In order to be effective, this structure had to be established and organised in peace. During the interwar period the provision of this framework was entirely the responsibility of the voluntary, part-time Territorial Army, the assumption was being on mobilisation each constituent unit would throw off a duplicate of itself, organised around a cadre of skilled personnel who had already been well trained in their role in peacetime.[10] These commanders, instructors and specialists would, thereafter, provide the leadership, training and technical expertise around which a cohesive army of volunteer or conscript troops could be quickly and efficiently formed. Achieving this task, however, was not without difficulty. Throughout the interwar period, the British army had neither the political nor social backing to prepare for a large-scale war, nor did it have any tangible prioritisation in economic and industrial rearmament, at least until the very eve of World War II. Overstretched by a multitude of commitments, stymied by political neglect and popular disinterest, and cut to the bone by successive defence cuts, it was not in the army's power to prepare adequately for every eventuality.

Nevertheless, there were certain areas regarding the organisational aspects of expansion that the military was responsible for, or at least was in a position to influence. Manpower itself was not considered an insurmountable problem, as the War Office always assumed that men would volunteer in a national emergency, and if they did not, conscription would be introduced in any case. In 1922, the Committee of Imperial Defence established two sub-committees to study the problems of military expansion, one to explore the issues surrounding national service and the other the supply of armaments and munitions. Their deliberations concluded that if Britain became involved in any future major war (defined as a conflict requiring 750,000 enlistments or more), conscription would have to follow. These broad principles would eventually be enacted in 1939.[11]

However, as the army's expansion over 1914–18 had demonstrated, this body of untrained manpower would count for little if there had been no prior preparation for its organisation and training. Therefore, if the army was to be capable of expansion, then it stood to reason that the machinery to enable this (the TA) had to be effective, available and utilisable across a range of commitments. This meant that the territorial cadres had to be efficient, well trained and could not be allowed to serve under restricted terms of service that interfered with their wartime role. In addition, its organisational framework of formations had to be organised, balanced, and structured in such a way as to be genuinely fit for purpose. Above all, there had to be a comprehensive and implementable policy governing expansion that both the army and the government could agree on. Yet, the degree of success with which the territorials and the interwar British army achieved these tasks has certainly been questioned.[12] By reviewing the efforts made to reform territorial terms and conditions of service, reorganise its framework for expansion and remodel its manpower into cadres, the enduring lessons of military reconstitution held in these examples can be brought out with greater clarity.

Ensuring Availability: Reforming TA Terms and Conditions of Service

The general staff was quick to accept that the failure to organise the army adequately for expansion prior to the outbreak of the conflict had seriously undermined Britain's early contribution to World War I. The reforming pre-1914 secretary for war, R. B. Haldane, had initially intended for the new Territorial Force to both support and expand the wider army, but fear of political opposition had forced him to compromise. As a result, the TF was only legally liable for home defence, and although it was hoped that individual territorials would volunteer to serve overseas in an emergency, only around seven per cent of territorials had agreed to an additional imperial service obligation by September 1913.[13]

This fact contributed to Kitchener's decision to establish the New Armies, which inevitably competed with territorial units for public support, equipment and volunteers. Territorial manpower also proved difficult to utilise in practice, as pre-war legislative safeguards ensured that individuals could not be compelled to transfer between units without their consent and neither could these units be amalgamated or disbanded. The fact that territorials could continue to volunteer for home service only until March 1915, and also accept their discharge when their enlistments of four years (plus one year of war service) expired, created further obvious difficulties.

None of these legal niceties reflected the manpower demands and realities of fighting World War I and were swept away in the wake of the 1916 Military Service Act. However, the painful memory of the improvised, ad hoc birth of the wartime national army left the general staff committed to avoiding a repeat of Kitchener's extemporised approach.[14] Indeed, initial planning sought a wholesale reform of the British army that radically departed from pre-war assumptions. Several committees were created in the months following the Armistice, all tasked with re-assessing the army's future organisation, administration and doctrine in light of wartime experience.[15] Most plans centred on the need for a new, fully-integrated, two-tier army, consisting of a small cohort of long-service, professional volunteers enlisting for imperial duties, over which would be grafted the much larger organisational structure necessary for a compulsory mass army.[16] Although their recommendations may have differed slightly in detail, they all agreed on one key point. Britain's security was inextricably linked to the maintenance of the balance of power in Europe, and the country could not afford to retreat into imperial isolation after Germany's defeat. As such, the ability to expand the army in order to intervene effectively against a modern, continental enemy was singled out as an enduring necessity.[17]

With this in mind, there was little support for simply reverting to the army's pre-war organisational structure. All agreed that the confusion and inefficiency of 1914 had illustrated the flaws in Haldane's separation of the regular and territorial, and few objected to the rational corollary that his pre-war scheme should be abolished. Instead, as the 1919 Committee on the Organization of the After-War Army argued, the Cardwell system of linked battalions, along with the regional Territorial Force structure, should be replaced with a new structure based on five corps areas, containing cadres of 20 divisions that, in an emergency, could be duplicated into a national army of 40 divisions.[18] However, such root and branch reform never had a realistic chance of implementation. Partly, this was due to the fact that all the plans depended on the presumed extension of compulsory military service into peacetime, which soon became a political impossibility given the pressure to demobilise. The decision to limit defence priorities in August 1919, the so-called 'ten-year rule' that prevented planning for a major war within that period, also militated against radical reform, as did the potential political costs of capriciously disregarding the military identity of an army that had only recently returned victorious from battle.[19]

A more pressing reason, however, was the reality that the army was simply too busy, engaged as it was with a list of global commitments that far outreached its ever-shrinking resources. The new world that emerged from the ashes of World War I was a dangerous, volatile place and, faced with a worsening 'crisis of Empire', the army had to guard against a myriad of security threats.[20] These included countering domestic unrest at home, suppressing smouldering insurgencies in Ireland and the newly mandated territories, and maintaining law and order in India and the colonies. This was in addition to new tasks that emerged at the war's end, such as maintaining interventionary forces in Russia and the Caucasus, and supplying various armies of occupation. As a result, and despite being recognised by the War Office 'obviously faulty', it soon became apparent that the army would be forced to retain its pre-war structure, at least in broad terms.[21] Nevertheless, the general staff remained adamant that the post-war army had to be re-modelled along the flexible lines necessary to meet the variety of possible commitments Britain now faced.

This process did not affect the regular army to any great degree. Rather, the problem was with how the army could be given depth. Ideally, the general staff sought to reorganise the army's reserve structure to achieve three primary functions. Firstly, it had to provide an organised framework for mass expansion on a compulsory basis; secondly, it had to offer a flexible source of trained formations to augment a medium-scale expedition on a voluntary basis. Thirdly, it should be capable of furnishing drafts to support a commitment of regular troops over and beyond what could be provided by the regular Army Reserve. All of these tasks necessitated differing scales of expansion, but none could be achieved with professional resources alone. The active strength of the regular army was only sufficient to manage its existing peacetime commitments, and as the war had seriously disrupted the normal inflow of men into its own regular reserve, the army would have struggled to deploy even a limited expeditionary force. Furthermore, the intention to abolish the Special Reserve meant that the army would also lack the draft-finding machinery to maintain it once committed.[22]

This made the establishment of an effective expansionary structure a priority, and the general staff was keen to base this around a new 'general purpose' Territorial Army Reserve. Doing so would have the advantage of utilising the old Territorial Force's pre-existing regional footprint and, hopefully, attract demobilised veterans, who had already been identified as a valuable but largely untapped source of trained manpower.[23] However, any reconstructed territorial organisation would have to offer clear advantages over the pre-war system and provide for a more functional, flexible and relevant role than simply home defence. This was in accordance with a broader intention to create an integrated force that brought regulars and territorials much closer together.[24]

Above all, the general staff was adamant that territorial personnel had to be considered available across a far wider spectrum of commitments, and its support was, therefore, conditional on the avoidance of any 'entangling agreements' that prevented the territorials from a making a broader contribution.[25] In line with this, the general staff were quick to confirm their preference for the territorial organisation to act as the sole machinery for future military expansion, as the Adjutant General, George Macdonogh, and the Chief of the Imperial General Staff, Henry Wilson, both considered it far preferable to any improvised setup similar to the New Armies.[26] Yet, in order to fulfil this role, the territorials had to accept an unambiguous and unrestricted obligation for overseas general service because without it the army would be incapable of maintaining and expanding any military commitment once the Regular Reserve was exhausted. Furthermore, and although they did eventually agree a compromise so that territorial units would only be considered available as formed sub-unit drafts within their own corps, the general staff continued to insist that once in theatre each individual would share the regular soldier's liability to be sent wherever he was needed.

This made perfect sense militarily, but the ensuing debate over the terms of a general service liability was not directed solely by arguments of military necessity but increasingly by the different priorities held by Wilson and the minister for war, Winston Churchill. Wilson was adamant that the territorials had to offer a clear military utility in order to justify a share of the army's shrinking budget, and this meant a clearly accepted responsibility to reinforce the expeditionary force as formed units and, ideally, to supplement the Regular Reserve by subsuming the draft-finding role previously imparted by the Special Reserve.[27] Churchill's priority, however, was to make the revived territorial movement a popular and political success. Although willing to concede that on purely military grounds the general staff's arguments were 'overwhelming,' he considered it 'essentially unfair to ask men who are not soldiers to take on a liability to be sent away to India, Egypt, Mesopotamia or the Black Sea for long periods whilst the mass of their fellow-countrymen pursue their ordinary avocations and bear no part whatever of the national burden.'[28] As such, he refused to impose on them a general service obligation, as he feared the terms would be thought so onerous that few would volunteer.[29] For Churchill, a poor response from the public would represent a political failure and be regarded as a highly damaging embarrassment for the government.[30]

Yet reinstating an obligation solely for home defence would completely undermine any ability the Territorial Army had to act as a viable framework for expansion. Furthermore, in Wilson's view, the absence of a usable reserve organisation would leave an alarming gap in the army's capabilities, and, therefore, threaten the entire security of Britain's possessions overseas.[31] With the views of the secretary of state and his advisers so at odds, it took nearly a year of debate and political wrangling before a compromise decision was reached. Accepting that the proposed home-defence role would be seen as 'simply playing with the force', the TA was formally recognised as the framework for all military expansion, and each volunteer was, thereafter, obliged to enlist for general service.[32] However, in order to reassure doubters that territorials would not be mobilised for any spurious reason, its actual despatch overseas required specific parliamentary approval. This formal act in itself would only be actionable after the regular Army Reserve had been called out and once a state of emergency had been declared. This was in addition to the official declaration that territorials would not be available as drafts for the regular army and they would only proceed abroad in their own formed units.[33]

In consequence, the prospect of utilising territorial troops in support of any scale of operation was a distinctly complicated undertaking. Furthermore, even though it was accepted that any future conscript national army would be raised through the TA framework, the guarantee on preserving unit integrity threatened to separate territorial personnel into a legally protected special class of reserve that would dangerously undermine a general mobilisation. As a later director-general of the TA warned, any wartime army would be inevitably 'divided rigidly into a large number of small compartments, each of which claims to retain the personnel with which it first started. It requires little imagination to call to mind the accidents of war, and the needs which must arise for employing personnel to better advantage in other compartments.'[34]

As a result, the army had managed on the surface to reorganise the territorials as a dedicated framework for expansion, but in practical terms, it was little better off than it had been in 1914.[35] As the Adjutant General pointed out, the intention to guarantee the integrity of each territorial sub-unit was both impractical and dangerous. If a regular unit sustained heavy casualties early in a campaign, it would be impossible to reinforce it with soldiers from a corresponding territorial formation. The experience of 1914–18 had demonstrated that fighting a war on such principles was unworkable. Indeed, Macdonogh declared that he would 'rather not have any Territorial Force at all than give a pledge which would bind the hands of the Military Authorities to that extent in the actual conduct of the war.'[36]

During the 1920s, the issue of the 'pledge' was held in abeyance, largely in order to get the territorial scheme up and running. However, the military arguments in favour of abolishing it were clear, and after several years of steady pressure, the War Office eventually managed to convince the TA County Associations that it should be withdrawn from all volunteers enlisting after May 1934 (although a later bureaucratic oversight meant that territorials were still assured they would proceed overseas in their own units).[37] As such, the War Office had finally managed to make a firm step towards freeing up the restrictions that constrained the use of reserve manpower, but it would not be until 1939, helped by the pressures of an impending war, that the last vestiges of the 'pledge' were finally removed.[38] At this point, the opportunity was also taken to amend the regulations to dilute one of the other long-held assurances, that the TA would not be used to provide drafts to regular units, which again could not be guaranteed under wartime pressures.[39] The general staff similarly pushed for the field force to assume the same embodiment obligation already undertaken by the Anti-Aircraft and Coast Defence Territorials. This would allow the entire TA to be called out under the authority of the secretary of state, without the necessity for a proclamation or calling out the Army Reserve first.[40] Although it was unlikely, these decisions would have been taken without the imminent threat of war, they also merely reflected the reality that in a modern conflict it was not possible to restrict the movement of manpower without also compromising efficiency.

The Sole Framework for Expansion: Reforming the Territorial Organisation

With the experience of 1914 fresh in War Office memory, establishing an efficient framework for future expansion was viewed as an important and enduring task, and the army was keen to absorb the knowledge gained during the war before the opportunity was lost. After all, as General Sir Ivor Maxse publicly warned:

> To-day we can still lay our plans with recent knowledge and experience of what is required, but in a few years' time, or in the dim future, when another war bursts upon us, you will all be

taken aback and just as surprised as you were in 1914 ... if we planned a bit more and thought seriously, it might be possible, without adding to the estimates of the Fighting Services in a perceptible degree, to produce a workable scheme. If we do not think about it we certainly shall not do so.[41]

Left having to tackle more pressing strategic problems with an ever-decreasing budget, the general staff certainly questioned the wisdom of investing too heavily in this contingency, but they still wanted to ensure the TA was capable of carrying it out in an emergency. In pursuance of this, the War Office pushed ahead with its plans to reorganise it in line with the proposed modernisation of the regular army, in order to further its main effort of 'remould[ing] the existing TF into a Territorial Army which would be scientifically proportioned according to the lessons learned in the late war'.[42] In consequence, each TA division was now to possess its full allocation of combat and support arms in peace, as well as an expanded allocation of army and corps troops. These also included several specialist units, such as bridging, motor machine gun and signals intelligence companies, which were intended to preserve capabilities that had been abolished from the regular army order of battle.[43]

However, this laudable aim proved hard to achieve in practice. In the absence of any additional financial investment, the required support units could only be raised through the conversion of existing surplus units. Over 1920–21, this largely concerned the mounted yeomanry, whose 55 regiments were to be reduced to ten to provide the TAs missing artillery batteries and armoured-car companies.[44] However, the yeomen's ability to mobilise political support (crucially to include the secretary of state for war) meant that, although most eventually agreed to convert, a total of 14 regiments stubbornly remained mounted. For the CIGS, Henry Wilson, the implications of them doing so were clear: 'In consequence, several TF divisions will go without RA, RE, etc. I told S of S that such action was unpardonable – but it will surely be done.'[45]

The influence that funding and politics had over the army's organisation also became apparent after mounting pressure to reduce government spending led to further economies being recommended by the Committee on National Expenditure under Sir John Geddes. Alarmed that the concomitant defence cuts were aimed primarily at the overstretched regulars, Wilson was desperate to ring-fence front-line capabilities as 'any reduction in these units must ... increase the risk that is being run [to imperial defence]. To adopt such a policy, while continuing to spend even 5 or 6 millions annually on the Territorial Army, which answers no essential purpose at the present time, is contrary to all sound military principles.'[46] Instead, Wilson called for economies to be carefully directed so as to protect front-line strengths, while preserving the reserve's core military efficiency as far as possible. Otherwise, as the quartermaster general warned the under-secretary of state at the War Office, 'the Territorial Army will cease to exist as a mobilisable force, and hence its actual value in a military sense is considerably discounted'.[47]

In the event, however, Wilson could protect neither the regulars nor the reserve. Although the TA retained its 14 divisions and, therefore, a superficially broad base for expansion, most of its service and support assets were abolished.[48] Furthermore, each infantry battalion was reduced to a peacetime establishment of 600 other ranks and 75 per cent of its officers, while artillery batteries were only authorised to man four guns instead of their wartime complement of six.[49] These reductions meant that the TA was bereft of the genuine depth and organisational cohesion necessary for it to function as a balanced framework for expansion. Its divisions could not, in truth, be regarded as effective formed bodies, and consistently disappointing recruiting figures meant that by 1924 they had only reached a strength representing 45 per cent of their war establishment. Neither can it be said that any serious thought had gone into how the process of expansion would actually be managed. No set instructions existed to help units plan how to recruit to war strength, absorb volunteers or conscripts, throw off a duplicate second or third line, and thereafter train and equip themselves to a deployable standard, all within the assumed six-month mobilisation window.[50]

Describing it at this stage as 'a bundle of uncoordinated good-will,' the Director-General of the TA, Hugh Jeudwine, felt compelled to complain that the TA's clear inability to carry out its expansionary role was undermining both its efficiency and morale, and insisted that the army should at least agree on certain key principles regarding policy.[51] This demand led the Army Council to form the TA Expansion Committee, which in 1925 decided that future military expansion would be undertaken in two set phases, whereby each existing territorial unit would throw off a cadre for a reserve unit on mobilisation but focus primarily on absorbing volunteers until conscription was introduced. Assuming that parliament would delay legislating for this measure for up to six months, it was only at this point that the reserve unit would itself throw off an additional cadre for a triplicate unit, at which point centralised training centres would have been set up to prepare a new national army.

The Expansion Committee's plan meant that the embodied TA could focus on bringing its existing first-line field divisions to war strength as quickly as possible, while at the same time leaving behind a framework of cadres to form up to 33 infantry and three cavalry divisions.[52] This was a sensible scheme that aimed to ensure that Britain's military expansion proceeded at a manageable and organised rate. Yet, it was predicated on the territorial divisions possessing a balanced order of battle, which, of course, they lacked. Without any prospect of increased investment, the general staff's preference was to streamline the TA by disbanding two to three divisions and re-directing the saving into organising and equipping the remaining formations properly.[53] The alternative was to reorganise the TA according to a set scale of readiness, whereby each division would be nominated and given a higher or lower establishment depending on the order in which it would proceed overseas. In this way, they could carry out the overall expansion scheme, but with only a select number of formations at proportionately less expense. The advantage of this was that it caused the minimum dislocation in peace, while producing the maximum result in war and keeping the overall organisation intact.[54]

However, while both options represented reasonable organisational solutions to the problem being faced, neither accounted for the possible psychological repercussions on serving territorial personnel. Fearing that both the wholesale abolition of divisions or the nomination of a favoured *corps d'elite* would seriously undermine morale, Jeudwine preferred to defer a decision until more funds became available.[55] The CIGS, the Earl of Cavan, regarded this as 'simply a policy of drift,' and argued that, as the government had publicly declared the TA as the basis of national expansion, it would now be almost a breach of faith if they did not enable the TA to function in its role.[56] Regardless of this, a final decision was held in abeyance and the TA continued to struggle against an organizational imbalance into the 1930s.[57]

Quantity or Quality? The Efficiency of the Territorial Cadres

Even as the debate over its organisation carried on, it became apparent that not everyone in the army believed that the TA's expansionary role made it necessary to establish it as a replica second line of the regulars. By the mid-1920s a clear counter-argument began to emerge. This entailed moving the territorials' role away from a quantitative approach, focused on manpower and organisational reform, and towards an emphasis on qualitative factors, notably the training efficiency and skill of key personnel. As expansion depended mainly on the availability of instructors and leaders, the Territorial Army, it was, therefore, argued, should focus accordingly on producing large numbers of officers, NCOs and specialists rather than a broad but ineffectual number of formations.[58] As such, instead of trying to organise it into a balanced second-line army these proposals envisaged restructuring the TA into a loose framework of cadres, maintained at a high level of efficiency but on a reduced, skeleton basis.

Reflecting as it did, the TA's inability to recruit to strength and the fact that any increase in funding was unlikely for the foreseeable future, restructuring the TA into a 'cadre for a nation in arms' was regarded by many as the most effective way to retain a practical expansionary capability.[59] This was predicated on the assumption that every territorial would be capable of immediately taking on a higher level of responsibility on mobilisation, swiftly becoming the command and instructional nucleus around which a conscripted national army would form. Yet this proved difficult to achieve. For one, territorials were only expected to train for the responsibilities of their actual rank, rather than for those above them.[60] Furthermore, there were never enough of them to give the cadres any effective depth. Restrictions on peacetime establishments meant that the majority of personnel in any territorial unit would have to be instantly promoted in order to provide the required wartime scale of commanders.[61] This meant that the selection and retention of skilled officers and

NCOs had to have priority, but those that did volunteer did not necessarily possess the right leadership, instructional and specialist skills to be effective. For example, territorial officers were still commissioned according to a social and character-based selection process (similar to the regular army), where suitability for command was regarded purely in terms of a public-school education and perhaps some limited instruction in an officers' training corps.[62] Once commissioned officers had only limited exposure to any training in command and leadership, and as promotion was more or less automatic, the standard and ability of officers could vary considerably, leading one territorial commander to identify a wide variety of capabilities, ranging from the 'War-trained' officer to the 'Enthusiast', the 'Average Worker', and, finally, the 'Slacker'.[63] At a more senior level, officers did not benefit from any real preparation for higher command or staff work, and there was little in the scheme of training to fit officers for their actual duties in war.[64]

Alongside officers, the cadres also relied on generating a large pool of NCOs and specialists, but despite their importance, the TA always struggled to generate enough of these, and when it did, the standard they achieved was also often disappointing.[65] NCOs were usually chosen from those who attended their drill halls on a regular basis, but this policy meant command appointments did not necessarily go to the best men.[66] It was also recognised that, even if an NCO was an effective leader or administrator, this did not necessarily make him a good instructor.[67] The general lack of instructional ability in the TA, particularly in the context of expansion, remained a pressing concern, leading one representative from the Lessons of the Great War Committee to doubt whether they were in any better position in 1933 than they had been in 1914:

> We know how rare the first-class trainer is in regular units – how can we expect to find him in the Territorial Army except in small quantities? The framing of its tactical schemes, umpiring and the general organization of collective training appear to be beyond the scope of the average Territorial Army unit.[68]

Although efforts were made to improve its standards as war approached, particularly in the allocation of regular army resources to support its training, the level of efficiency achieved by the territorial cadres remained a problem.

It is also clear that the TA lacked a clear policy to direct its preparations and, therefore, neither committed fully to a cadre organisation or that of a deployable second line. As a result, many territorials were unsure as to what immediate ends they were training for and had similar doubts as to what standards they had to achieve during the annual training cycle.[69] This led to a wide disparity of opinion over how the force should be organised and how training should be carried out.

Territorials had to wait until the early 1930s before the *Training Regulations 1934* stipulated that 'the role of the Territorial Army, in addition to that of providing the sole means of expansion to form a national army, includes the liability of supporting the Regular Army overseas in the event of war.[70] However, it was clear these two specified tasks required quite different approaches. For example, while instructing the TA to concentrate on the training of its cadres made sense for its role as the 'sole means of expansion,' a skeleton framework did little to meet the TA's additional 'liability of supporting the Regular Army overseas,' which required balanced formations of fully equipped and trained men.

This confusion of purpose reflects the different opinions held by the general staff and the wider army regarding the best ways of managing its expansion. As the need to rearm, and the possible requirement to deploy another army to the continent, became apparent during the 1930s, the focus swung back towards preparing the TA. The CIGS, Field Marshal Sir Archibald Montgomery-Massingberd, regarded the TA as a true second-line army that had to expand quickly to support the field force in the important build-up phase following an initial mobile campaign, in line with his conception of how a European campaign would develop.[71] In accordance with the mobilisation timetable set out in his revised 'Western Plan', his primary focus was on accelerating the TA's readiness to deploy as quickly as possible. This involved introducing measures designed to reduce the manpower gap between the territorial peace and war establishments, establishing a TA Reserve and nominating and prioritising each division to their field force echelons in advance.[72]

This policy was directly at odds with that of his successor, Sir Cyril Deverell, who differentiated between the role of the regular army, designed for immediate service in any part of the world, and the territorials, which he saw as exclusively for a war of mass. Deverell had always preferred to remodel the TA solely as a force of specialists, commanders and instructors.[73] Instead of replicating the regular army in balanced formations, Deverell wanted the TA organised according to the requirements of a national war, forming specialist support battalions and tank units while expanding the technical arms at the expense of the infantry. This necessitated a hollow cadre organisation, focused on producing leaders and instructors and only retaining sufficient rank and file to practice the former in training technique and the art of command. For Deverell, the key to mobilisation and expansion was in improving the TA's readiness to act as an instructional training group, rather than expanding its manpower pool and broadening its organisation.[74]

This lack of consensus did little to help the army prepare itself for war, although by 1934 the real impediment in this regard came from the political reluctance to make a tangible ground commitment to the defence of western Europe. The ensuing debate over the direction of British military policy, culminating in the defence review undertaken by the Minister for the Co-ordination of Defence, Sir Thomas Inskip, and the consequential reorientation of strategic priority away from the continent, ostensibly removed the need for the army to consider expansion on any scale. However, although the government's decision over 1937–38 to limit its liabilities had serious ramifications on rearming the army with modern equipment, the general staff continued planning for a larger commitment, especially because in its view war with Germany would make this unavoidable.[75] This led to considerable efforts being made to enhance the TA's war fighting potential and its readiness to support the regular army wherever it was deployed, including against a modern enemy in Europe.[76]

As a result the TA's organisational framework managed to survive this 'limited liability' phase largely intact, at least with regard to its ability to expand. Furthermore, over 1938, strenuous efforts were made to modernise the force and reorganise it once more into a balanced 'general purpose' force.[77] In pursuing this, it benefited from a far greater degree of interest from the public, enabling the TA to come close to approaching its establishment strength for the first time (Table 6.1).

Consequently, by early 1939, the War Office had significantly accelerated the rate in which the Territorial Army could be mobilised and removed most of the residual limitations placed on its use. In addition, the subsequent reversal of government policy back in favour of a continental commitment finally gave the War Office authority to start rearming the TA.78 By preparing the first territorial echelon in peace, the field force was assured a degree of depth and resilience, and the decision would also pave the way for further expansion, should full-scale war prove unavoidable.

Table 6.1 Comparative strengths of the territorial divisions (all ranks) on 1 October 1938

Division	Peace Est.	Strength	Strength to Est. (%)
55th (West Lancs)	9500	9601	101.1
51st (Highland)	9906	9977	100.7
49th (West Riding)	9864	9590	97.2
50th (Northumbrian)	8875	8566	96.5
42nd (East Lancs)	9857	9476	96.1
48th (South Midland)	9242	8678	93.9
53rd (Welsh)	9857	9225	93.6
52nd (Lowland)	9879	9127	93.4
54th (East Anglian)	9856	9060	91.9
London Division	9991	8937	89.5
43rd (Wessex)	9099	8030	88.2
44th (Home Counties)	9772	8066	82.5
1st Anti-Aircraft	22,669	21,401	94.4
2nd Anti-Aircraft	25,529	20,721	81.2
Total TA Divs.	163,896	150,455	91.8

Source: "Army Notes" in RUSI Journal, Vol. 84 (1939), p. 884.

Unfortunately, the positive results of these reforms were considerably undermined from mid-1939 onwards. This was largely due to the fact that the War Office lost full control over the TA's reform programme during this period. Although new logistic and support units were being raised, the inability to control the direction of voluntary enlistments began to significantly unbalance the distribution of the TA's manpower, leading to a surfeit of infantry and a large deficit amongst the support arms and services.[79] Furthermore, the cadre system struggled to process this influx of men. Between the start of April and the end of May, the TA absorbed 152,000 volunteers, but these were almost entirely untrained and inexperienced – in June 1939, over 56 per cent of the Territorial Infantry had served less than six months.[80] The desperate need to find additional NCOs meant that promotion had to be accelerated regardless of qualifications – one territorial gunner found himself promoted to sergeant overnight, and in some cases, men simply volunteered to become their unit's NCOs.[81]

This unregulated process of expansion was further exacerbated by a decision to expand the TA's size without any real consideration of its impact on wartime manpower priorities.[82] In an effort to demonstrate political resolve, the government decided in March 1939 to raise the TA establishment to 170,000 and then immediately double it to 340,000. The decision has generally been denigrated as a hastily conceived and poorly implemented scheme, with little thought being given to practical military realities.[83] This may be true, although it can also be argued that what the proposal really amounted to was the bringing forward into peacetime of the expansion that was set to occur anyway on mobilisation. In this case, each unit would have to throw off a second-line duplicate, and doing so in peacetime would be easier than attempting it during the first rush of war.[84]

However, it did inevitably lead to a mismatched and tiered organisation of 'first' and 'second' line formations. The War Office did not offer units any detailed instructions on how to manage their duplication, leaving it up to their commanders to determine. The London Division, for example, decided to simply divide itself equally, transferring half of its manpower and equipment to the new 2nd London Division. Its territorial commander, Claude Liardet, subsequently considered this process to have been:

> A shocking business, rape of a decent Div, training hard, half of officers, NCOs and specialists and vehicles handed over to a non-existent formation, but had to be trained, organized and equipped by its parent, who was jolly bust at that time endeavoring to be efficient.[85]

Organisationally, duplicating the TA may well have been logical for the purposes of fighting a war of mass in the long term, but in the short term it certainly added more practical difficulties to an ever-lengthening list of shortages and limitations. The pressure this put on units actually led to a marked drop in territorial efficiency by the declaration of war.[86]

The reality of the situation was that by the outbreak of war the Territorial Army, like much of Britain's defence services, was caught in transition. Required to expand at short notice at an impossible rate, there were too many men to train, with too few instructors, too little equipment and too little time. After mobilisation, units had to spend at least a month reorganising their first and second lines, combing out those in reserved occupations, exchanging those too young to serve overseas and absorbing conscripts called up by the limited Military Training Act and its successor, the universal National Service (Armed Forces) Act.[87] Alongside the general lack of experienced personnel and the shortage of modern equipment, facilities and regular army support, the training and preparation of this expanded army was heavily disrupted.[88]

Nevertheless, without the territorial system the army would have been incapable of playing any role in the ground war at all. In numerical terms alone, the TA's contribution to Britain's mobilisation was considerable, as outlined in Table 6.2. Territorials, therefore, represented just short of half the army's entire manpower strength and more than double the number of those serving on active attestation.

Territorial formations also dominated the early-war army in organisational terms. In September 1939, Britain had on paper a force of 33 divisions, of which two were armoured and seven regular infantry divisions, whilst 24 were either 'First' or 'Second Line' territorial divisions. The TA also initially contributed 12 tank brigades and Anti-Aircraft Command was almost entirely territorial.[89] All further expansion was based on the Territorial Army, and every wartime recruit, whether volunteer or conscript, was deemed to have enlisted in the TA.[90] The Territorial Army also provided the larger share of the wartime army's junior leadership, at least initially. Between September 1939 and January 1940, the army commissioned 1,617 territorials, against 393 men from the regular army and 207 from the militia.[91] This was, however, balanced by the relative inadequacy of territorial senior commanders; a factor that led the CIGS to calculate that as many as 55 per cent of all territorial COs were unfit for active command.[92]

Table 6.2 Manpower in the British army on mobilisation (3 September 1939)

	Officers	Other ranks
Regular	15,000	217,000
Reserves	12,000	173,000
Militia	N/A	34,000
Territorial Army	19,000	409,000
Territorial Reserve	8,000	13,000
Total	54,000	846,000

Source: LHCMA ADAM MSS 3/1, Notes for S. of S. Estimates Speech: AG Department, 15 February 1941.

However, by 1940, whether a soldier was serving on a territorial or regular attestation was increasingly irrelevant. The general staff had always stressed that fighting a national war required the raising of a national army. As the CIGS, George Milne, had iterated as early as 1928, once war was declared 'there will be only one Army. I wish to make this point clear. There is no distinction between the soldier who serves all the year round and the Territorial soldier.'[93] As a result, territorials, regulars and militia conscripts were soon deliberately integrated together as policy. In order to enhance professional and administrative ability in general, a programme of 'stiffening' territorial units with regular personnel was begun soon after mobilisation, and in France, one territorial battalion in each territorial brigade was substituted with a regular unit.[94] This was part of a process that sought to eventually remove any distinction between individual British soldiers. As the Adjutant General, General Gordon-Finlayson, declared in December 1939:

> ... although nothing should be done to discourage Territorials and the Territorial spirit, there should be no need to emphasise distinctions between Regulars, Territorials and Militia during the present War; rather it should be borne in upon everybody that the nation is now fighting for its life, and that the Armed Forces concerned constitute one National Army in which every individual, whether Regular, Territorial or Militia, is determined to do his best for the common end.[95]

By providing a viable framework for expansion, the peacetime Territorial Army had established the building blocks of this national army and, as such, played a vital role in Britain's contribution to final victory.

Conclusion

Between the end of World War I and the outbreak of World War II, Britain's ability to expand the strength of its ground forces relied entirely on its voluntary citizen reserve, the Territorial Army. Learning from its arduous experience between 1914 and 1918, the army was well aware of the problems it faced in managing large-scale expansion. As such, it quickly managed to identify many of the solutions and the measures that needed to be established in advance in order to ensure an efficient transition from a peacetime footing to a state of national mobilisation.

In the first instance, it recognised that the peacetime terms and conditions of service governing reserve manpower had to be flexible and appropriate for the purposes of expansion. Taking on board the lessons of 1914–18, the general staff understood that manpower had to be available without restriction. The utility of the pre-war territorial force had been hindered by the various legal constraints controlling its use and strenuous efforts were made to ensure such restrictions were not carried over into the post-bellum army. In doing so, they were only partially successful. Although interwar territorials all signed an obligation for general service in an emergency, the necessity for attaining formal parliamentary sanction and the 'pledge' on unit integrity and drafting was at odds with its role as the framework for a national army, and undermined the universality that underpinned any general mobilisation. The War Office did eventually manage to rid itself of all the residual restrictions in territorial terms of service, but it had taken a concerted effort over 20 years. Arguably, these are issues that should have been insisted upon in 1919, even if doing so risked the re-establishment of the Territorial Army.

Similarly, the army knew that a framework for expansion had to be organised appropriately for the task and balanced between combat and support arms. The general staff intended to re-establish the TA as a fully equipped second-line army, structured along modern lines as a replica of the regular organisation. Yet budget cuts, poor recruiting and the difficulties encountered in converting surplus arms to those required resulted in the interwar TA consisting mainly of infantry and artillery, with only a scattering of vital logistic, technical and support units. How to find these missing units was a problem the War Office struggled with throughout the interwar period, despite recognising that a modern army relies as much on its 'tail' as its 'teeth'.

Within the Territorial Army itself, it was accepted that its cadres had to attain a high level of peacetime efficiency if they were to train, support and lead a wartime national army. In order to do this quickly and efficiently, the TA was obliged to prepare its commanders, instructors and specialists in advance. Its successful expansion would, therefore, depend on the depth and efficiency these cadres could generate in peacetime. However, under the voluntary system it proved extremely difficult for the territorial cadres to achieve a high standard and the accelerated rate of expansion from 1938 strained them almost to breaking point. The general staff accepted that improving this standard depended on the greater availability of training resources and professional assistance, but this was not always forthcoming or effectively applied.

Lastly, the British example demonstrates the importance of formulating and disseminating a policy for expansion that is clear, concise and implementable. The War Office consistently stated that the Territorial Army was the sole framework for military expansion. However, there remained lingering doubts as to the sincerity of this statement. This was seemingly supported by the lack of any firm guidance informing territorial units of how they should plan for their expansionary role. During a period when reserve service was far from universally popular or was even viewed as relevant, providing clearer instructions would have both facilitated the TA in its practical preparations, as well as boosted confidence in a voluntary organisation that at times doubted whether its role was truly considered to be of national importance.

However, it remains certain that the expansionary system the army had in place by 1939 was superior to that of 1914. It enabled Britain to plan and subsequently mobilise its resources in a far more effective manner and without a reliance on the desperate improvisation and wasteful inefficiency that characterised the New Armies.

During the interwar years, the War Office and general staff always regarded the Territorial Army's role as a framework of expansion an essential element in Britain's broader military capabilities. Although the priority afforded to this role varied according to the strategic focus at any one time, they understood that this was still a task that had to be taken seriously. This simply reflected the fact that in an era of total war a military's ability to reconstitute the mass necessary to conduct a modern industrial conflict was of fundamental importance. As a result, the TA continued to provide a valuable function; one that the regular army alone was incapable of fulfilling. With this being the case, it is to be commended that the interwar general staff recognised that, 'The Territorial Army is the Army. It is the only Army we have got in the modern sense of the term.'[96]

Notes

1   MOD, Army Reserve Sub-Strategy: Enclosure 1 to ECAB/G(17)010, 16 March 2017.
2   Hew Strachan, "The British Way in Warfare" in David Chandler and Ian Beckett, (eds), *The Oxford History of the British Army* (Oxford, 1994), p. 409.
3   Ian F. W. Beckett, *The Amateur Military Tradition, 1558–1945* (Manchester, 1991).
4   K. Jeffery, "The Post-war Army" in Ian F. W. Beckett and Keith Simpson (eds), *A Nation in Arms: A Social Study of the British Army in the First World War* (Manchester, 1985), Table 8.1, p. 214.
5   Brian Bond, "The Army between the Two World Wars, 1918–1939" in Chandler and Beckett, *British Army*, p. 257.
6   Shelford Bidwell and Dominick Graham, *Fire-power: British Army Weapons and Theories of War, 1904–1945* (London, 1982), p. 146.
7   David. French, *Raising Churchill's Army* (Oxford, 2000), pp. 13–19; D. French, "Doctrine and Organization in the British Army" in *The Historical Journal*, Vol. 44, No. 2 (June, 2001), pp. 497–515.
8   TNA WO 33/1297, Report of the Committee on the Lessons of the Great War, Main Report, p. 79, October 1932.
9   H. Strachan, "The British Way in Warfare", p. 408.
10   The Territorial Field Army was reduced to 12 divisions in 1935 after two were converted into the anti-aircraft role.
11   P. Dennis, *Decision by Default: Peacetime Conscription and British Defence 1919–39* (London, 1972), especially pp. 16–17.
12   B. Bond, *British Military Policy between the Two World Wars* (Oxford, 1980) p. 27; B. Bond, "The British Armed Force, 1918–39" in A. Millett and W. Murray (eds), *Military Effectiveness Volume 2: The Interwar Period* (London, 1990), p. 114; F. W. Perry, *The Commonwealth Armies: Manpower and Organisation in Two World Wars*, (Manchester, 1988), p. 41.
13   I. F. W. Beckett, "The Territorial Force" in I. F. W. Beckett and K. Simpson (eds), *A Nation in Arms: A Social Study of the British Army in the First World War* (Manchester, 1985), p. 129.
14   TNA WO 32/11246, Minute by AG, 24 March 1919; DCIGS to AG, 26 March 1919.
15   D. French (Oxford, 2001), pp. 500–3.
16   TNA WO 106/356, Army Reorganization Committee Report, 30 June 1917; TNA WO 32/11357, Minute by DCIGS, 22 Nov 1918 and War Office to Maj. Gen. Bird, 27 November 1918; WO 32/11356, Minute by DDSD, 27 November 1918; WO 32/11356, Minute by DCIGS, c.25 November 1918, Minute by AG, 26 November 1918; WO 237/2, Army Reorganization

Committee 1919, Abstract of Recommendations; WO 32/11357, Bird to Lynden-Bell, 15 July 1919; D. French, Doctrine and Organization in the British Army (2001), p. 501.

17 TNA WO 106/356, Army Reorganization Committee Report, 30 June 1917; WO 237/2, Army Reorganization Committee 1919, Abstract of Recommendations; WO 237/13, Report of the Committee on the Organization of After-War Army, July 1919.

18 TNA WO 237/13, Report of the Committee on the Organization of After-War Army, July 1919.

19 B. Bond, British Military Policy (1980), p. 23; G. Spillan, "Manpower Problems in the British Army, 1918–1939: The balancing of resources and commitments" (University of Oxford, DPhil thesis, 1985) p. 72.

20 For the extent of the commitment see K. Jeffery, The British Army and the Crisis of Empire, 1918–22 (Manchester, 1984).

21 TNA WO 32/11246, Report by Deputy Director of Military Operations, The Reconstitution of the Territorial Force at the Present Time, 12 March 1919.

22 TNA WO 32/3675, Hamilton-Gordon to Macdonogh, 22 July 1919, Macdonogh to Vesey, 24 July 1919; WO 32/3676, Report by Director of Organization, 25 November 1919; Parl. Papers, Cmd 565: Memorandum by the Secretary of State for War relating to the Army Estimates for 1920–21, p. 10; WO 32/3675, Minute by AG.1, 12 July 1919.

23 TNA WO 32/11246, Proposal for Reconstituting the TF by DGTVF, 24 February 1919, Minute by AG, 1 March 1919.

24 TNA WO 32/11790, Churchill to Harington, Masterson Smith, Stevenson and Creedy, 12 April 1919; WO 32/11790, DCIGS to Secretary of State, 14 April 1919; WO 32/2681, Minutes by Lee, Scarborough, Geddes, Wilson and Churchill, 9 January 1920.

25 TNA WO 32/11246, Report by D.DMO, The Reconstitution of the Territorial Force at the Present Time, 12 March 1919.

26 TNA WO 32/11246, Minute by AG, 24 March 1919; DCIGS to AG, 26 March 1919.

27 TNA CAB 24/87 GT.8039, The Future of the Army, 7 August 1919; WO 32/2681, Statement by DCIGS, 14 August 1919; Suggested Obligations of Service, 22 October 1919.

28 TNA CAB 24/95 CP.388 Liability of Territorial Force for General Service, 5 Jan 1920.

29 Churchill believed by imposing the obligation they may only attract 50,000 volunteers for a 190,000 establishment. See TNA WO 32/2681, Churchill to TF Conference, 13 January 1920.

30 TNA WO 32/2681, Conference between the S. of S., U.S. of S., DGTF and CIGS, 23 Oct 1919; CAB 24/95 CP.388, Liability of Territorial Force for General Service, 5 January 1920.

31 IWM, Wilson MSS 18 B/17, Wilson to Churchill, 6 October 1919.

32 TNA WO 32/2681, Minutes of the Sub-Committee on the Re-Organization of the Territorial Force, Geddes to Davies, 17 January 1920.

33 TNA CAB 23/20, Conference on the Future Organization of the Territorial Force, 27 January 1920. See also WO 32/2681, Memorandum by Creedy, 5 February 1920.

34 TNA WO 32/2678, Note on 'Pledge' for Meeting of T.A.A. Secretaries, 7 July 1932, compiled by the DGTA and DF(b), July 1932.

35 TNA WO 32/2678, Memorandum by DRO, Disadvantages of Existing Pledge, no date but around July 1932.

36 TNA WO 32/2681, Minute by Macdonogh, 23 January 1920.

37 TNA WO 32/2678, Statement by the Adjutant General to the Forces, 15 February 1933; P. Dennis, The Territorial Army, 1906–1940 (Woodbridge, 1987), p. 145; I. F. W. Beckett, The Amateur Military Tradition (1991), p. 253.

38 TNA CAB 23/283 CP.53(39), Proposals to secure the removal of a restrictive undertaking affecting service in the Territorial Army, 24 February 1939; Hansard, HC Deb 08 March 1939 Vol. 344, c. 2181; P. Dennis (1987), p. 244.

39 TNA WO 32/4562, PUS to S. of S., 17 March 1939.

40 TNA CAB 53/44 COS 838(DC), Acceleration of Mobilisation – Draft Report, 6 February 1939; CAB 2/8 CID 347th Meeting, 16 February 1939; CAB 4/29 CID Paper No.1526-B, Acceleration of Mobilisation, February 1939; CAB 54/2 DCOS 33rd Meeting, 30 January 1939; WO 32/4652, War Office to all Commands and TA Associations, 3 April 1939; CAB 4/29 CID Paper No.1538-B, Acceleration of Mobilisation, 9 March 1939; WO 32/4682, Memo by the Minister for Co-ordination [of Defence], 24 February 1939.

41 General Sir I. Maxse, "The Territorial Army: Based on Suggestions put forward by the Writers of the Gold Medal Essays, 1924 (lecture)" in *RUSI Journal*, Vol. 71, No. 484 (November 1926), p. 664.

42 TNA WO 32/11257, War Office Memorandum on the Re-organization of the TF, no date but May 1922.

43 TNA CAB 24/95 CP.371, Future Organization of the Territorial Force, 29 December 1919.

44 Of the 55 yeomanry regiments, only ten needed to remain mounted.

45 Quoted in C. E. Callwell, *Field Marshal Sir Henry Wilson: His Life and Diaries* (London, 1927), two volumes, Vol. II. p. 323.

46 TNA WO 32/11306, Note by CIGS, 12 August 1921.

47 TNA WO 32/11257, QMG to U.S. of S., 12 August 1921.

48 TNA WO 32/11257, Conference held in DO's Room to discuss reductions which might be made in the Territorial Force, 30 July 1921.

49 P. Dennis (1987), p. 98. Recruiting for the TA would also be capped at 60 per cent as an economy measure.

50 TNA WO 32/2856, Peace Organization of the Territorial Army, Memorandum by DGTA, 14 March 1924; see also WO 163/30, Army Council Précis No.1186 (Revised), The Peace Organization of the Territorial Army: Appendix.

51 TNA WO 32/2856, The Expansion of the Territorial Army in War, no date but May 1924; DSD to CIGS, 3 June 1924; DGTA to DRO and DSD, 22 May and 4 June 1924.

52 TNA WO 33/1088, First Report of the Territorial Army Expansion Committee, 4 August 1925.

53 TNA WO 32/2857, CIGS to PUS, 30 Sept 1925.

54 TNA WO 33/1088, Majority View, 8 August 1925.

55 *Ibid.*

56 TNA WO 163/31, Army Council Précis No. 1231, Expansion of the Territorial Army, October 1925; WO 32/2857 CIGS to PUS, 30 September 1925.

57 TNA WO 33/3218, Report of the Committee on the Provision of New Units for the Territorial Army on Mobilization, 26 March 1934; WO 33/3323, Interim Report of the Re-Constituted Committee on the Provision of New Units for the Territorial Army on Mobilization, 21 December 1934; WO 32/3485, Second Interim Report of Strathcona Committee on the Provision of New Units for the TA on Mobilization, 21 November 1935.

58 TNA WO 32/2857, U.S. of S. to PUS, 6 October 1925; AG to PUS, 11 Nov 1925; WO 163/31, Army Council Précis No.1234, Expansion of the Territorial Army, November 1925.

59 Surrey History Centre, 5th Earl of Onslow MSS 5337/11/(25), Unpublished Memoir Manuscript: Onslow to Milne, 4 May 1926.

60 TNA WO 278/75, Report on the Staff conference, 1934.

61 For example, an infantry battalion in 1935 was held at a peace establishment of 437, of whom no fewer than 217 were required as commanders on mobilisation. TNA WO 32/2680, The Organization and Administration of the Territorial Army: Impression of the TA by Maj. Gen. C. G. Liddell, GOC of the 47th (2nd London) Division, TA, around October 1935.

62 D. French, *Raising Churchill's Army* (2000) p. 50; J. Crang, *The British Army and the People's War 1939–1945* (Manchester, 2000), pp. 21–22; TNA WO 279/70, Report of the Staff Conference,

13–16 January 1930: Appendix A – 'Standard of Education'; Captain G. E. Grimsdale, "The Territorial Army and its Expansion for War" in *Army Quarterly*, Vol. X, No. 2 (July, 1925), p. 360; TNA WO 279/70, Report on the Staff Conference, 13–16 January 1930, Comment by Lt Col. Newth.

63 LHCMA Kirke MSS 19/4, The Territorial Army in Peace, Notes by Col. Liardet, around 1936.

64 TNA WO 279/75, Report on the Staff Conference, 8–12 January 1934, Comment by Maj. Gen. Dick-Cunyngham.

65 TNA WO 231/207, Memorandum on Training carried out during the collective training period 1925; WO 231/208, Memorandum on Army Training: Collective training period 1926, 29 November 1926; WO 231/210, Memorandum on Army Training: Collective Training Period 1927.

66 TNA WO 32/4610, GOCinC Scottish Command to War Office, 25 November 1938; Major F. M. Bladon, "Arma Tuentur Pacem" in *Army Quarterly*, Vol. XXXI, No. 1 (October 1938), pp. 55–56.

67 TNA WO 279/70, Report on the Staff Conference, 13–16 January 1930: Comment by Col. Clive; WO 32/2680, The Organization and Administration of the Territorial Army, around October 1935; LHCMA Liddell Hart MSS 1/232/16, Deverell to Liddell Hart, 29 December 1936.

68 TNA WO 33/1308, Supplementary Report on the Staff Conference, 9–11 January 1933, Comment by Maj. Gen. Armitage.

69 TNA WO 279/75, Report on the Staff Conference, 8–12 January 1934; WO 32/2679, Report on the Territorial Army by the Director General, October 1935.

70 War Office, *Training Regulations 1934*, Chapter 1, Section 4, paragraph 15.

71 TNA WO 32/3486, Revision of Field Force to Improve Preparedness, Note by CIGS, 7 February 1934; CAB 16/109 DRC 6th Meeting, 23 January 1934; WO 32/4612, Part I: Organization of the Field Force, 9 September 1935.

72 TNA WO 32/4244, Committee on the Readiness of the TA on Mobilization: First Interim Report, 21 November 1935; WO 163/42, Army Council Précis No.1394, The Readiness of the Territorial Army on Mobilization; WO 32/2679, Report by the Director General of the Territorial Army, 1935, Minute by Strathcona, 18 October 1935; WO 32/4246, Memorandum on the Readiness of the Territorial Army (Other Ranks) on Mobilization, 1936.

73 TNA WO 33/1308, Supplementary Report on the Staff Conference, 9–11 January 1933, Comments by GOC Eastern Command.

74 TNA WO 32/4246, Minute by CIGS, 6 May 1936.

75 TNA CAB 53/37 COS.707, Staff Conversations with France and Belgium, 8 April 1938; CAB 53/42 COS.795, Staff Conversations with France, 18 November 1938; CAB 2/8 CID 340th Meeting, 1 December 1938; CAB 53/40 COS.747(JP), Appreciation of the Situation in the Event of War against Germany in April 1939, Note by JPC, 15 July 1938.

76 TNA WO 32/10326, Limitations to the Possible Expansion of the British Army in War, 18 July 1938; B. Bond, *Chief of Staff: the diaries of Lt-Gen. Sir Henry Pownall, Vol. 1 1933–1940* (London, 1972), p. 126; D. French, *Raising Churchill's Army* (2000), p. 37.

77 TNA WO 32/4611 DGTA to CIGS, 20 May 1938.

78 TNA CAB 23/97/5 CC.5(39), Cabinet Conclusions, 2 February 1939; CAB 23/97/8 CC.8(39), Cabinet Conclusions, 22 February 1939; CAB 24/283 CP.49(39), The State of Preparedness of the Army in Relation to its Role: Memorandum by the Prime Minister, 18 February 1939.

79 TNA WO 32/4651, Man Power in Relation to War, Memorandum by AG, 16 May 1939.

80 Brig. K. J. Drewienkiewicz, "Examine the build-up, early training and employment of the Territorial Army in the lead-up to, and the early days of, the Second World War" (Royal College of Defence Studies, dissertation, 1992) Annex E: TA Strength in Infantry and AA Units in June 1939.

81 B. Price, *What did you do in the war, Grandpa? Memories of a Young Gunner: Two weeks' Territorial Camp which lasted seven years 1939–1946* (Woolhampton, 1989), p. 10; J. Colquhoun, *Action*

Front! – *A History of 'C' Battery HAC in War and Peace* (London, 1992) p. 3; B. Sheridan, *What did you do in the War, Dad?* (Lewes, 1993), p. 15.

82 TNA WO 277/12, *Manpower Problems 1939–1945* (London, 1949), p. 2.

83 I. Beckett, *The Amateur Military Tradition* (1991) p. 257; W. Philpott and M. Alexander, "The French and the British Field Force: Moral Support or Material Contribution?" in *The Journal of Military History*, Vol. 72 No. 3, (July, 2007), p. 765; M. Dockrill, *British Establishment Perspectives on France, 1936–40* (London, 1999), pp. 132–33; B. Bond, "Leslie Hore-Belisha at the War Office" in I. Beckett and J. Gooch (eds), *Politicians and Defence: Studies in the Formulation of British Defence Policy, 1845–1970*, (Manchester, 1981), p. 122; 'The army between the Two World Wars 1918–1939,' in D. Chandler and I. Beckett, (eds) *The Oxford History of the British Army* (Oxford, 1944) p. 267; B. Bond, *British Military Policy* (1980), p. 306.

84 B. Bond, (ed.) *Chief of Staff*, (1972) p. 197, entry for 3 April 1939.

85 LHCMA Liddell Hart MSS 1/445, Liardet to Liddell Hart, 14 August 1965.

86 K. J. Drewienkiewicz, Examine the build-up, early training and employment of the Territorial Army (1992), p. 12.

87 LHCMA Adam MSS 3/2, Paper by AG on Use of Manpower in the Army, 21 November 1941.

88 K. J. Drewienkiewicz, Examine the build-up, early training and employment of the Territorial Army (1992) p. 47; TNA WO 163/49 OS.11, Memorandum by the CIGS on the Training of III Corps, Appendix A – Report by GOC 3 Corps, 21 January 1940.

89 D. French, *Raising Churchill's Army* (2000) p. 187.

90 *Hansard*, HC Deb, 5 December 1939, Vol. 355, c.467W.

91 *Hansard*, HC Deb, 16 January 1940, Vol. 356, c.7.

92 IWM Dunlop MSS 74/164/8, Report No. 8 South Midlands, 25th to 28th October 1939; TNA WO 163/48, Army Council Meeting, 29 March 1940; WO 163/49 OS.44, Memorandum by CIGS on the Employment of Territorial Army Officers reported upon as Unfit to Command in War, March 1940.

93 TNA WO 32/2672, Address by the CIGS to the Central Council, Territorial Army Association, 23 May 1928.

94 TNA WO 163/47, Army Council Meeting, 27 September 1939; WO 163/48, Army Council Meeting, 9 October 1939; CAB 53/52 COS.947, Reinforcement for Garrisons Abroad, 19 July 1939; WO 163/47, Army Council Meeting, 12 September 1939; WO 193/19, Swapping TA for Regulars in India, 26 October 1939; quoted in K. J. Drewienkiewicz, Examine the build-up, early training and employment of the Territorial Army (1992), p 27; W. S. Churchill, *The Second World War Volume 1: The Gathering Storm* (London, 1948), p. 437; B. Bond, *Chief of Staff* (1972), p. 303, entry for 25 April 1940.

95 IWM Dunlop MSS 74/164/8 AG to DRO (through DAG(T), 1 Dec 1939.

96 TNA WO 33/1308, Supplementary Report on the Staff Conference, 9–11 January 1933, Comment by Lt Gen. Percy Radcliffe.

CHAPTER 7

Rising to the Occasion

US Army Expansion in the World Wars (1900–45)

Alexander A. Falbo-Wild

Reflecting upon the European influence within the US army during the late modern era, one might picture densely packed kepi-sporting ranks commanded with Jominian offensive élan at Antietam. Or one might envision the budding professionalism of the officer corps, following the establishment of Fort Leavenworth as America's early emulation of the *Kriegsakademie*.[1] However, the American model for *mobilisation* is of neither French nor German inspiration but British. Inheriting Britain's long-standing suspicion of large standing armies meant that American culture and, therefore, the US Army were predisposed to improvise expansion to meet the challenges of both world wars. Although mobilisation initially presented significant drawbacks in deployment readiness and engagement, in both 1917 and 1941, the United States successfully raised from a core regular force, augmented by national guardsmen, reservists and draftees, two citizen-soldier armies which were continental in size and expeditionary in character.

America's Road to a Citizen Army

When the United States declared war on Germany on 6 April 1917, the US Army was composed of two main elements; the regular army and the National Guard. The regular army consisted of full-time professional soldiers who occupied outposts and garrisons across the country. It also occasionally conducted expeditions to serve American interests abroad, especially in the western hemisphere. The National Guard, whose origins could be traced to the colonial militias created by the English settlers of North America, was a domestically oriented institution of locally recruited part-time soldiers, whose units served at the pleasure of their respective state governors. The American president also possessed the power to place the National Guard under direct federal control including assignment overseas.

However, these combined forces totalled approximately 291,880 troops in April 1917. To build a behemoth army able to survive *and* succeed on the Western Front in Europe, President Woodrow Wilson and Congress chose conscription with the ratification of the Selective Service Act on 18 May 1917. By 11 November 1918, at the signing of the war's Armistice, over four million men were in uniform. A growth by a factor of 17. Of the total wartime figure, 72 per cent were produced from the draft.[2]

What is perhaps most remarkable about this staggering expansion, is the nation's lack of comparable precedent and cultural hostility towards compulsory military service. In 1917, America's only experience with such a comprehensive level of conscription were four federal drafts between 1863–65. Even so, only 6 per cent of the total Union Army strength in the American Civil War came from these drafts.[3] Despite the totality and modernity showcased in that conflict, the US Army relied primarily upon volunteers and the militia throughout the war and well into the 1880s. Yet, at the dawn of the 20th century, American policymakers soon recognised the need for recruitment and expansion reform, even if they refused to embrace the international movement towards standing citizen-armies.

By the 1890s, the pressure of imperial competition and national security concerns eroded European military fears of popular involvement in war in favour of an ever-improving, pre-emptive posture. The tonic to the conception of the 'armed mob' was the emergence of the Prussian universal military service system. The system's appeal lay in the ability to harness the manpower of the state across the social strata for massive reserve-based armies. France's stunning defeat in 1871 at the hands of Prussia convinced the world of its potential. Before the end of the 19th century, most European states could double the size of their large active duty armies with a mass of trained citizen-soldier reservists awaiting a mobilisation order. The conservative nightmare of the radical egalitarian horde, exemplified by France's *levée en masse* in 1792, had thus transfigured into the patriotic flower of the nation, vigilant and invested. Military service, therefore, became part of the essence of citizenship in Europe.[4]

Of the world's major powers, only Great Britain and the United States ignored this trend, relying instead on their navies to secure strategy and project power throughout the period.[5] Geographic consideration, mainly in the form of oceanic isolation, certainly guided this policy. But, in the American case, isolation stood as only one in an arsenal of arguments wielded by a powerful and growing American 'navalist' lobby of politicians, business magnates and editors, supported by the maritime theories of Admiral Alfred T. Mahan.[6] A grand surface fleet complimented America's economic interests. Although costly, a cutting-edge navy was argued to be cheaper than a mass citizen-army. It garnered diplomatic prestige, whilst guarding America's sea commerce and spheres of influence. If direct intervention was required to deter foreign incursion or to quell indigenous unrest within America's territories, the US Navy possessed an organic specialist expeditionary force in the US Marine Corps.

Naval battle also carried a romantic Nelsonian ideal, where a decisive engagement could win a war in an afternoon. Mahan championed this aesthetic quality of high-seas engagement in much of his work.[7] Finally, applying the latest technologies to shrink oceans and encourage greater trade in thought, capital and materiel resources embodied the late-19th century's *zeitgeist* of human progress. A large peacetime army, by contrast, represented profligacy and belligerence, and the American Gilded Age duly passed it by. However unpopular it may have been, the urgent need for military mobilisation reform was underscored by America's war with Spain in 1898, which became the catalyst for a process of modernisation lasting until 1920.

The US army began the war in April 1898 with roughly 28,000 soldiers. That same month, Congress authorised the number to be doubled. However, the regular army's stringent physical recruitment standards left thousands of vacancies. In accordance with American military tradition, President William McKinley called for volunteers to fill them. Popular enthusiasm brimmed to avenge the alleged Spanish sabotage of the USS *Maine* in Havana Harbor (America's *causus beli*) and over 207,000 volunteers were inducted.[8] The bulk of these troops, however, never reached Cuban or Philippine shores as the US War Department was utterly overwhelmed with providing them equipment, transportation and logistics. Regular officers sought a measured expansion of the army. But the national enthusiasm for the war, reflected in the volume of enlistments along with the rapidly unfolding strategic events, dashed their hopes for an orderly process. Shortly after the war's end, the public outcry at the War Department's gross inefficiency – including shipments of contaminated tinned meat rations and surplus wool tunics from the Civil War to a tropical theatre – prompted both investigations and legislative revisions to army policy. These reforms became the basis for what would become Wilson's army of 1917–18.[9]

The Root Reforms and the Progressive Army (1902–16)

The spearhead for the modernisation of the American army took the form of a shrewd, eloquent and vigorous conservative lawyer who served as the secretary of war from 1899–1904; Elihu Root. Having represented corporate firms in private practice and later the state of New York as its Southern District Attorney, Root was quite experienced in the art of negotiation and legislation. Enjoying the support of both President Theodore Roosevelt and progressive army officers, he was thoroughly primed to navigate the War Department's internal sectarianism and bureaucratic inertia. To this end, Root's agenda was twofold: the professionalisation of the army's officer corps and the creation of a designated national reserve for a more efficient wartime expansion. Both courses hinged upon the professionalisation of military education.

Modern warfare increasingly demanded a synergy of managerial and tactical skill, and the army possessed no institutions designed to address this development. Thus, in 1901, Root ordered the creation of the Army War College. It was not initially an academic institution in the way of the British Staff College at Camberly or the German *Kriegsakademie*. Rather, it was charged with gathering the brightest minds in the army to design plans for immediate strategic problems, with a focus on the western hemisphere. Unlike its naval counterpart, the war college did not focus on long-term procurement, military theory and geo-strategic planning.[10] But, by the 1910s, it evolved into a more educational format due through the efforts of pedagogically minded officers such as Arthur L. Wagner, Tasker Bliss and William H. Carter. The war college's first students attended in 1904 and it became a place for officers to test their strategic theories with high-level war games.[11] Regarding the latter, Root also mandated in 1903 the engagement of large-scale military manoeuvres for the first time in the country's history. The war college's early years did impact the American Expeditionary Forces (AEF) of 1917–18, because several of its ablest commanders were graduates, including lieutenant colonels Hunter Liggett (class of 1910) and Fox Conner (class of 1911). Liggett eventually led the US First Army in late 1918, whilst Fox Conner served on John J. Pershing's AEF operations (G3) staff. Both were highly regarded for their intellectual abilities.[12]

Root further concentrated on educational reform with the development of an army collegiate system stemming from his political progressivism. He viewed mass education as a means to a meritocratic society and was determined that the army should benefit likewise. The United States Military Academy occupied the first tier, providing a foundational education to future officers. Next, graduates would enter their branches and attend the various service schools. The best students would proceed to the General Service and Staff College at Fort Leavenworth, re-designated from the Infantry and Cavalry School in 1902. At Fort Leavenworth, students learned the art of operations, combined arms warfare and staff work. Finally, distinguished graduates of the Staff College would advance to the Army War College.[13] These academic reforms served Root's drive for greater command efficiency through centralisation. His inspiration derived from big businesses and corporate power structures placing emphasis on executive decisions within a streamlined administration.

It should be noted that Root did not necessarily advocate such centralisation comprehensively, i.e. as the tactical or operational *modus operandi*. Rather, these reforms ensured that the strategic levels of command were clarified and strengthened with an eye to effectively translate the war's political objectives into military ones. The progressivist management theories of the American industrial consultant Frederick Taylor were indeed rooted in philosopher Max Weber's work on professionalisation and therefore of German origin.[14] But the net effect of their use served a wider British expansion model for war emergencies. With the establishment of a structure to manifest the army's brain trust, Root then turned to the matter of consolidating the chain of command to expedite its decision making.

In 1900, the War Department's bureau chiefs (the Army Signal Corps, Engineer Corps, Quarter Master Corps and others) acted independently to the point of dysfunction, as was demonstrated in the 1898 war with Spain. There also existed the confusing title of Commander of the Army (the US Army's most senior rank at the time) which allowed previous generals to presume they possessed the authority to ignore or argue with their civilian superiors. Thus, in January 1903, Root tabled his most significant reform to Congress with the creation of the army general staff and the position of army chief of staff. Bureau chiefs could no longer interface directly and independently with civilian administration and leadership. Everything was channelled up to the general staff. The chief of staff then reported to the secretary of war who took orders from the president, constitutionally designated as the commander-in-chief.

Internal resistance to the general staff structure was stout. By 1910, the War Department bureaux confined the general staff's work to exclusively military matters and in a counselling capacity. Although Root's protégé, Henry L. Stimson, successfully established the centralised authority of the chief of staff during his time as secretary of war from 1911–13, the War Department's habit of an informal high command crept back into practice after 1914. This parallel command eventually led to the infamous and unresolved bickering between generals John J. Pershing as commander-in-chief of the AEF and Peyton C. March as army chief of staff, throughout World War I. The question of supremacy in practice was not firmly resolved within the War Department until General George C. Marshall's reorganisation plan of 1942, which will be explored further on.[15]

Centralisation of command and professional military education were not the only issues which the bureaux chiefs resisted. A week prior to the introduction of the bill to create the general staff, Root addressed the question of a primary reserve in the draft Militia Act of 1903 (also known as the Dick Act). Root, along with the War Department, desired a reserve under direct federal control. The regular army, especially, held the militia concept in contempt, and viewed the guard as an ill-disciplined and poorly equipped ragtag of amateurs whose leadership was rife with nepotism and local politics. However, Root knew that the proposal to raise a federal national reserve would likely garner even more opposition than his other reforms, risking public outrage if such a system required conscription. Such opposition came in the form of the National Guard Association (NGA); an interest group which lobbied guard affairs in Congress. However, one of Root's congressional allies, Representative Charles Dick of Ohio, who also chaired the House Militia Affairs Committee, drafted a solution.[16] Dick's compromise between Root and the NGA was to make the guard America's official national reserve. The caveat was that guardsmen could be federalised for nine months within US borders for national defence and to enforce martial law. They were also subject to increased oversight by the regular army's standards, including training, doctrine, equipment and organisation. In return, the guard would receive federal funding and a renewed mandate within the national defence scheme, which meant a diminishment of their much-despised role as strike breakers in local industrial disputes. By 1908, the NGA successfully lobbied Congress to lift the restriction on the National Guard's overseas deployment as well.[17]

As the armies of the Entente and Central Powers mobilised and converged across the plains of eastern and western Europe in the late summer of 1914, the question of America's eventual involvement and national preparedness dominated domestic political discourse. These debates were characterised by an air of isolationism throughout the population, particularly in the agrarian south. President Wilson, sworn-in in March 1913, was similarly inclined towards anti-militarism and possessed a distaste for what he perceived as imperial European intrigue. Progressives, on the other hand, desired extensive preparations for war if not outright entry into the Entente alliance. Despite arguments in the press and by politicians about the 'Prussian' character of universal military service, the general staff throughout 1915–16 fought for the establishment of a programme like the European citizen-army schemes, often described as Universal Military Training (UMT). What distinguished the American UMT concept from its European counterpart was length of service. Instead of a year's training and three years' active service, as found in French, German and Russian models, UMT consisted of six months' training with no active service afterward until mobilisation. Ostensibly, UMT sought to unify the population with such qualities as education, military discipline and comradeship, whilst providing a pool of trained men with a rudimentary knowledge of soldiering. Proponents included Roosevelt, Root, General Leonard Wood (Army Chief of Staff 1910–14) and, eventually, Wilson himself. Yet the public, press and much of the army remained adamant that UMT was a blow to American principles of liberty. Irish and German immigrant communities were especially loath to be involved in European struggles *and* on the side of the British. Despite Wilson's professed neutrality – a platform which also won him re-election in 1916 – the sinking of RMS *Lusitania* and Germany's return to its unrestricted submarine warfare policy gradually softened Wilson's stance.

Debates over the army's readiness to fight overseas was abruptly sidelined by the question of whether it was even strong enough to defend America's frontiers. On the evening of 8 March 1916, the ongoing Mexican Civil War spilled over into the US when a 500-man guerrilla force, led by Francisco 'Pancho' Villa, raided Columbus, New Mexico, along with its military post, Camp Furlong. The town's defenders, 353 troopers of the US 13th Cavalry Regiment, repulsed the marauders and incurred minor casualties in the ensuing action. By 15 March, Wilson's immediate orders for a response operation assembled just 4800 regular troops at Columbus under General Pershing, who then pursued Villa into north-east Mexico. Although Pershing's logistics base martialled roughly 2500 tonnes of supplies delivered by a motorised transport fleet, which grew five-fold during the campaign, the overall personnel mobilisation figures left much to be desired.[18] The majority of the regular army's total 108,399 soldiers in early 1916 were dispersed across the Philippines, Hawaii, and the newly completed Panama Canal Zone. This left only 23 per cent located within the continental United States.[19] The problem was keenly felt when a second incursion was made at Glenn Springs, Texas, on 6 May. The Texas, New Mexico, and Arizona National Guards were then federalised three days later. Unfortunately, despite the Root reform's improvements to the guard, the latter did not uphold regular standards in several key areas, including physical fitness. In reports for 14 mid-west states, an average of 15.5 per cent of recruits failed to meet federal standards and were rejected.[20] When Wilson federalised the Arizona, New Mexico, and Texas guards, they could barely field 4000 men. Although Wilson finally federalised the entire National Guard in June, it was not until August that 110,000 guardsmen could be deployed to the 1900-mile long Mexican-American border. Overall, this lacklustre mobilisation confirmed for the War Department that the guard simply could not function as the nation's primary reserve force.

Part of the problem was that the guard's mobilisation for the Mexican expedition was carried out simultaneously with the passing of the National Defense Act of 1916. Signed into law on 3 June, the act furthered Root's initiatives and increased the regular army strength to 175,000 men over the next five years. The numbers of the National Guard were also significantly enhanced from 100,000 to 400,000 over a similar timescale. This initially created much confusion over the methods and structure for guard expansion whilst it was preparing for border operations.[21]

But the two crucial developments of the law resided in the augmentation of federal powers over the guard and industry. Whilst the 1908 amendment allowed the guard to be sent overseas, the 1916 amendment required guardsmen to pledge a state and federal oath, with a service contract specifying three years of active duty and three years in reserve; a system not wholly unlike that found in continental Europe, aside from the part-time weekend drill nature of the guard.[22] The War Department also agreed to wholly fund and supply the guard for all its needs. The penalty for non-compliance to regular standards was the withdrawal of federal funding. Essentially, the 1916 act placed the National Guard at the federal government's call, with the regular army theoretically maintaining oversight as to its readiness.[23] As for industry, the new law granted the president the ability 'to place an order with any individual, firm, association, company, corporation, or organized manufacturing industry for such product or material as may be required' that could be manufactured by those respective entities.[24]

It is critical to understand, however, that the US Army in 1916, within the wider context of the World War I, still operated under many of the 19th century's agrarian mentalities, which kept it a small and comparatively under-armed constabulary. Many officers within the War Department and throughout the army resisted the culture of reform and dismissed developments like professional military education as merely a passing trend. Meanwhile, as the entrenched European armies were experimenting with tanks, complex artillery barrage schemes, photographic aerial reconnaissance, wireless transmissions and decentralised infantry platoon tactics by late 1916, the US Army Ordnance Department had still not procured a principal heavy machinegun.[25] The primacy of the militia/volunteer tradition also remained firmly planted in both the civilian and military mainstream into 1917. However, the culmination of the Root Reforms provided the essential internal mechanisms, framework and federal authority for the War Department to mobilise for a continental struggle. It is debatable whether American foreign policy was well served by the Mexican expedition or if a small war was needed to shock American defence policy into action before entering World War I. But the army correctly viewed the Mexican expedition as a valuable learning experience and actively drew lessons from it as the AEF headed for the Western Front.[26]

Getting an Army Over There (1917–18)

In February 1917, both Wilson and his secretary of war, Newton D. Baker (1916–21), believed that when America joined the Allies in the war, the militia/volunteer expansion model would be inadequate to raise the needed army numbers in time. In a strategy similar to that of Britain's Liberal government in 1914, Wilson wished to steer the eventual peace proceedings with a late but decisive military victory.[27] The only realistic way to earn such a place at the peace table amongst the bloodied European nations was a massive army raised as quickly as possible and then committed to operations in the main theatre. This realisation pointed to a draft. Wilson subsequently ordered Baker to ready a conscription bill to that end. Shortly after war was declared on 6 April, Wilson's concern was confirmed when the army only managed to recruit 86,405 men that month. The result in and of itself was good. But the strategic pressures faced by the Entente in 1917 and the renewed German U-boat offensive in the Atlantic made the reliance upon the traditional expansion format impossible.[28] Furthermore, Wilson believed that the draft was the best chance of preserving an orderly social and economic transition into war. By comparison, Britain's early mobilisation phase, mainly governed by volunteerism, saw scores of munitions workers and skilled labourers attempt to join the colours in 1914. This was harmful for shipyards and other essential industries that depended on skilled and un-skilled manpower retention. Wilson firmly held that early conscription would prevent such a situation through a measured selection process. Subsequent events proved him correct.[29]

Yet, there was another reason for Wilson's preference for conscription. He feared the interference of Theodore Roosevelt. The popular ex-president remained actively involved in politics since his tenure in the White House and was an outspoken critic of isolationism and neutrality since 1914. Wilson was not simply gripped by politician's paranoia. Writing to Senator Henry Cabot Lodge on 22 March 1917, Roosevelt described an offer he made to the French government to recruit and lead 'an expeditionary infantry division to France under the American flag' should they agree to finance the formation. In the event of rejection, the proposal would be extended to the Canadians as well.[30] To Wilson and the War Department, Roosevelt's meddling in the mobilisation scheme threatened to polarise and politicise the army through his personal recruitment efforts and possibly those of his political allies. Roosevelt also pushed the administration to place him in command of the AEF. But the War Department and the White House were united in their belief that Roosevelt's dilettante soldiering experience was wholly unsuitable for the challenges of the AEF commander-in chief and that his combative personality could also pose a direct challenge to the army chief of staff, secretary of war and even Wilson himself. Despite these difficulties, which were compounded by the urgency of expanding the army for the war in Europe, Wilson ultimately sidestepped the whole matter with a selective service draft designated for the duration of the war.

On 27 April, the Selective Service Act of 1917 was presented before Congress by Representative Julius Kahn of California. Passed on 18 May, the bill became the most comprehensive compulsory service law in American history at that time. The legislation called for all able-bodied males between the ages of 21–31 to register with their local draft board on 5 June 1917.[31] The 4648 five-man draft boards were located within 155 districts across the country and were supervised by their respective state governors. Importantly, the ability to hire substitutes – a major factor in causing class tension over the obligation of service during the Civil War – was eliminated. Deferments sought on medical, occupational or familial grounds were adjudicated by the local boards of appeal, granting exemption on a case-by-case basis, with Wilson acting as the final arbiter in some instances.[32] There was apprehension from the White House and the War Department over the reception of such an unprecedented level of conscription. Consequently, many of the administrative aspects were discreetly completed in anticipation of congressional approval. However, their worst fears never came to pass and 9,925,751 men signed up for the first registration with no great civil unrest. Two more successful registrations in 1918, with an amendment expanding the age range from 18–45, brought the total figure to 24,234,021 for the war. These men were divided into five classes that grouped the pool of registrants with various deferments. This method helped prioritise the sequencing of the call to duty with registrant draft numbers chosen by a central lottery in Washington DC. The draft effectively threaded many political and military difficulties as fairly as possible in timely fashion.[33]

However, there remained thorny opposition in the form of out-spoken isolationists, agrarian politicians, socialist party leaders (such as Eugene Debs), and German and Irish immigrant populations. The argument over UMT largely faded by March 1917 and the debate boiled down to a question of conscription versus volunteerism. Recalling the fierce and embarrassing resistance to Union drafts throughout the north during the American Civil War and the egregious media indiscretion toward military plans in the Spanish-American War, national security concerns quickly presented a challenge to the preservation of the constitutional right to free speech.

The Wilson administration passed several executive orders from 1915–18, which included the creation of agencies and committees of propaganda and censorship. The Committee for Public Information (created 14 April 1917), for example, guided the self-censorship policies of newspapers, which were either patriotic or pragmatically opting for compliance over compulsion.[34] This was essential work as these publications printed headlines and features regarding the procedures and consequences of the Selective Service Act. On 30 May, a headline in the *Los Angeles Times* stated, 'Uncle Sam's Mailed Fist for Anti-Draft Agitators' whilst a pair of front-page articles in the 1 June edition of *The New York Times* went 'New Police Arms Awe Socialists' and 'Draft Shirkers Barred in Flight.'[35] Legislation also played an integral role in suppressing dissension. As an amendment to the Espionage Act of 1917, the Sedition Act, passed on 16 May 1918, ensured great federal latitude and elasticity in the interpretation of what passed for freedom of speech versus treason. Roughly a month later, Debbs famously addressed a convocation of the Socialist Party of America in Canton, Ohio. His fiery oration against selective service and what he argued was the population's ambivalence to American militarism found him indicted, and later convicted, with a 10-year prison sentence under the new law.[36] Despite such instances of vocal criticisms, however, conscription never faced determined opposition nor was seriously impeded. More importantly, these statutes and organisations converted public isolationist indifference into an ideological crusade, for the safeguarding and international proliferation of democratic institutions.

In July 1917, as the first influx of conscripts arrived at camps and bases across the country, the army reorganised its fighting formations. This was the point at which the selective service draft numbers were transformed into combat power for the AEF (see Diagram 7.1). The key semi-autonomous fighting formation around which both sustained operations and a cultural identity could be built was the division. Upon entry into the war, the division was also the metric for Wilson's commitment to the Allies and the foundation of the fighting strength of the AEF. Although divisions had existed since the Civil War, they were usually composite formations which shunted their units and sub-units (e.g. brigades, regiments and battalions) between other divisions within a corps command. Experiments toward a fixed divisional organisation were successfully made from 1911–16, but the first permanent entities were created in May 1917.[37]

The American infantry division of World War I consisted of 27,120 men led by approximately 1000 officers distributed into two infantry brigades of two regiments per brigade, an artillery brigade with three artillery regiments and integral headquarters troops, machine-gun, signal, engineer, medical, and train (munitions, sanitary, etc.) companies and battalions.[38] This was twice the size of the typical British, French or German division and the structure was the same across the regular army, National Guard and newly formed national army divisions. The latter were composed of draftees from regional recruitment zones, which approximately coincided with

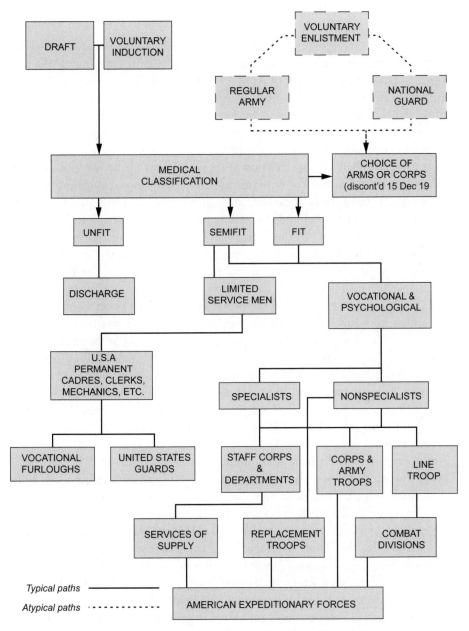

Diagram 7.1 The Selective Service to AEF System (1917–19).[39]

National Guard recruitment areas. Based upon their experiences in the Spanish America War, army planners designed the division as a massive formation capable of operating as independently as possible. Firepower and logistical endurance were preferred over tactical agility.

Whilst the process of selective service efficiently provided the needed manpower to populate these divisions, there existed no clear plan for deploying them to Europe. Initial steps were taken in April 1917 when the War Department devised a temporary programme which first aimed to get as many men as possible into training camps. However, failures in National Guard recruitment figures, adequate equipment procurement and the redistribution of personnel throughout the regular, National Guard, and national army formations, led to an overall revision in the process. The so-called 'Thirty-Division Plan' was drawn up by the end of 1917, which attempted to balance the Entente's urgent need for more troops and Wilson's desire to get an identifiably American force into battle. This was a joint directive designed by the general staff and the AEF's General Headquarters. It proposed to send 30 divisions (roughly 1.3 million men) to France by the end of 1918. This plan was interrupted by the German army's final bid for victory in the spring of 1918. In response, the War Department, under pressure from the Entente and the strategic situation, produced the 'Eighty-Division Plan' which was finalised on 25 July 1918. The plan tripled the projected AEF figure to an astonishing 3.3 million men by 1 July 1919, with 52 divisions (2.3 million men) set to arrive in France by 31 December 1918. Based upon the rate of troop transfers in late 1918, this directive was not altogether impossible. The 'Eighty-Division Plan' sought to reinforce the AEF at a rate of 250,000 troops per month from July 1918 through to the new year. In execution, the average rate was maintained at approximately 258,000. But it is uncertain if this figure could have been sustained into 1919 as the trend from July–October 1918 demonstrated a steady 60 per cent decline over the period.[40]

And then there was the issue of shipping, which was critical in 1917 as German U-boats reached the apex of their efficacy during the war. British tonnage was being sunk at such volumes and rates that there was grave concern within the British Admiralty as to whether the Royal Navy could survive the year intact. The US Navy and Merchant Marine, however, were unprepared for the task of shipping the troop figures allotted for the 'Thirty-Division Plan', let alone the 'Eighty-Division Plan'. This placed Washington in an awkward position of demanding the support of the already taxed Royal Navy, whilst the British government argued for the immediate deployment of American combat personnel. The British, facing a manpower crisis of their own in late 1917, were mainly interested in getting infantry and machine-gun battalions integrated into existing British Expeditionary Force (BEF) divisions. The French also possessed similar ideas, which were, perhaps, less outspoken. Their chief concern was simply to get American troops to the Western Front in the hopes of rejuvenating critically low French morale following the catastrophic failure of the Nivelle Offensive in April 1917. Ultimately, the task of transporting American troops to France was split by the US navy (45 per cent) and Royal Navy (49 per cent), with various Entente naval forces assisting (6 per cent).[41] Additionally, the quantities transported steadily increased throughout 1917–18 as the Anglo-American naval coalition began successfully employing convoy formations.

In the end, the Selective Service Act registered 24 million men for the draft. Of these, 2.8 million were inducted with a further 878,485 volunteers. The US army's total strength on 11 November 1918 stood at 3.7 million, with a total of 4 million inducted over the course of the war. Out of the total 64 army divisions created during the conflict, the AEF possessed 42 divisions, 29 of which saw action. Put another way, 65 per cent of the AEF's 1.9 million men was combat strength.[42] Although the war ended before the AEF could lead the Allied offensive of 1919, its expansion and contribution to the coalition's campaigns in such a condensed space of time, with a method so contradictory to America's liberal society, is a remarkable achievement.

The Return to a Constabulary (1919–39)

The end of World War I proved almost as chaotic as its beginning for the american army. With the prospect of a great 1919 AEF-led offensive dashed, the War Department was confronted by a precipitous demobilisation. To that effect, Pershing immediately issued orders to facilitate the return of the two million men in France with 25,000 repatriated in November 1918 and a further 124,000 through December.[43] And although the war did not diplomatically terminate with the armistice, the cessation of hostilities qualified in the minds of most of the troops in the AEF and the American public as the conclusion of the 'duration'.

Despite this sentiment and its concordant socio-political pressure, Secretary Baker and the War Department asked Congress for funding an army of 509,909 troops in a bill introduced in the new year.[44] Three factors contributed to the request. First, it was uncertain what might occur should the German government reject the terms of Versailles. Although militarily defeated on the Western Front, the German Army was not annihilated in 1918 as it was later in 1945. A reasonably large AEF was potentially needed in the case of either a national uprising or a resumption of military hostilities to whatever degree. The British, for example, took the possibility seriously enough to continue their naval blockade well into 1919 to ensure German submission. Second, there were ongoing military commitments. An 8000-man AEF expedition deployed in 1918 to bolster White Russian forces at Murmansk and in Siberia was actively engaged against Red Bolshevik forces in Russia's civil war. Meanwhile, in Germany, eight divisions of the US Third Army centred around Coblenz occupied the Rhineland with over 200,000 troops. A further two divisions were based in

Luxembourg with the US Second Army.[45] The bases sustaining these operations also required manpower. Third, there remained the question of completing the army's Progressive Era reforms. It was hoped by capitalising on the public's high regard for the existing mass-citizen army that the process of creating a large peacetime army might be better facilitated.

Relevant to these considerations was the issue of service contracts. Most of the AEF and wider army consisted of conscripts. Their obligation for four months of service following the end of the war meant that most of these soldiers would be discharged by the spring of 1919. The army's wartime mixture of draftees into regular and guard units further complicated matters with uneven reductions across formations. With no volunteers to replace the coming conscript exodus (due to the ongoing recruitment ban since mid-1918), the regular army was particularly confronted by an acute manpower dilemma in 1919. The War Department's request to the House of Military Affairs Committee for 500,000 men was only a temporary solution, but the number was deemed excessive and reduced to only 175,000 when the bill was passed on 22 February 1919.[46] As a means of keeping a strong peacetime force, the 1916 proposition of UMT was resurrected by the general staff and a handful of senators. However, the idea was again stonewalled by Congress whose views were echoed by ardent pacifist and anti-militarist editors. Even the chief of staff favoured emergency conscription over UMT and deleted the latter from the War Department's bill. The overall situation was not helped by the conclusion of the 65th Congress on 1 March, with no further hearings tabled until the start of a new Congress on 19 May. Thus, historians have aptly described the American army of 1919–20 as 'an army in limbo'.[47]

Meanwhile, it shrank 31 per cent from January–June 1919.[48] To counter this rapid depletion of personnel, General March (still chief of staff) ordered the resumption of recruitment on 12 February, which took effect on 1 March. With a total of 513 recruiting stations erected across 56 recruitment districts nationwide, the army began a drive to maintain the congressionally authorised size of 175,000 men. This effort included adopting commercial advertising tactics (still in use today) with the largest recruitment budget in the army's history at that time of $185,000.[49] Whilst there was initial enthusiasm, recruitment eventually dropped by the winter of 1919 to 9000 men per month; a 56 per cent decrease since the previous summer. This figure had to contend with the loss of 644,580 discharges for the year, at an average rate of 54,000 per month.[50] Running headlong into a manpower crisis with a speculative strategic posture, the War Department remained aimless, policy wise, until the passing of the National Defense Act of 1920.

The act effectively completed two decades of military reform and utilised the experience of a world war. Its three primary achievements were: the reorganisation of the reserves; the augmented involvement of the National Guard in War Department affairs; and the creation of a procurement link between the military and industry.

It first outlined that the components of the army were to consist of the regular army, the National Guard and the organized reserve. Regular and guard strengths were increased to 280,000 and 400,000 respectively, whilst the organized reserve was unlimited in size. This latter component effectively regrouped the Reserve Officer Corps, Reserve Officer Training Corps and Enlisted Reserve Corps into an administrative body without strictly amalgamating them. More importantly, many of the national army divisions formed in 1917–18 (such as the 77th, 82nd and 90th) were retained in structure and lineage on paper throughout the 1920s–30s. This included their regional recruitment departments and training camps. The experiment, however, was a disappointment during the interwar period for only the divisional staffs could be maintained at full strength, whilst roughly a few hundred enlisted personnel populated the rest of the formation. This was tied to the low pay and stagnant promotion prospects for a peacetime enlisted man versus an officer who could at least use his leadership rank for distinction in a civilian job interview. As the Great Depression hit America in the autumn of 1929, this problem only worsened well into the 1930s. But the retention of these formations on an 'inactive' basis meant that when war came in 1941, the army could martial its massive infusion of drafted manpower into fighting organisations efficiently.

The implications of the act for the National Guard were even greater. Since 1903, the guard gradually fell within the federal purview. However, guard officers remained largely ignorant of War Department affairs due to routine exclusion. The new legislation allowed guard officers to serve on the general staff and stipulated that only guard officers be placed as chief of the National Militia Bureau. This theoretically ensured that guard interests were represented within the War Department, whilst regulars were better able to supervise and interact with guard formations in training.[51] Although nepotism and local popularity continued to play a role in the appointment of National Guard formations, with many officers too old or inexperienced to carry out combat operations abroad, this was not always the case. Nor was nepotism necessarily a negative aspect of guard staffing.

For example, Major General Robert S. Beightler was appointed to command the 37th Infantry Division in 1940 by his good friend and Governor of Ohio, John W. Bricker. Beightler had served in combat during World War I and later became a civil engineer and entrepreneur. A top graduate of the general staff and Command College in 1926 and then the Army War College in 1930, he also served on the general staff in 1932, gaining valuable experience before returning to his Ohio National Guard post as a brigade commander in 1936. He was the only American commander to raise, train and lead the same division throughout the duration of World War II.[52]

However, the most comprehensive aspect of the new law was the establishment of the Army Industrial College.[53] Raising the needed manpower for the AEF stood in stark contrast to the mobilisation of industry for the US military. Whilst American factories were adequately supplying Entente contracts for raw materiels, munitions and equipment, the experience of adjusting to US military requirements left much to be desired. Although military-industrial complexes had been in existence throughout Europe since the late-19th century, 1924 marked its emergence in America with the Army Industrial College. This institution grew from its nine initial students to an annual average of 45 by the late 1930s. Unlike the Army War College, the Army Industrial College was an academic institution from the outset. Its mission was essentially to train Army officers in all aspects necessary to the 'procurement of all military supplies in time of war and to the assurance of adequate provisions for the mobilisation of material and industrial organisation essential to wartime needs'.[54] The college ensured that the army was provided with a dynamic means of interfacing with industry, which was absent during World War I. This included the coordination of army and navy interests through permitting Navy and Marine Corps officer's admittance to the college and through the establishment of the joint Army and Navy Munitions Board. This entity then allowed the various bureaux and service branches to handle the specific requirements, whilst resolving and administering the overall effort.[55]

Just as the Spanish-American War inspired the civilian-led reforms of the 1900s, World War I galvanised the army into poring over its seemingly endless lessons. Discontent with following the same 1917 mobilisation plan in the event of another major war, the War Department developed no less than seven distinct mobilisation plans between 1921–39. Whilst it is beyond the scope of this chapter to examine them in any detail, it should be said that the work sought much greater integration in all aspects of the nation's mobilisation and expansion for war. Unlike previous conflicts, where the army not only shrunk but shelved its experiences to be possibly

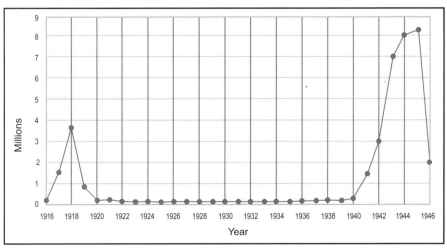

Graph 7.1 Total per annum strength of the US army (1916–46).[56]

reconsidered later, the 1920s–30s witnessed a flurry of War Department activity to maintain army preparedness.

Overall, the interwar period witnessed the army return to a constabulary populated by an all-volunteer model, annually averaging 228,000 men.[57] As the Great Depression gripped the nation, military expenditure was not high on the list of priorities for the average citizen and his elected representatives. And, as Europe and Asia emitted the early tremors of World War II, isolationism regained popularity. However, the provisions of the National Defense Act of 1920 worked silently toward structuring the American army for another global conflict. Although the legacy of World War I faded from public memory, it routinely guided the War Department throughout the interwar period.

Raising an Army for Rainbow 5 (1940–45)

By June 1939, the War Department's strategic focus centred upon a looming conflict with Japan. The latter's 1937 invasion of China and subsequent juggernaut through east Asia, definitively clashed with ongoing American foreign policy objectives in the western hemisphere. However, consideration was soon made by the War Department for the possibility of a major two-front war with the inception of the Rainbow catalogue of strategic directives. Numbered 1–5, they posited multiple scenarios which reacted to foreign aggression. Rainbow 1 was a low-intensity military defensive posture designed to protect the 'spirit' of Monroe Doctrine. Rainbow 2 added to the former directive with diplomatic, military and materiel support for allied democratic Pacific nations engaged in hostilities. Rainbow 3 was a more assertive combination of 1 and 2, additionally featuring the deployment of military task forces for a Pacific oriented offensive. Rainbow 4 extended the directive of 3, with specifically allocated task forces to South America and the eastern Atlantic as needed. Rainbow 5, by contrast, entirely reoriented the primacy of the Pacific offensive to the Atlantic, with task forces sent to Europe and/or Africa in an alliance with France and Great Britain, for the defeat of Germany and Italy. For much of 1939–40, Rainbows 2 and 3 were given top priority by the War Department. The ascendency of Rainbow 5, however, was the product of France's shocking collapse and Britain's survival throughout 1940–41. Therefore, Rainbow 5 became the chief guiding strategic principle for the expansion and deployment of the US army in World War II.[58]

Following the German invasion of Poland on 1 September 1939, both the War Department and President Franklin D. Roosevelt recognised the need to better prepare the armed forces. Conscription was once again considered, but Roosevelt was sceptical of the American public's willingness to expand the military to a war footing, especially in peacetime. Thus, an executive order was quietly issued (concurrently with a national emergency declaration) on 8 September authorising the growth of 17,000 troops for the regular army and 43,000 for the National Guard.[59] This was wholly inadequate for the prospective task of engaging the Axis powers or undertaking all but the first of the Rainbow directives, and by the spring of 1940, the American army ranked 19th in the world. This statistic, which placed it between the Portuguese and Romanian armies in terms of size, is often used to illustrate the woefully unprepared state of the army and War Department amid an increasingly Axis dominated world.[60] And rightly so, for the deliberation of the Roosevelt administration over popular support and civic cooperation to conscript for another world war had reached a critical impasse as the Germans occupied Paris and bombed London. The problem was not Roosevelt's wish to enter the war nor confusion over the best means to expand the army. It was a matter of trust and communication between the presidential administration and the nation's citizens.

Ironically, it was civilian executive leaders of the Military Training Camps Association who proposed an unprecedented peacetime draft through a new selective service act. This association originated from the pre- World War I Plattsburg Camp concept, which basically offered civilians military training with no induction into the army nor service obligation. Discussions were held in Congress throughout the summer with the peacetime draft warmly received, and on 16 September, Congress passed the Selective Service Act of 1940. It contained many of the same elements of the 1917 draft, such as localised draft boards, a centralised federal lottery and deferment classifications. All able-bodied male citizens between the ages of 21–36 were tasked to register on or by 16 October 1940. Their tenure would last a year before discharge and no more than 900,000 men could populate the army at any one time. Lastly, this draft forbid overseas deployment of these conscripts except for assignment to US territorial possessions. Despite widespread isolationist sentiment, the existential threat posed by the Axis powers kept the public's hostility to the draft minimal in comparison to opposition in World War I. Ultimately, 16 million men registered by 16 October and they were assigned first to fill out understrength regular and National Guard formations, the latter of which were mobilised by the War Department in June 1940 for one full year of active duty training in their respective states starting 16 September 1940. Although they were not yet called to Federal service, guardsmen were effectively put on standby for that eventuality which ultimately arrived on 3 February 1941.

As expected, the draft was successful in growing manpower figures as the army's total strength from 30 June 1940 to 30 June 1941 was raised from 264,118 to 1,455,565 men.[61] However, trouble appeared that summer when rumours of service extension circulated. Enlisted guardsmen were particularly vocal in their displeasure with discipline rapidly deteriorating and morale plummeting. Whilst many of the cases were due to home sickness and/or an aversion to military service, most "spirits were low merely because they were bored."[62] But the scandalous reports which emerged across printed journalism about the National Guard's declining status compelled the Army to face the situation. The War Department and the general staff possessed no solution for such a massive demobilisation and the army chief of staff, General George C. Marshall, articulated to Congress the peril of gutting army strength at such a critical moment. The prospect of calling the men back was daunting, verging on prohibitive. An extension of the draft was the only course. But deciding on that course was a close shave. The Selective Service Extension Act cleared the Senate well enough, but the House was historically split with 202 against and 203 in favour of the extension. Thus, the strategic direction of the army's (and the nation's) preparedness was determined by a *single* vote on 12 August 1941. By the time the Japanese attacked Pearl Harbor in December, 1,686,403 men were in the army and counting; 16 per cent of these were in the US Army Air Forces.[63] This latter percentage became increasingly important as the air force expanded for its strategic bombing campaigns throughout 1943–45.

Once again, the infantry division provided the core organisational building block for the army's ground combat power. Many of the old divisions from World War I were also reconstituted in both the National Guard and national army. Regular divisions typically remained in continuous service during the interwar period, whilst National Guard divisions drilled on weekends at the unit level until the Louisiana Maneuvers in June 1941 brought several guard divisions together as complete formations. The two national army divisions (92nd and 93rd) which were composed of segregated soldiers of African-American decent were also recreated. African-American soldiers were also subject to selective service as they had been in 1917–18, whilst the War Department sought to maintain their numbers in proportion to the overall African-American population within the US. Ultimately, they represented 10.5 per cent of the total drafted figure which met the War Department's expectations. However, no serious attempt at integration was made during the war and they were frequently assigned to support units until a manpower crisis in mid-1944 compelled the army to increase their assignment to combat units.[64]

Once regular and guard divisions were brought to strength by selective service, national army divisions were allocated cadres of regular officers and NCOs numbering some 1900 men who arrived five days before the flow of some 13,000 soldiers to complete the division's personnel strength.[65] Divisions also began to evolve into specialisations by 1942, with the standard infantry and cavalry types being accompanied by airborne, armoured, mountain and motorised divisions. These concepts were based on observations from both Allied and Axis operations during 1940. And early estimations differed significantly from execution, despite the consistency between the projected and actual army personnel growth figures.[66] Unfortunately, these evaluations were grossly inefficient with time and materiel resources. Some concepts, such as the tank destroyer battalion, which was meant to cheaply counter an enemy preponderance of armour, proved innovative even if unnecessary by 1943–44.[67] But others, like the motorised divisions were wholly redundant and occupied the training of five divisions from 1942–43, delaying their deployment as infantry divisions. Mountain divisions were another disappointment, although not because they were superfluous. The War Department planned to create ten mountain divisions but ultimately raised only one, the 10th Mountain Division. Although activated in July 1943, the division only came into action in Italy in January 1945. This egregious delay meant that a much-needed capability was unavailable during the intense mountain campaigns in Italy and south-eastern France throughout 1943–45.

The most important change, however, came in the form of a reorganisation which 'triangularised' the old AEF modelled formation (see Diagram 7.2) in September 1939.[68] This design sought flexibility and mobility, with a minimal reduction in firepower. The triangular division removed the infantry and artillery brigades altogether and arranged the fighting infantry divisional strength into three infantry regiments and four field artillery battalions. Additionally, the support troops now included attached anti-aircraft gun batteries, tank battalions and mechanised cavalry reconnaissance troops. This allowed for divisions to more easily create smaller regimental sized task forces if needed. Thus, divisions were reduced from the 1918 strength of 28,000 to roughly 15,000 in 1943. Despite the army's two-fold expansion over the World War I total size, the combat fighting elements became smaller, logistically streamlined and more flexible for mobile operations. There were difficulties within the National Guard divisions as the triangularisation resulted in the loss of an infantry regiment which was usually reassigned to another division. But the overall transformation was smooth and division morale generally remained intact.

Soldiers serving in the regular army or National Guard frequently found themselves using weaponry and equipment which was cutting edge (or even outdated) in 1918. In many cases, soldiers trained without these items if a shortage was encountered. Stove pipes stood in for mortars and lorries posed as enemy tanks during the training and manoeuvres of 1940–41. Field artillery battalions were still equipped

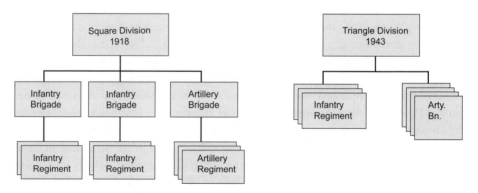

Diagram 7.2 US army infantry division combat elements compared 1918 and 1943.[69]

with French guns from World War I, the famous 75s, and only 66 medium tanks were available to the newly created armoured divisions in June 1941.[70] However, American industry was already producing equipment and technologies for the Allies with distribution through the Lend-Lease programme begun in March 1941. By 1943, the trouble in supplying the Pacific and European theatres lay with a shipping shortage. But the problem was eventually resolved to the extent that the Normandy invasion's American assault force of 130,000 troops (US First Army) in June 1944 was supported with a prepared 90,000 tonnes of supplies. Within three months, over 1.3 million American soldiers were ashore and operating in France with the latest equipment of American manufacture. US industry produced over a billion artillery shells during the war and roughly 88,000 tanks (49,000 of the M4 Sherman medium tank variety) were produced from 1940–45, supplying 16 US armoured divisions (which possessed 263 tanks per division by 1945) plus other nations' tank forces, too. This was a significant advancement from the situation in 1918 where not a single shell fired during the AEF's Argonne campaign was American made nor did a single American-made tank see action.[71]

Finally, the administrative and command structural problems of the general staff were ironed out in General Marshall's 1942 reorganisation plan. Unfortunately, the War Department bureaucracies reverted to pre-1917 fiefdoms during the lull of peacetime. As one official history put it, '[General] Marshall's role as general manager of the department was interfering with his duties as the President's adviser on military strategy and operations.'[72] The central issue ailing the general staff was one of executive congestion. At the end of 1941, Marshall had 60 War Department bureaux reporting to him on a range of detailed operational matters often requiring his decision. This was the result of the unfinished centralisation process of the Root Reforms interrupted by World War I. Taking cues once more from the corporate world, Marshall brilliantly flattened the general staff hierarchy to increase liaison between bureaux in a decentralised manner. To do this, he reduced staff personnel and procedures and closed redundant bureaux where their functions could be better performed elsewhere. He authorised direct communication between departments and generally trusted these entities to handle their administrative work. Most significantly, he created three major organisations to deal with a range of issues for the expanding army; the Army Ground Forces (AGF), the Army Air Forces (AAF) and the Army Service Forces (ASF). The AGF was responsible for training and organising soldiers into units and formations. The AAF performed similar work for army flying personnel, whilst the ASF dealt with administration and logistics. The effect of these changes reduced Marshall's paperwork by roughly 95 per cent almost instantly.[73] This allowed him not only to focus on strategic matters, but to consolidate his executive power through delegation.

The Second World War marked the culmination of everything the United States learned about mass mobilisation for modern total war. Of the 8.2 million men inducted by the army, 6.9 million were deployed overseas. In accordance with Rainbow 5, 4.3 million went to Europe and the Mediterranean, whilst 2.5 million operated in the Pacific and Burmese theatres. The scope of effort dwarfed the unprecedented achievement of World War I of 4 million men. The army's total strength in 1918 was doubled by 1945, whilst it was expedited overseas in a two-front war with bountiful quantities of quality equipment by 1944; a 12,000-mile coverage spanning the United States. It was not a perfect venture, especially in the early days in Tunisia or on New Guinea. But the degree of complexity and gargantuan scale managed from 1941–45 was a testament to both the improvisation skills of the American army and the lessons it gleaned from its first major international excursion in 1917–18.[74]

Rising to the Occasion: The Modern Anglo-American Mobilisation Model

In its essence, the primary Anglo-American mobilisation model was, and continues to be, improvisation. In the two catastrophic diplomatic breakdowns of the 20th century that resulted in the world wars, the British and American empires effectively interrupted their peacetime activities to raise four mass citizen-armies, primarily through conscription; something which struck at the very core of their liberal societies and traditions. In 1914, the only significant encounters with mass warfare that either nation possessed were their respective civil wars. But colonial experience and observations in Europe and Asia throughout the late-19th century inspired major reforms of command, organisation, technology, tactical doctrine and national reserves.

The two nations also possessed a similar approach to the issue of a second-line defence between the British Territorial Force and the National Guard. Recruited locally by counties in Britain and states in the US, these formations provided a ready flow of personnel for defence of the homeland, whilst contributing to the earliest contingents deployed to the front. However, the ferocity and totality of the world wars demonstrated, particularly for America, that this concept was problematic if the guard was expected to be the sole national reserve. Britain maintained the militia/volunteer model until the British government finally resorted to conscription in 1916. But neither country waited to institute a draft in World War II.

One could argue that Germany, France, Russia and others faced complex mobilisation obstacles and raised their armies around core regular strengths. But the figures for these armies averaged 600,000 troops within their peacetime universal service schemes and they faced no seas to cross for their deployment. However, the distances arguably worked in Britain and America's favour because it took roughly a year during World War I for their armies to reach a combat strength of one million men, thereby compensating for their personnel and industrial unpreparedness.[75]

Such a policy practised by continental powers would be catastrophic given the immediacy of initial border contact. But the central common thread between the two countries was the paradoxical desire to suspend liberties in wartime to preserve them in peacetime. The mass compulsory mobilisation programmes and co-opting of industry for military means symbolised the apex of total war in the human experience thus far.

Notes

1   Ronald J. Barr, *The Progressive Army: US Army Command and Administration, 1870–1914* (London: Macmillan Press, 1998), p. 13.

2   US Provost Marshal General, *Second Report to the Secretary of War on the Operations of the Selective Service System* (Washington, DC, 1919), p. 227. See Table 80.

3   Marvin A. Kreidberg and Merton G. Henry, *History of the Military Mobilization in the United States Army 1775–1945* (Washington, DC: Department of the Army, 1955), p. 108.

4   Dennis E. Showalter, "The Prusso-German RMA, 1840–1871" in MacGregor Knox and Williamson Murray (eds), *The Dynamics of Military Revolution 1300–2050* (New York: Cambridge University Press, 2001), p, 94, p. 110; Manfred Messerschmidt, "The Military Elites in Germany since 1870: Comparisons and Contrasts with the French Officer Corps" in Klaus-Jügen Müller (ed.), *The Military in Politics and Society in France and Germany in the Twentieth Century* (Oxford, UK: Berg, 1995), p. 48. It should be noted that this global phenomenon was neither systematically applied nor identical in detail from country to country. See Roger Chickering, "World War I and the Theory of Total War: Reflections on the British and German Cases 1914–1915" in Roger Chickering and Stig Förster (eds), *Great War, Total War: Combat and Mobilization on the Western Front, 1914–1918* (Washington, DC: German Historical Institute, 2000), pp. 37–6.

5   Julian Go, *Patterns of Empire: The British and American Empires, 1688 to the Present* (New York, NY: Cambridge University Press, 2011), pp. 40–41. See Figure 1.3 for the remarkable similarity in the fiscal-military spending expenditures of both empires through the long 19th century.

6   Gordon Carpenter O'Gara, *Roosevelt and the Rise of the Modern Navy* (New York: Greenwood Press, 1963), pp. 8–9; Russel F. Weigley, *The American Way of War: A History of United States Military Strategy and Policy* (Bloomington: Indiana University Press, 1973), p. 181; Barr, *The Progressive Army*, p. 10.

7   Weigley, *The American Way of War*, p. 192.

8   Kreidberg and Henry, *History of Military Mobilization*, p. 163.

9   David F. Trask, *The War with Spain in 1898* (New York, N.Y: Macmillan Press, 1981), 154–55, 485; For an analysis on the strategic effect of War Department unpreparedness see, Joseph Smith, "'At the Place, at the Wrong Time and with the Wrong Enemy': US Military Strategy towards Cuba in 1898," in *The Crisis of 1898: Colonial Redistribution and Nationalist Mobilization*, ed. Angel Smith and Emma Davila-Cox (London: Macmillan Press, 1999).

10   James E. Hewes Jr, *From Root to McNamara: Army Organization and Administration, 1900–1963* (Washington: Center of Military History, US Army, 1975), p. 12.

11   One of whom was Captain John J. Pershing who briefly attended the college until reassigned.

12   Paul F. Braim, *The Test of Battle: The American Expeditionary Forces in the Argonne Campaign* (Newark: University of Delaware Press, 1987), p. 47, p. 50. Conner also became a mentor to the likes of Eisenhower and Marshall.

13   T. R. Brereton, *Educating the U.S. Army: Arthur L. Wagner and Reform, 1875–1905* (Lincoln: University of Nebraska Press, 2000), p. 95, pp. 102–3; Barr, *The Progressive Army*, p. 144.

14   Hewes Jr, *From Root to McNamara*, pp. 18–19; Thomas X. Hammes, *The Sling and the Stone: On War in the 21st Century* (Voyageur Press, 2006), p. 233; Barr, *The Progressive Army*, p. 182, p. 190; Irmgard Steinisch, "Different Path to War: A Comparative Study of Militarism and Imperialism in the United States and Germany, 1871–1914" in Manfred F. Boemeke, Roger Chickering, Stig Förster (eds), *Anticipating Total War: The German and American Experiences, 1871–1914* (Cambridge: Cambridge University Press, 1999), pp. 37–38.

15   Brian Neumann, "A Question of Authority: Reassessing the March-Pershing 'Feud' in the First World War" in *The Journal of Military History*, Vol. 73, No. 4 (14 October 2009): p. 1140; Hewes Jr., *From Root to McNamara*, pp. 69–70, p. 76.

16   Dick was also a veteran of the Spanish-American War.

17   "Militia Act", 4316 S, Section 5 (1908).

18   William Scheck, "World War I: American Expeditionary Forces Get Motorized Transportation" in *Military History Magazine* (June 1997) https://www.historynet.com/world-war-i-american-expeditionary-forces-get-motorized-transportation.htm; Julie Prieto, *The Mexican Expedition 1916–1917* (Washington, DC: Center of Military History, US Army, 2016), p. 24, p. 67; War Department, *War Department Annual Reports, 1917*, Vol. I (Washington, DC: Government Printing Office, 1918), pp. 313–14.

19   Prieto, *The Mexican Expedition*, p. 21.

20   Kreidberg and Henry, *History of Military Mobilization*, p. 200.

21   "National Defense Act of 1916," 12766 H.R. Sections 2 and 62 (1916); Julie Prieto, *The Mexican Expedition 1916–1917* (Washington, D.C.: Center of Military History, U.S. Army, 2016), p. 59; John Whiteclay Chambers II, *To Raise an Army: The Draft Comes to Modern America* (New York: Free Press, 1987), p. 118; Kreidberg and. Henry, *History of the Military Mobilization*, pp.198–99.

22   "National Defense Act of 1916", 12766 H.R., Sections 70 and 73 (1916).

23   "National Defense Act of 1916", 12766 H.R., Sections 61 and 67 (1916).

24   "National Defense Act", 12766 H.R., Section 120 (1916).

25   James A. Huston, *The Sinews of War: Army Logistics 1775–1953* (Washington, DC: Center of Military History, US Army, 1966), p. 321.

26   War Department, *War Department Annual Reports, 1917*, I:10; John M. Cyrulik, "A Strategic Examination of the Punitive Expedition into Mexico, 1916–1917" (U.S. Army Command and General Staff College, 2003), pp. 82–83, Defense Technical Information Center, http://www.dtic.mil/dtic/tr/fulltext/u2/a416074.pdf.

27   David French, "The Meaning of Attrition, 1914–16" in *The English Historical Review*, Vo. 103, No. 407 (April 1988), p. 386, p. 388.

28   US Provost Marshal General, *Second Report to the Secretary of War on the Operations of the Selective Service System* (Washington, D.C., 1919), 227. See Table 80.

29   R. J. Q. Adams, "Delivering the Goods: Reappraising the Ministry of Munitions: 1915–1916" in *Albion: A Quarterly Journal Concerned with British Studies*, Vol. 7, No. 3 (1975), p. 238, p. 240; Chambers II, *To Raise an Army*, p. 118, p. 126. It should be noted that British conscription in 1916 did not necessarily solve the problem of manpower allocation between industry and the military. See the Maurice Debate.

30   Theodore Roosevelt, *The Letters of Theodore Roosevelt: Days of Armageddon, 1914–1919*, Elting Elgmore Morison (ed.), Vol. VIII (Cambridge: Harvard University Press, 1954), p. 1165.

31   "Selective Service Act", 3545 H.R., Section 5 (1917).

32   Kreidberg and Henry, *History of Military Mobilization*, p. 260. See Chart 10 for organisational scheme.

33   U.S. Provost Marshal General, *Second Report to the Secretary of War*, p. 31.

34   Kreidberg and Henry, *History of Military Mobilization*, p. 347.

35 Associated Press Night Wire, "Uncle Sam's Mailed Fist for Anti-Draft Agitators" in *Los Angeles Times* (30 May 1917), pp. 1–2; "Draft Shirkers Barred in Flight" in *The New York Times* (1 June 1917), pp. 1–2; "New Police Arms Awe Socialists2 in *The New York Times* (1 June 1917), p. 1–2.

36 This sentence was later commuted by the Harding Administration as 'time served' rather than a pardon.

37 John B. Wilson, *Maneuver and Firepower: The Evolution of Divisions and Separate Brigades* (Washington, DC: Center of Military History, US Army, 1998). See Chapters 1 and 2 for the most thorough exploration in the evolution of the US Army division before the World War I.

38 Wilson, *Maneuver and Firepower,* 56. See Chart 4.

39 Center of Military History, Order of Battle of the United States Land Forces in the World War Zone of the Interior, Vol. 3 (Washington, DC: Center of Military History, US Army, 1988), p. 55. See original Chart 14.

40 Leonard Porter Ayres, *The War with Germany: A Statistical Overview* (Washington: Government Printing Office, 1919), p. 15; Kreidberg and Henry, *History of Military Mobilization,* p. 307.

41 Ayres, *The War with Germany,* p. 43.

42 American Battle Monuments Commission, *American Armies and Battlefields in Europe,* (Washington, D.C.: Center of Military History, U.S. Army, 1992), p. 502; Wilson, *Maneuver and Firepower,* p. 73.

43 American Battle Monuments Commission, *American Armies and Battlefields,* p. 492.

44 Robert K. Griffith Jr, *Men Wanted for the U.S. Army: American's Experience with an All-Volunteer Army Between the World Wars* (Westport: Greenwood Press, 1982), p. 9.

45 American Battle Monuments Commission, *American Armies and Battlefields,* p. 482, p. 489.

46 Griffith Jr, *Men Wanted for the U.S. Army,* p. 11.

47 *Ibid.,* p. 29; Edward Coffman, *The Regulars: The American Army 1898–1941* (Cambridge: Belknap Press of Harvard University Press, 2004), Chapter 7. It should be noted that Coffman also used the phrase for his chapter broadly covering the army's 1920s experience.

48 US Provost Marshal General, *Second Report to the Secretary of War,* p. 282.

49 Griffith Jr, *Men Wanted for the U.S. Army,* p. 31. Based on the US Bureau of Labour Statistic's 2.6 per cent annual inflation rate; this is roughly $2.3 million in 2018 monies.

50 Kreidberg and Henry, *History of Military Mobilization,* p. 379.

51 Since the inception of the National Militia Bureau in 1903, this post was filled by Regular officers.

52 William M. Donnelly, "Keeping the Buckeye in the Buckeye Division: Major General Robert S. Beightler and the 37th Infantry Division, 1940–1945" in *Ohio History: The Scholarly Journal of the Ohio Historical Society,* Vol. 106, (Winter–Spring 1997), p. 42, p. 46; Stanley A. Frankel, *The 37th Infantry Division in World War II* (Washington: Infantry Journal Press, 1949), p. 4.

53 Now the Dwight D. Eisenhower School for National Security and Resource Strategy.

54 Kreidberg and Henry, *History of Military Mobilization,* 497–98. Quoting the War Department's *General Orders* No. 7, 5 February 1924.

55 Huston, *Sinews of War,* pp. 405–6.

56 Kreidberg and Henry, History of Military Mobilization, p. 379. See Table 51.

57 *Ibid.,* p. 379. Calculated on the figures compiled from Table 51.

58 Weigley, *The American Way of War,* pp. 313–14.

59 Kreidberg and Henry, *History of Military Mobilization,* p. 555.

60 Rick Atkinson, *An Army at Dawn: The War in North Africa, 1942–1943* (New York: Henry Holt & Co., 2002), p. 8; George C. Marshall, *Biennial Reports of the Chief of Staff of the United States Army to the Secretary of War* (Washington, DC: Center of Military History, US Army, 1996), p. v; The 'Special Relationship' between Great Britain and the United States Began with FDR, Roosevelt Institute, 22 July 2010, http://rooseveltinstitute.org/special-relationship-between-great-britain-and-united-states-began-fdr

61 Kreidberg and Henry, *History of Military Mobilization*, p. 590. See Table 58.

62 Joseph Balkoski, *Beyond the Beachhead: The 29th Infantry Division in Normandy* (Mechanicsburg, PA: Stackpole Books, 1999), p. 22; Frankel, *The 37th Infantry Division in World War II*, pp. 20–21.

63 *Ibid.*, p. 593, p. 597. See Table 60.

64 *Ibid*, p. 644.

65 Wilson, *Maneuver and Firepower*, p. 170.

66 Kreidberg and Henry, *History of Military Mobilization*, p. 623. See Table 65.

67 Robert S. Cameron, *Mobility, Shock, and Firepower: The Emergence of the U.S. Army's Armor Branch, 1917–1945* (Washington, DC: Center of Military History, 2008), pp. 432–33.

68 Wilson, *Maneuver and Firepower*, p. 137, p. 143.

69 Wilson, Maneuver and Firepower. See Charts 4 and 19. The diagram here illustrates only the essential combat arms of infantry and artillery.

70 George F. Howe, *The Battle History of the 1st Armored Division, 'Old Ironsides'* (Washington: Combat Forces Press, 1954), p. 9; Balkoski, *Beyond the Beachhead*, p. 23; Homer R. Ankrum, *Dogfaces Who Smiled Through Tears: The 34th Red Bull Infantry Division in World War II* (Lake Mills, Iowa: Graphic Pub Co, 1987), p. 40.

71 American Battle Monuments Commission, *American Armies and Battlefields*, p. 504; Ayres, *The War with Germany*, p. 80; Huston, *Sinews of War*, p. 479; Cameron, *Mobility, Shock, and Firepower*, p. 462. It should be noted that production was ramping up as 778 Renault FT-17 Light tanks were built by the end of March 1919. Heavy tank production was also well underway with half of an order of 1500 tanks completed by the Armistice.

72 Hewes Jr., *From Root to McNamara*, p. 63.

73 *Ibid.*, p. 68.

74 Huston, *Sinews of War*, p. 559.

75 Ayres, *The War with Germany*, p. 14. See Diagram 1.

CHAPTER 8

'This Sacred Trust'

Enlarging Armies with Local Forces (1878–1945)

Dr Robert Johnson

'I know with what readiness my loyal and brave Indian soldiers are prepared to fulfil this sacred trust on the field of battle, shoulder to shoulder with their comrades from the Empire.'[1]

KING GEORGE V, 1914

'L'armee d'Afrique … a donné surtout l'exemple de toutes les vertus militaires, et mérité par là de prendre place a cote de ces armées dévouées'[2]

LE DUC D'ORLÉANS, 1852

At the outbreak of major war, despite the relative confidence in small professional forces to hold on long enough to ensure general mobilisation, there is often a shortage in the manpower with the requisite skills. In 1914, and again in 1939, the manpower crises were acute, the presence of relatively large colonial armies enabled Western European powers to fill the gap. In recent conflicts in the early-21st century, local forces have been important elements in creating legitimacy for a newly established government and conducting low-intensity operations. Local forces have often been employed to cut costs, augment manpower in challenging environments and engage in 'small wars', but historically, there was an equally important function for regular and auxiliary troops drawn from colonial forces in major wars.

La Force Noir played an important part in France's military efforts in 1914–17 on the Western Front, while Britain made extensive use of colonial troops in the campaigns in Africa, brought a division of Indian army regulars to France and Flanders in 1914 and several Indian divisions were deployed to the Middle East. Commonwealth troops were vital in these campaigns too. In World War II, Indian Army and Commonwealth regulars took on even more substantial tasks in North Africa and South East Asia, once again covering gaps in the order of battle of the British regular army in that critical period before full mobilisation could take effect.

French colonial troops, concealed during the Vichy years as armed constabulary, fought in Italy and liberated southern France.

The experience of rapid expeditionary deployment for these colonial and Commonwealth forces was not entirely smooth. There were a variety of administrative and logistical problems, shortcomings in transport and shipping, a lack of heavy weapons, inappropriate tactical and training protocols, weaknesses in doctrine and staff work, and the shock of being thrust into a conflict characterised, in the first year or so, by tactical and operational setbacks.

This chapter highlights the value, significance and weaknesses of the use of local regular forces in the period before and during full national mobilisation, drawing out the implications for those considering comparable schemes in the 21st century. It consists of sections that highlight the covering of the gap between the professional forces' holding actions and national mobilisation, evaluations of the system and their implications.

The Indian Army in the Late-19th Century

The defence of India was, in common with other parts of the British Empire, a naval responsibility, but the landward frontiers of south Asia were nevertheless vulnerable to antagonised tribal groups, hostile potentates and rival European powers. The chief concern of the late-19th century was the gradual approach of Russian forces as they annexed central Asia. The proximity of a larger Russian army caused considerable anxiety, and efforts were made to keep their influence out of neighbouring Afghanistan, Persia and Tibet. General Frederick Sleigh Roberts, the Commander-in-Chief in India in the 1890s, developed a scheme of defence known as the Scientific Frontier, which posited that standing forces, the majority of which were from India, would hold the passes of the Hindu Kush until reinforcements could be despatched from Britain.

The strength of the Indian Army was in its ability to garrison every part of the subcontinent, despatch troops to pacify the frontiers and, if necessary, deploy independent brigades overseas. Before World War I, there were 39 regiments of cavalry (not including contingents of bodyguards), 95 single-battalion regiments of infantry, 12 single-battalion Pioneer regiments and 11 double-battalion regiments (39th Garwhals and the ten Gurkha regiments).[3] There were three units of sappers and miners (for engineer operations), mountain artillery, ordnance units, logistics teams, medical units and administrators. There were the auxiliaries: Imperial Service Troops, militias, levies and scouts, who provided some regional and frontier security, especially to British political officers and the various Indian constabularies. There was also a pool of European and Anglo-Indian volunteers who could be called on to protect installations such as the railways, and there were still sizeable private armies controlled by the princely states under British supervision, such as the Hyderabad

Contingent, the Central India Horse or the local units of the other princely states such as Malwa, Erinpura and Deoli, where the quality varied between anachronistic retainers to more modernised troops.

The Indian Army had built up an expertise in the leadership of local forces over many decades. In 1914, each infantry battalion had 12 European officers, and subordinated to them, regardless of experience, were 17 Indian Officers carrying the Viceroy's Commission. Together, they commanded 729 ranks and 42 civilian 'commissariat' followers. In the cavalry, the proportions were the same. Unlike the French colonial forces, which were expected to learn French, all British officers spoke the local languages of their soldiers.[4] This was not simply because the officer needed to be sure of communications in combat but also because the officer was regarded as the neutral arbiter in any local disputes.[5]

There was more to the ethos of the British officer corps in India than languages, however. In the Indian cavalry, the legacy of being 'irregular' and under the personal command of pioneering individuals gave rise to an attitude that praised initiative, carried disdain for the rest of the army and cherished the horses above all else. The fact that *sowars* (troopers) owned their own mounts made the men particularly attentive to the endurance of their animals. In the Indian infantry, the atmosphere between officers and men was respectful and less prejudiced than the class hierarchy of British regiments. Claude Auchinleck wrote: 'there was no question of ordering them about – they were yeomen really and that made all the difference'.[6] The emphasis on personal leadership led to a tendency to lead from the front in combat, but that had its own attractions for young British officers. The appeal of command in the Indian Army was so high that, in 1913, of the top 25 cadets at the Royal Military Academy Sandhurst, 20 of them opted to join the Indian Army.[7]

In 1878, after Russian forces overran the eastern Balkans and seemed poised to seize Constantinople, the Royal Navy was despatched to protect the Ottoman capital, while the British army was mobilised. An Indian contingent was also deployed to the Mediterranean to demonstrate the linked nature of Britain's imperial defence. But Russia too recognised the connected nature of British defence, and, as preparations for opening routes to India in the event of war, the Tsar's envoys opened negotiations with the Persians and the Afghans. The most positive response came from Amir Sher Ali in Kabul, and Britain moved quickly to suppress the Afghans and deter Russian encroachments across the Hindu Kush with an invasion and temporary occupation. Nevertheless, a German-brokered agreement in Berlin prevented the outbreak of an Anglo-Russian war in Europe.

Russian annexations of central Asia continued, and in 1885, war again seemed likely when the Afghans, now under British protection, were attacked at Penjdeh by a Russian brigade.[8] The Royal Navy were despatched to commence operations against Vladivostok, while the reserves were called up in Britain. In India, a large-scale exercise was staged, and there were further preparations for war. Former Indian soldiers volunteered for service and recruitment increased. But, once again, war was averted by diplomacy.

For their part, the Russians realised they did not have the infrastructure in place to support any force larger than corps strength in central Asia, and they commenced a railway building programme to defend and reinforce their southern flank. The Indian Army also discovered that its weakness was in transport and logistics, but there were difficulties in staff work and large formation manoeuvres.[9] The Indian Army's scale of artillery was also inadequate because, after the Mutiny of 1857, only British personnel were permitted to serve field batteries. Indian troops served mountain artillery, which was sufficient for the low-intensity frontier campaigns but not against a modern European army. The Indian Army was, therefore, reformed in 1903 by Lord Kitchener and provided with heavy and field artillery, while British regiments were brigaded with two or more Indian ones. The arrangement was known by the name 'the Army in India' and independent brigades were formed to make overseas service easier. The only problem was in the size of the deployable force, which in 1914 proved to be far too small for the sheer scale of the war that came. The assumptions had been based on the largest conflict Britain had had to fight to that date, which took place in South Africa.

The South African War (1899–1902)

The South African War was of particular interest to European armies at the turn of the century since it matched an army of European-descent armed with modern weapons, namely the Afrikaners, against the British colonial army. There were unexpected results. The first surprise was that Afrikaners launched an immediate offensive and invested three settlements of Kimberley, Ladysmith and Mafeking. The sieges were the result of a second surprise: British forces being defeated in the field, with the most humiliating period being 'Black Week' in late 1899. It was clear that the numbers available to restore the situation were limited, since Britain had only a small volunteer army. Yet, there was an understanding, from the outset, that this was to be a 'white man's war', given the ethnicity of the Afrikaners, which ruled out the use of colonial troops. The result was a significant mobilisation of reserves and the raising of volunteer battalions, Imperial Yeomanry cavalry units and Commonwealth units.

Despite the understanding, black troops did play a part in the conflict. In 1900, British reinforcements overwhelmed the Afrikaner field armies and relieved the besieged towns, but some Afrikaner fighters, nevertheless, refused to accept defeat and waged a guerrilla war for a further two years until their food, ammunition and, crucially, horses, ran out. The British established cordons across South Africa and combed the countryside looking for guerrillas. To prevent the insurgents getting supplies from the sympathetic population, farms were burned, livestock seized and civilians moved into temporary internment camps. Black labour was crucial in the construction tasks in this campaign, building camps and the blockhouses that crossed the veldt, digging trenches, repairing railway bridges and tracks, building dams, constructing roads, and portering equipment and supplies.[10] Black men were also employed in providing transport, driving cattle, horse management and other labouring associated with the provision of supplies. By 1902, there were some 20,000 African workers on the railways providing manual labour. It is estimated at least 14,000 worked as transport drivers. In total, the British army may have employed as many as 100,000 black men in labouring tasks during the conflict. In addition, there were thousands of workers recruited for the war industries. But blacks were also armed, despite official denials, because the manpower requirements were so large.

Gradually, it emerged that, during the period of guerrilla war that developed after 1900, the British had provided arms for 10,053 blacks and employed these men in a variety of roles. These included scouts, guides, cattle guards and, crucially, watchmen on the lines of blockhouses that criss-crossed the country to prevent the movement of insurgents. The British authorities argued that it was essential to arm them for their own safety. During the war, the Afrikaners had made it their policy to shoot armed or unarmed Africans they caught serving with the British. The British government estimated that between November 1901 and January 1902, there were 235 reported murders of unarmed Africans by Afrikaner guerrillas in the field. The deaths, the government claimed, vindicated their decision to arm the blacks for their own protection.

At Mafeking, black men were armed and formed part of the perimeter defence of the town. The black population of Mafeking was larger than the white and they occupied a separate settlement to the south-west of the railway junction, known locally as the Stadt. The majority of the population were Baralong who had claims to local land, which they hoped, by joining the British, they would be able to possess. There were several hundred Mfengu who had moved from the Eastern Cape and settled at Mafeking some years before. There was also a community of Cape Coloureds and these provided many of the craftsman, artisans, railway workers or police in the town. The remaining black population was simply referred to as refugees because they came from a variety of backgrounds from across southern Africa. When the siege began, on 13 October 1899, 400 picked black men with arms were tasked to defend the south-western approaches to the town, while another 100 formed picquets. The refugees' contingent, approximately 300 strong, were nicknamed the 'Black Watch' and one of the areas they were designated to protect was known as the brick fields, a sector that was the scene of some determined actions, as it developed into maze of trenches and dugouts. Blacks also joined the Town Guard, a flying reserve that could plug any gap in the defences.

It was difficult for the British and the Europeans to draw conclusive lessons from the South African War, which was not thought to typify modern warfare in the same way that the subsequent Russo-Japanese War did. In Britain, there were reforms to mobilisation and the creation of an expeditionary force. For operations, the indicators seemed to be that bold offensive action, as practised by the British and later by the Japanese, was most likely to produce success. Few paid attention to the role of black troops, which had been regarded as mere auxiliaries, but this was not the deduction in France, which had recruited its own large-scale, regular black force.

La Force Noir

Despite the existence of the *Armée Coloniale*, the regular army in Algeria, the French believed from the outset that the colony would become a source of military labour for its colonial armies, and some authorities believed that all of North Africa, and indeed the entire Near East, would become as important to France as India was to Britain.[11] In 1832, the French established three battalions of infantry *legere d'Afrique* and three battalions of locally recruited *tirailleurs indigenes*.[12] By 1841, there were four regiments of *chasseurs d'Afrique* and three cavalry regiments known as *spahis*. By 1873, the collective *Armée d'Afrique* became an established part of the order of battle of the metropolitan French army and was titled XIX Corps. Units containing indigenous personnel were known by their origin, as *tirailleurs sénégalais*, *tirailleurs malgaches* or, in the case of South East Asia, as *tirailleurs indochinois,* but the exception was that all West African forces were known by the collective title *tirailleurs sénégalais*; to reflect the seniority of the original French colonial forces that were drawn from Senegal.[13]

As always, manpower demands grew exponentially as colonial responsibilities increased. Colonial campaigns required the support of large numbers of transport animals, porters and mule drivers. In 1894, French planners believed that, to conquer Madagascar, they would require between 18,000 and 20,000 porters and mule drivers in support of an expeditionary force of just 12,000 men. In the event, the introduction of lightweight carts reduced the numbers required to 7000, but it still created a vulnerable caravan 'tail' for the army. Management of the logistics and transport system also proved a far greater challenge. When the French requisitioned 35,000 camels to supply the Tuat Expedition of 1901–2, some 25,000 died because the French troops did not know how to manage this livestock, and locals had not been employed to reduce costs. Local expertise was, therefore, a crucial element in operations.

The use of local forces could create confusion on campaign. In 1881, in the Sud-Oranais region of Algeria during the Bou-Amama revolt, a French force lost 72 soldiers killed and wounded, and most of their baggage and transport, when Arab horsemen, mistaken for French-led *goum* mounted auxiliaries, were not engaged as they approached. In the western Sudan, the French dependence on tribal levies or badly disciplined Senegalese, led to far greater devastation than anticipated.

Of the French column which captured Segou in 1890, only 50 were European, since there were 500 regular native soldiers and the remaining 3000 men in the column were porters and auxiliaries provided by their African partners. These local troops were quick to abandon the firing line to obtain loot or female slaves. In 1898, the Voulet-Chanonine expedition ended with significant destruction and a mutiny, which caused a scandal in France. There were, therefore, serious doubts about the reliability of local military labour. A far greater problem was the loyalty of auxiliaries, particularly those that were irregulars. In 1890, the French established a Battalion of *tirailleurs soudanais*, but African porters who were conscripted to support operations had to be chained together on the march to prevent desertion.

By 1914, the French colonial army had grown to 42,100 white and 88,108 native troops. The Algerian Garrison was equivalent of two army corps just before World War I broke out. This was important when there was such anxiety about the demographic growth of Germany, which, potentially, could give them additional reservists to overwhelm the French army. In his book *Force Noire* in 1910, General Mangin had urged his countrymen to draw more manpower from the colonies, but George Clemenceau, the Prime Minister, disagreed, believing that colonial expansion wasted the critical resources required to develop an army to confront Germany on the north-eastern frontier of the country. In France, resistance to colonial military expansion was magnified by even minor setbacks in the field. In 1894, at Timbuktu, a French camp was attacked by the Tuaregs. The position was overrun and 13 French officers and NCOs, and 68 native soldiers were killed. The reaction in France was protest at the ugly realities of the so-called 'civilising mission'.[14]

Nevertheless, as anxiety about a European war increased, selective conscription was applied to the Muslim population of Algeria to comb the colony for recruits in May 1913. But, from an eligible annual cohort of 45,000, only 2000 conscripts a year were obtained, and it remained overwhelmingly a volunteer force. In 1914, the Army of Africa in Algeria and Tunisia comprised nine regiments of Algerian *tirailleurs*, four of *Zouaves*, six of *Chasseurs d'Afrique*, four of *Spahis* and two of the Foreign Legion. In Morocco, there were a further 19 battalions of *tirailleurs* and nine of *Zouaves*, along with detachments of the Foreign Legion and the African Light Infantry. A large proportion of these troops were sent immediately to serve in France in World War I. Some 33,000 Muslim Algerians served as the Spahis, *Tirailleurs* and other units of the Army of Africa. During the course of the war, a further 137,000 enlisted, either as volunteers (57,000) or as conscripts (80,000). They proved to be an important augmentation in World War I.

World War I

The French government regarded its North African colonial possessions as metropolitan departments of France and, given the demographic advantage of its chief rival, Germany, it saw the recruitment of French African soldiers as pragmatic and necessary. By extension, it considered the use of colonial soldiers from elsewhere in the continent to be entirely consistent. Part of Germany's objection to increasing French influence in Morocco in the 1910s had been that the country offered the French: 'excellent raw materials the soldiers and therefore additional divisions with which to fight Germany in the future.'[15] Faced with large numbers of Russian troops to the east and potentially millions of French and African soldiers in the west, Germany too looked towards the Ottoman Empire and the Middle East as a potential reservoir of military manpower of its own.

In Britain, the recruitment of colonial personnel, already a key feature of their imperial garrisons, was extended. India provided 1.3 million volunteer soldiers, but such was the scale of demand for men by 1918 that the British authorities were considering conscription in the sub-continent. In Egypt, a voluntary system of acquiring both military and manual labour was retained, but the conscription of labourers in rural areas, along with their animals, generated resentment and fuelled unrest in 1919, just as it did in the Punjab, a traditional recruiting area. The British War Cabinet also considered the use of Japanese troops, which could be used in India as an internal security force in order to release more British and Indian soldiers from garrison duty in the subcontinent, while China was encouraged to contribute more labouring manpower.[16] The Chinese government was eager to join the war so as to show it was a worthy nation that should not be dismembered between the colonial powers, and offering labourers was a first step in that process, which greatly assisted the British war effort. But what the War Office wanted was fighting men, and they looked to employ more black troops. Commander J. C. Wedgwood, who had served at Gallipoli and compiled a report on manpower in the Mesopotamia Campaign for parliament, noted: 'I am only too anxious to get all I can and have been scouring the world to find out where they can be raised.'[17] The government of South Africa strenuously resisted the endless demands for more manpower, fearing its effects on the economy of the country and also its political implications.[18] What they and many other colonial authorities feared was the exposure of men to the realities of Europe, which might break the mystique of their power and fuel aspirations for liberation.

France faced an acute manpower crisis, particularly when, at the end of 1914, it had already suffered a million casualties. Of all the French troops in World War I, some 9 per cent were non-French, which represented 500,000 men from the colonies, with a further quarter of a million labourers. Some 160,000 men came from West Africa alone, but to obtain this number had required considerable coercion.[19] A combination of taxation, forced labour, and recruitment efforts for the army led to unrest in Dahomey and other areas; paradoxically, this required French forces to suppress the unrest.[20] New methods were, therefore, required to raise manpower. In Senegal, chiefs were paid for each man they could bring in, which replicated a system of acquiring slaves in a former era. Approximately 100,000 labourers were found from Indochina, largely by force, which led to lingering resentment and ultimately political mobilisation against France in subsequent generations. Another tactic was to encourage voluntary enlistment through the example of men already serving. One Senegalese sub-lieutenant, decorated for courage, announced to all new recruits: 'You are the first among the blacks, for the French, first among the whites, have conferred this distinction upon you.'[21] General Mangin, the enthusiast for colonial soldiers, believed that black troops, given their innate warlike qualities, could accomplish more than French soldiers on the Western Front in offensive operations and he was keen to praise their achievements.[22] The 2nd Colonial Corps of General Mangin's 6th Army on the Chemin des Dames attacked the sector between Cerny and the Ferme d'Hurtebise on 16 April 1917, but the combination of exposed terrain, German defensive fire and officer casualties meant the attack failed, leading to subsequent condemnation in racialised terms.

There was real excitement in France about the arrival of Britain's Indian troops in 1914. Amongst the British authorities, there was more of a sense of relief when it was found that Indian troops were willing to stand against a European adversary. One officer, H. V. Lewis, attached to the 129th Baluchis, commented: 'Our men are very cool under fire, [and] don't seem to mind a bit, I think.' He praised particularly their skills in night patrolling.[23] Another officer was more concerned by press sensationalism which had raised expectations about: 'The marvels of night scouting, surprise attacks and *kukuri* work which would be performed by Indians.' He did not think they could be considered equals of the British soldier, for if they were 'India would not be a British dependency.'[24] As historian V. G. Kiernan put it: 'Britain wanted to think it's native troops good enough to help win the war, but not good enough to be able to break away from the Empire.'[25] General Lewis had noted at the time that: 'The general opinion was that an Indian victory over white troops would have a bad effect on India.'[26]

The chief concern in the early months of the war was that the Muslim soldiers might respond to the Ottoman caliph's call to jihad in November 1914 and desert or mutiny. There were isolated incidents, but nothing of the magnitude that many had feared. One group of the 10th Baluchis *en route* to Mesopotamia shot their officer and were subsequently redirected for service in Burma. The Germans and the Ottomans attempted to distribute propaganda leaflets into Egypt to subvert the local troops there and also to Senegalese Muslim troops in French service in Gallipoli. Small numbers went over to the Ottomans during the static periods on the Tigris in 1915, and there was some indication that the 5th Light Infantry mutinied at Singapore because of the influence of a radical imam. But the numbers were small and the incidents unconnected. As the tide of the war turned in the Allies favour, the numbers of incidents declined.

At the tactical level, certain experienced regiments of the Indian Army, such as the Frontier Force and the various battalions of the Gurkhas, were highly accomplished, able to use field craft to great effect and were skilled in the precise use of fire to defeat guerrilla fighters on the frontiers. However, units with little experience of mountain warfare were often unsuited to the modern conditions of combat.

At the higher command level, an Indian Army general staff was created in 1903 to manage the complexities of training, military policy, operations, plans, intelligence and deployments. However, while relieving the commander-in-chief India of many tasks, the general headquarters had still to manage a high volume of minor administrative matters and there was no clear chain of command to the divisional level. Divisional commanders were burdened with administering not only their three infantry brigades, a cavalry regiment, and their artillery and pioneers but also all the additional formations in their area of responsibility, including militias and volunteers, even though these would not be the units under their command in wartime. Moreover, while there was a surplus of this additional manpower, there was a paucity of vital ancillary services, including medical and administrative staff. Worst of all, there were far too few staff in each headquarters. In 1906, 'A' staff of the general branch, directed by the chief of staff, were concerned with training, discipline and personnel; while 'Q' staff were concerned with equipment and supply. The following year, a staff college was established at Quetta, ending older systems of patronage or dependence on the British Staff College at Camberley. The only tragedy of this reform was that it was too late to produce senior staff-trained officers before the outbreak of war in 1914.

The Indian Army of 1914 was a long-service professional, force but one of its fundamental flaws was that it lacked sufficient trained reserves to be able to regenerate itself in the event of significant casualties. Frontier fighting had required well-trained units with the cohesion to withstand demoralising insurgency, but casualties had, on the whole, been light.[27] Service in Indian regiments tended to deter the rapid turnover of personnel and, therefore, it was hard to generate a large cadre of reservists. To qualify for a pension, soldiers had to serve 25 years. By contrast, three-year short-service men, who could take opportunities for periodic retraining, were few and far between, and in any case, insufficiently trained to be useful. Often, sickness and civilian employment rendered ex-soldiers unfit for further military service. The result was an army of some experience in mountain warfare and cohesive, with a strong sense of its exclusive identity, but without any notion of formation level operations or high-intensity European war, and unable to draw on a large pool of trained reservists.

Four expeditionary forces were mobilised, far more than had been planned for. The scheme for mobilisation and deployment functioned well enough and India had two infantry divisions and one cavalry brigade available for immediate operations.[28] But the requirement to expand this deployment rapidly caused disruption and overwhelmed the depots. The Lahore and Meerut Divisions (Force 'A') were assembled and despatched urgently to France. Indian Expeditionary Forces B and C, barely at brigade strength, went to East Africa, ostensibly to secure the coast and neutralise the German naval threat to shipping in the Indian Ocean, but also to protect the British railways into Kenya for which there was insufficient manpower for defence.

There were problems from the outset.[29] The call-up occurred in August when most personnel were on leave and, in an age before information technologies, it took time to make contact with everyone, especially those up in the hills. The depot system, which was supposed to operate as the rear link for deploying units, handling call-ups, reservists, pensions and discharges was completely overwhelmed and remained chaotic well into 1915. While units made their way to Bombay relatively quickly, the entire force was deficient in artillery and possessed only two machine guns per battalion.[30] Insufficient numbers of troop ships meant 30 vessels had to be hurriedly converted. The most significant problem was the ability to sustain enduring operations for the Indian Corps when it had to fit into a new and unfamiliar logistics system.[31] Force A had disembarked briefly at Suez before setting off for France where it was issued with the newer Mark III Lee Enfield Rifle, conducted marches, organised stores, was allocated liaison officers and established a camp. Transport was provided in the form of London butchers' carts, but apart from the distribution of some greatcoats, the troops wore their light tropical uniforms and had ration scales with which they were unaccustomed.

The Indian regiments were soon thrown into action as the British Army tried to stem the German advance towards the Channel in late 1914. The intensity of the fighting, sometimes at close quarters, exceeded anything the Indian army had trained for. The Poona Horse *sowars*, for example, did not initially take cover in their unfamiliar dismounted role as they had little training in infantry tactics or trench warfare. Their casualties were severe. Abysmal autumn weather and the evident confusion of troops unused to the environment added to the disorientation.[32] From personal accounts, we know that some officers struggled to keep their men in place. Captain 'Roly' Grimshaw (Poona Horse) came across some Gurkhas attempting to seek out Germans in no man's land on their own initiative, while others were clearly shirking in culverts, ditches and ruins. He explained that 'the sight which met the eyes at daybreak was perfectly revolting … corpses choked the trenches … fragments of human beings everywhere. Most of the dead seemed to have been bayoneted, but some had their heads blown clean off.'[33] Sikhs and Pathans were described as having lost turbans, revealing their long hair, matted with mud. All ranks were terribly filthy and often exhausted. Some Gurkhas discarded their boots, complaining that sore feet were worse inside their footwear. If the open fighting was not severe enough, there were other unseen and unexpected enemies: a German mine detonated under the Indian lines killed 200 and induced profound shock.

In the spring of 1915, the Indian Corps had new equipment and much needed winter clothing, along with rifle grenades, Mills bombs, mortars and trench periscopes. Morale improved. Nevertheless, what the corps lacked was artillery and, without a superior weight of fire support, it could not operate against defended positions alone. However, as the Indian Corps proved at Neuve Chappelle, when supported with sufficient firepower, it could perform as well as any other combat formation.

In April and May 1915, at Festubert and Aubers Ridge, the Indian Army was unsuccessful. Explanations were sought in terms of inadequate artillery support, shell shortages and criticism of Indian army staff work.[34] Senior Indian Army officers have since been criticised for valuing seniority over merit, failing to have sufficient numbers put through staff college and being unfamiliar with the large formation manoeuvres that characterised European warfare. Yet, as elsewhere during the World War I, the relentless mathematics of modern warfare, together with the engineering capabilities of the German army, was the true cause of failure. New and unexpected technologies played their part too. In April 1915, the Germans used poison gas to the north-east of Ypres and the Lahore Division was thrust into the gap in the line. Despite their counter-attack, they were checked by German fire.[35] The supporting Ferozepur Brigade was then subjected to a retaliatory gas attack, which, for troops without any respirators or protection, inflicted severe casualties.

The main concern became the loss of British officers.[36] Some officers posted into the Indian regiments to replace the casualties did not speak the language of the soldiers. Losses in the Viceroy's Commissioned Officers were also severe. Familiar faces, who knew the men well, were often now gone.[37] Moreover, Indian units had to be reinforced with drafts, and although efforts were made to replace class companies with men of the same background, this had not been possible in the confusion of the early months of the war.[38] Despite the larger numbers of reinforcements available by June 1915, the cohesion of the corps could no longer be guaranteed.[39] The decision was, therefore, taken to move the Indian infantry out of France and relocate them in Middle Eastern theatres where communications with India were shorter and, for those from the plains of India at least, the climate more familiar.[40] In any case, the expansion of the campaigns in the Middle East demanded more manpower.[41] The cavalry stayed on in France and took part in the larger actions of the war on the Somme, although without success. The unique composition of the Indian army, while a strength on frontier operations, had suffered severely under the pressures of very heavy losses and the conditions in Europe.[42]

In the Middle Eastern campaigns, the Indian army suffered just as severely at first, with heavy casualties on the Tigris and at Gallipoli. But in 1917, the Egyptian Expeditionary Force (EEF) in Palestine was comprehensively 'Indianised' so that the proportion of effort by the Indian army was higher. As the manpower crisis became more acute towards the end of the war, the Prime Minister, David Lloyd George, made a direct appeal to India. He wanted more men in the spring of 1918 to halt the final German offensive on the Western Front. In April, the All-India War Conference, with the viceroy, pledged to provide half a million more troops that year, of which the Punjab would provide 200,000.[43] After the war, when it was imperative to reduce costs, the cheaper Indian army provided the garrison forces for Palestine, Transjordan and Mesopotamia. The outbreak of revolts across Iraq in 1920 necessitated the emergency deployment of 85,000 Indian troops, many of them new men because the veterans of the war had served their time.[44] Some Muslim troops were, nevertheless, unhappy about the long service away from home and the defeat of the Ottoman empire. The abolition of the Ottoman caliphate in 1922 did little to improve their morale.

In 1918, at the Armistice, almost one million Indian troops were serving overseas.[45] Despite a few episodes of unrest, including the mutiny in Singapore in 1915, the majority of the Indian army had remained cohesive and loyal to the British. This was all the more remarkable when one considers the unexpected and hasty expansion between 1914 and 1917, the acute problems of supply and logistics that had characterised the operations in Mesopotamia and Gallipoli, and the shocking conditions of the first months of the war in Europe. Crucially, measures were put in place to improve the performance of the army in time for the next major war, in 1939.

World War II

The sheer variety of nationalities, ethnicities and communities, and the plethora of formations and categories of units serving Britain in World War II was astonishing. The entire process was not only orchestrated from London but was compelled to react to – and adapt to – three hostile powers that had long prepared for the conflict. The fact that this great complexity of forces was militarily successful, along with critical allies like the United States, is even more remarkable. Despite widespread criticism from many of its Africa and Asian subjects, the British could also quietly refer to the absence of violent internal unrest, with the exception of India in the years 1943–44, and they regarded the cohesion of the empire as a vindication of their achievements and pre-war efforts.

Initially, the British made use of their colonial and partnered forces in a defensive role, but it did not take long to shift to a counter offensive. When Amman, the capital of Transjordan, was bombed by Vichy aircraft in 1940, it was an indication of how vulnerable the British Empire was in the Middle East, which was a strategically vital source of oil for the British war effort.[46] The British mobilised the Transjordan Frontier Force (TJFF), increasing its strength from a small pre-war *gendarmerie* to a competent military brigade of 8000 men.[47] The Arab Legion, the emir's own force commanded by Brigadier Glubb Pasha, similarly expanded to 5000 men and remained under British command for the duration of the war. During the conflict, the TJFF comprised three cavalry and two mechanised squadrons, while a 'line of communications' squadron was raised to protect the routes between Haifa and Baghdad. Transjordan also provided support services in the form of repair workshops, hospitals and a training depot. When, in 1941, the British garrison at RAF Habbaniya was attacked by pro-Nazi Iraqis, the TJFF was on standby to relieve it, although at the last minute it was never despatched. The force did, however, take part in the Syrian campaign from June 1941, where it secured routes for supplies along the Haifa–Damascus railway and roads. It was then employed in internal security tasks in Syria to maintain law and order, before providing the border security force along the Turkish frontier. Meanwhile, the experienced reconnaissance capabilities of the Arab Legion's Desert Mechanised Force meant that it was selected to lead British troops into Iraq. It pushed along the Euphrates and closed off the Mosul road, before moving on to Baghdad. The Arab Legion also provided reconnaissance during the Syrian campaign, particularly in the attack on Palmyra and afterwards provided internal security during a period of widespread unrest. These forces, therefore, provided a number of roles and usefully freed up other regular units for offensive operations elsewhere.

In South East Asia before the war, the only fighting force available was the Burma Rifles, which was organised along the lines of a standard Indian Army regiment. Its role was primarily internal security because it was not envisaged that Burma would ever become a theatre of operations against an external power. In 1940, the Burma Rifles were expanded from four to six battalions and an officer cadet school was established at Maymyo to train British, Burmese and Anglo-Burmese candidates. A seventh battalion was formed from the civil and military police and an eighth from the Burma Frontier Force. The rest of the Burma Frontier Force consisted of five battalions of Burma Military Police, providing frontier security. Two more battalions were raised as a training establishment. An 11th and 12th Battalion were established for the security of lines of communication, while the 13th and 14th Battalions were raised to protect the local Shan states and provide internal security. The entire formation was known as the 1st Burma Division from July 1941, but they lacked the experience or equipment, especially artillery support or anti-aircraft defence, to match the Japanese invaders. To make matters worse, the Burmans were strongly disliked by many of the other Burmese communities, who were reluctant to cooperate. The only other forces that could augment the Burma Rifles were the 17th and 7th Indian Divisions. At the last minute, the British 7th Armoured Brigade arrived, but these forces were insufficient to turn the tide against the Japanese 15th Army.

There was rather more success in resisting the Japanese amongst the Malayan People's Anti-Japanese Army, which was supported by the Special Operations Executive (SOE). Major Freddy Spencer Chapman, of SOE, was particularly prominent in facilitating anti-Japanese guerrilla activity, often with Chinese Malays. In 1945, the Malayan People's Anti-Japanese Army numbered 7000 and came to dominate large parts of the country, but they also provided crucial intelligence and reconnaissance. In 1944, SOE Force 136 created its own country section for Malaya and, by making contact with Ceylon, brought in new agents, radio equipment and munitions. The organisation provided its own propaganda facilities and made anti-Japanese radio broadcasts. Guerrillas were supplied by airdrops provided by the RAF. The system was so successful that similar units, which specialised in operations deep inside enemy occupied territory were established, some carrying out missions as far afield as Indochina and Laos.[48]

At the outbreak of war, the forces available to the British in Africa were very modest indeed.[49] The Royal West African Frontier Force (RWAFF) was 4400 strong; the King's African Rifles (KAR) was 2900; the Somaliland Camel Corps (SCC) was 600; the Sudan Defence Force (SDF) was 4500; and the Northern Rhodesia Regiment (NRR) was 430.[50] By 1945, these formations had grown to over half a million strong. The King's African Rifles and Royal West African Frontier Force fought in East Africa, Madagascar and Burma, and provided internal security in Africa itself. In Burma, 120,000 East and West African soldiers were employed against the Japanese, including the 22nd (East Africa) Infantry Brigade. Ultimately, this brigade actually saw service in East Africa, Italian Somaliland, Abyssinia, Madagascar, Ceylon and Burma. To meet the immense labouring demands of the war, the African Pioneer Corps, part of the British Army's Royal Pioneer Corps, employed tens of thousands of men from across the African territories and moved them into the Middle East and southern Europe as part of a 100,000-strong logistics force in support of the Eighth Army.[51] Africans also saw service in the Royal Navy and the Royal Air Force. The Royal Navy Volunteer Reserves formed units in Gambia, Kenya, Tanganyika and Nigeria. Some 3500 Nigerians served in the Royal Navy and an even larger number in the Merchant Navy. Thousands of West Africans provided the ground staff for British airbases. Many more provided the physical labour to support war industries and the supply of the armed forces during the conflict.

In May 1941, the 26th (East African) Brigade took responsibility for the blockade of Vichy-French Somaliland and they were assisted by local Somali fighters. In May 1942, these auxiliaries, which had increased to a strength of six companies, were formally designated the Somaliland Scouts. The brigade's subsequent operations were conducted over a wide area and involved the use of auxiliaries of the Mounted Police and local *arbagnoch*, as well as 'scouts' and 'irregulars' from Northern Kenya, Somalia and Somaliland. These forces joined the combined operations against the Italians and assisted in overrunning all the territory in East Africa that had been occupied. This offered a degree of strategic depth to operations against the Italians in North Africa.

In West Africa, the War Office took control from the Colonial Office in June 1940 and established the West Africa Command. This organisation assumed responsibility for recruiting, training, supplying and moving some 200,000 soldiers drawn from across the region. Under its jurisdiction, the Royal West Africa Frontier Force (RWAFF) was expanded rapidly. In October 1941, the RWAFF stood at 42,000, but by 1942, it had more than doubled in size to 92,000; a significant force with which to garrison the region and supply troops to operations elsewhere. The Royal

Navy and the Royal Air Force also recruited extensively from West Africa, as they did in the Caribbean, Pacific and Indian Ocean.

During World War II, the Indian Army expanded from 200,000 to more than 2.5 million men, without even the imposition of conscription.[52] It was organised into more than 10 divisions. However, severe equipment shortages meant that few of these divisions were ready for modern mechanised warfare. The first deployments involved the 5th and 11th Indian Infantry Brigades being sent to Egypt in the defence of Suez, with the 7th Indian Infantry Brigade following soon after. These three brigades formed the nucleus of the 4th Indian Division. This was the first formation to see active service in the war and was amongst the most accomplished. In this early stage of the conflict, the division conducted rigorous training in desert warfare prior to their deployment into Libya under the command of General Sir Archibald Wavell. His force of some 31,000 was outnumbered by the Italians at a ratio of more than two to one but, after three days of intense fighting in December 1940, more than 20,000 Italian prisoners were taken and four Italian divisions were destroyed for a loss of approximately 700 casualties. Following this success, 4th Indian Division was redeployed to Sudan, where it joined the newly arrived 5th Indian Division. By now, these formations were mechanised, but their advantages were neutralised by the mountainous nature of the terrain in southern Abyssinia through which they were fighting. The Italians contested the ridges and defiles with determination, but both Indian divisions prevailed and the Italians surrendered in mid-1941.

In March 1941, when the pro-German Iraqi army staged a *coup d'état*, the 20th Indian Brigade of the 10th Indian Division was redirected to Basra where, fortunately, the Iraqi Army showed no signs of resistance. The 10th Division moved on to Baghdad and secured the oil fields around Mosul, while the 21st Indian Brigade advanced into western Syria to support British operations there. The 5th Indian Brigade also participated in the capture of Damascus.[53] German agents also attempted to orchestrate the takeover or destruction of the Persian oilfields, so the 8th and 10th Indian Divisions were redeployed from Iraq to secure southern Iran. British forces also occupied Teheran. Two entire divisions were required for internal security duties in the areas of the Middle East that had come under British occupation.

Until this point in the war, most of the training of the Indian Army had been for mechanised warfare in the desert, so it came as a profound shock when the Japanese mounted offensives through the jungles of Burma and Malaya. The III Indian Corps had formed a defensive line in northern Malaya but had found itself outflanked by more fluid Japanese forces. A similar problem confronted forces sent to Burma. Fortunately, those that had escaped the disaster at Singapore were able to bring valuable lessons about jungle fighting to the newly formed divisions. Nevertheless, there was no disguising the crushing defeat of the Allies in this region. Burma Corps, which included the 17th Indian Division, was cut off in Rangoon having suffered heavy casualties in January 1942.

To restore morale, the British made a concerted effort to improve the welfare of their Indian troops. Particular attention was paid to maintain morale through radio programmes, army publications, entertainers visiting the fronts and an acknowledgement that, after the war, self-government was only a matter of time. In 1942, there were promises of representative government and dominion status after the war, but this did not stop the orchestration of the Quit India movement.[54] A widespread civil disobedience campaign was supposed to persuade the British to abandon India.[55] Disruptions to the food supply caused acute shortages in some areas. Telephone lines, post offices, courts, revenue offices and even police stations were the targets for attack and arson. In extreme cases, railway tracks were torn up. At its height, the Quit India campaign required an entire British division to be diverted to Bombay to quash the unrest. Fortunately, the disturbances were suppressed before the Japanese could capitalise on them, and British and Indian reinforcements reached the eastern frontier successfully to stem the subsequent Japanese offensive.

Indian troops were critical in augmenting Allied manpower in the fighting of 1942–45. In North Africa, the 4th Indian Division participated in the battle of El Alamein and pursued the Afrika Korps to the Murrah Line and beyond. There was particularly bitter fighting around Wadi Akarit, but, soon after, the Germans were driven out of North Africa for good. General Montgomery's verdict was that the 4th Indian Division was amongst his most experienced and best formations. The 4th Indian Division took part in the attempts to take Monte Cassino, which the Germans had turned into a line of almost impregnable positions. The first attacks involving Indian troops were a failure. When the 1/9th Gurkhas succeeded in capturing Hangman's Hill, regarded by the Germans as 'key terrain', they were subjected to intense counter-attacks, but the Allies held on in desperate conditions, which led to a stalemate. In the sustained fighting, the division suffered 4000 casualties. The 8th Indian Division was also deployed to Italy, and in November 1943, this formation fought its way across the Trigno river. It went on to cross the Sangre river, battled its way through fortified villages and crossed the Moro river before winter called its advance to a halt.

Before the fighting in Italy was concluded, the 4th Indian Division, which had already done so much in the conflict, was redeployed to Greece to intervene in the civil war that had broken out when the Germans withdrew; a task that otherwise would have fallen to hard pressed British troops. In April 1945, just weeks before the war ended in Europe, the 8th and 10th Indian Divisions were still involved in difficult operations to cross the Senio river. The Germans continued to contest every mile until the very end.

By late 1944, Field Marshal William Slim had broken the Japanese forces in northern Burma. In December that year, his army's counteroffensive began and the 19th and 20th Indian Divisions were amongst those who crossed the Chindwin river. The Japanese held their positions determinedly, forcing Slim to manoeuvre his brigades and divisions in and around the Japanese formations. The Japanese also conducted resolute counter-attacks, and the terrain, with its dense vegetation, necessitated more fighting at close quarters. By March 1945, Meiktila was in British hands, but the Japanese continued to contest and counter-attack every advance. By now, the Indian army had perfected jungle fighting and combined-arms operations. When the landscape opened up, around Rangoon, Indian units quickly adapted and reverted to a more mobile mechanised warfare. Rangoon was even captured with an amphibious assault on 3 May 1945. Throughout World War II, Britain had been able to call upon large numbers of imperial and Commonwealth troops, including specialist units, to augment its war effort.

Evaluating the System

The value of indigenous forces to British and French mobilisation was twofold. First, the raising of local forces released regulars from world-wide bases who were needed urgently in other theatres. Second, regular Caribbean, African, Asian and Pacific forces could themselves serve in European and global theatres of operations. Nevertheless, western powers cannot today call upon other nations to provide forces, except as voluntary members of coalitions, and the size of contingents that have been offered, since decolonization, have been far smaller than those of the colonial period. Commonwealth nations have been more willing to join coalitions where Britain is a participant, but invariably, the real motive has been to be aligned to the United States or to demonstrate their own national values. In a major conflict, the United States, Britain and France could call upon other nations to assist them, and one can imagine how such coalition partners would be willing to act as peacekeepers in cleared areas or protect ground, air and sea lines of communications. Some nations, such as Australia, Canada and New Zealand, would be more likely to continue their policy of deploying contingents as part of a broad western effort. Where their own regions are affected, these contingents would also be large and have the distinct advantage of being inter-operable with the United States, the United Kingdom and the rest of NATO.

The historical cases indicate that there are still relevant implications for augmenting forces in the event of a major war. The first ramification is that local forces will accept military service on their own terms, where there is a coincidence of interests. Colonial recruitment only succeeded where these conditions were met, particularly when it came to pay and conditions of service. Unrest was common where African and Asian personnel perceived their interests were being infringed. Second, it is also clear that these locally recruited forces performed far better when they possessed sound logistics and modern weaponry, as these affected morale as well as capability. There was a significant improvement in the morale of the Indian army, for example, when they received the same heavy weapons, armour, ships and aircraft as British forces during World War II. Their sense of professional pride was enhanced, and there was greater confidence in being more than a match for the Japanese in operations in Burma with the better arms and equipment they received. Today, if coalition partner nations sent contingents, they are far more likely to be 'light forces', that is, short of heavy weapons and equipment. There are exceptions, of course, but as the British found with the King's African Rifles and the Indian Army in the world wars, the heavier equipment was in short supply, which limited their role.

It was understandable that, during and after the wars, Indian Army officers would emphasise the excellent examples of courage and determination shown by Indian units and their soldiers.[56] Critics have tended to stress the unequal nature of the partnership, ideological or physical subjugation and their failures. Champions and critics alike had their agendas.[57] In recent years, these have been replaced with new historiographical trends. There have been efforts to show that the Indian Army was merely an issue of race and coercion, apparently representing the organising principles of the British Empire. The problem with this interpretation is it was clearly not the way the soldiers and officers of the Indian army saw it themselves at the time.[58] They were organised primarily as an army, with a distinct cultural emphasis that could and often did generate fierce loyalty, competitiveness and *esprit de corps*. However, before World War I, it was an army built around certain assumptions about the character of the war they would be called upon to fight. No one could have foreseen the demands that were to be placed upon it, and we should remember that the Indian army was pitched hastily into a conflict, without the luxury of preparation, to hold the line in France, replace shattered divisions or secure vulnerable parts of the empire. Although largely withdrawn from France and Flanders, from 1917, the Indian army that took the offensive in Palestine, Mesopotamia and Africa was a significantly different organisation from that in 1914. Better equipped, seasoned and expanded, with better staffs, intelligence, logistics and *materiel*, it would go on to provide a great contribution to Allied victory in all these theatres. In the interwar years, the problem of preparation was tackled to some extent by a programme of mechanisation. The mechanised Indian army gave Britain the flexibility to operate in the campaigns in East Africa, North Africa and the Middle East at same time. The Indian Army was also the most crucial element in the campaign in Burma in 1944–45. The implication here is the longevity of the relationship was important, enabling a long-term scheme of development to be implemented, while ensuring inter-operability in a crisis. This would be a good example of the value of the concept of persistent engagement, currently favoured by the British armed forces.

Leadership has always been important in the process of rapid mobilisation and was no less so when it came to the direction, management, and guidance of locally raised forces. For colonial armies, the major vulnerability was the insufficient numbers of qualified young officers or experienced local officers to the replace the casualties they suffered. The question seems less relevant to a modern scenario where coalition nations would have their own officer corps, except for the problem of suitably qualified staffs used to operating a higher headquarters. With smaller contingents, it is unlikely the officers will have experience of divisional or corps command or work in a western establishment. It is here that 'defence engagement' has a part to play, offering officers from partner nations the opportunity to serve as divisional and corps staff, in command roles, in maritime headquarters, in an expeditionary air cell or as part of a large-scale exercise.

Exercises, both as a command post set-up and physically, can also be extraordinarily useful in exposing the difficulties of mobilisation and deployment. When the Indian Army tried to mobilise for World War I, its depot system was overwhelmed and the small mobilisation scheme of two infantry brigades and a cavalry brigade was clearly inadequate. Fortunately, plans for expansion were in place, and improvised depots were established; a feature that can be replicated in exercises today. World War I mobilisation also exposed the deficiencies in certain skill sets, including staff work, and some identification of these was required. In the interwar years, staff college courses were updated and mobilisation schemes identified most of the specialist skills that would be required. Private schools of the period tended to emphasise leadership too and could be said to have fitted a cadre with a relevant sense of mission command, although much of their curricula neglected the needs of a modernised technical and industrial economy. Skills associated with special forces had to be improvised, although local knowledge was invaluable in South East Asia between 1941 and 1945.

The final implication of the mobilisation of forces to fill the gap is the likelihood of political opposition, especially in the event of a major war. In World War I, there were political objections about empowered and experienced military personnel demanding more on their return from conflict, and the war raised the level of consciousness of civil and political rights. There were criticisms about the reliability of local forces, but this was more often due to the lack of equipment, munitions and training caused by the rapid mobilisation. In World War II, Indian nationalists' Quit India campaign of civil disobedience tied down British and Indian troops at a crucial period prior to a major Japanese offensive. After 1945, anti-colonialism accelerated the abandonment of the imperial military system for Britain and France, but the Korean War was the first significant test of a voluntarily associated international force operating as a coalition. In the event of a major war, if the national interests of a number of states were affected, it would be this model, not a colonial one, that would be implemented. Nevertheless, it is worth reflecting that in the supreme crises of 1914 and 1939, Britain and France could automatically mobilise and deploy significant numbers of inter-operable forces from outside of Europe, an asset that is no longer available. The circumstances of a future major war would clearly be radically different, which suggests that an effort today to create voluntary alliances like NATO in other parts of the world, rather than being dependent on *ad hoc* coalitions, has great significance.

Notes

1 Major C. C. Jackson, Lieutenant Colonel G. D. Martin, and Colonel H. H. Smith, *The History of the 4th Battalion 16th Punjab Regiment* (London, 1931), p. 41.

2 'The army of Africa has given an example of the military virtues and merits a place amongst the most dedicated armies', preface to le duc d'Orléans, *Campagnes de l'armée d'Afrique, 1835–1839* (Paris: Michel Levy, 1852).

3 TNA 58-D, CAB 6/2, Redistribution of the Army in India, 1904, Committee of Imperial Defence.

4 George Morton-Jack, *The Indian Army on the Western Front: India's Expeditionary Force to France and Belgium in the First World War* (Cambridge: Cambridge University Press, 2014), p. 3.

5 There were two examinations, with further training in specialist languages as required.

6 Auchinleck served with the 62nd Punjabis and was decorated for his dedication and courage in actions at Suez, the Hanna, Kut and in northern Mesopotamia between 1915 and 1919. Charles Allen, *Plain Tales From the Raj* (London: Andre Deutsch-Penguin, 1975), pp. 239–40.

7 Charles Chenevix Trench, *The Indian Army and the King's Enemies, 1900–1947* (London: Thames and Hudson, 1988), p. 25.

8 Robert Johnson, "The Penjdeh Incident, 1885" in *Archives*, Vol. 24, No. 100 (1999), pp. 28–48.

9 Robert Johnson, "'Russians at the Gates of India': Planning the Strategic Defence of India, 1884–1899" in *Journal of Military History*, Vol. 67 (USA: Virginia Military Institute, July 2003), pp. 697–743.

10 Peter Warwick, *Black People and the South African War, 1899–1902* (Cambridge University Press, 1983), pp. 19–27; 137–41.

11 Anthony Clayton, *France, Soldiers and Africa* (London: Brassey's Defence Publishers, 1988), p. 61; CEHD (Centre d'Etudes d'Histoire de la Défense), *Les troupes de Marine dans l'armée de Terre: Un siècle d'histoire (1900–2000)*, (Paris: Lavauzelle, 2001).

12 Robert Hure, *L'Armée d'Afrique: 1830–1962* (Paris: Charles-Lavauzelle, 1977), p. 20.

13 Shelby Cullom Davis, *Reservoirs of Men: A History of the Black Troops of French West Africa* (Westport, Conn.: Negro Universities Press, 1970), p. 73.

14 V. G. Kiernan, *Colonial Empires and Armies, 1815–1960* (Stroud: Sutton, 1998), p. 101.

15 Frederich von Bernhardi, *Germany and the Next War* (London, 1918), p. 90, p. 146; S. P. Davis, *Reservoirs of Men: A History of Black Troops of French Africa* (Chambéry, 1934), Chapter 4.

16 V. Rothwell, "The British Government and Japanese Military Assistance, 1914–1918" in *History* (February, 1971), pp. 39–43.

17 V. G. Kiernan, *Colonial Empires and Armies*, p. 184.

18 IWM Documents Collection, 16598, Private papers of Josiah Wedgwood, 1st Baron Wedgwood of Burlaston, DSO, letter of 29 September 1916.

19 J. D. Hargreaves, *The End of Colonial Rule in West Africa* (London: Historical Association, 1976), p. 14.

20 M. Crowder, *Revolt in Bussa* (London, 1973), pp. 114–15, pp. 146–49.

21 Commandant F. Ingold, *Les Troupes Noir au Combat* (Paris, 1940), pp. 97–8.

22 V. G. Kiernan, *Colonial Empires and Armies*, p. 185.

23 IWM Documents Collection, 2531, Private papers of Major General H. V. Lewis, letters dated 26 October 1914 and 29 June 1915; Philip Mason, *A Matter of Honour*, (London: Jonathan Cape), p. 413.

24 IWM Documents Collection, 10942, Lieutenant Colonel K. H. Henderson, papers, memoir, pp. 117–20.

25 V. G. Kiernan, *Colonial Empires and Armies*, p. 186.

26 IWM Documents Collection, 2531, Lewis, letter, 1 September 1914.

27 The most significant losses of the frontier wars occurred in the 1897–98 Pathan Rising. On the Tirah expedition, some 287 were killed and a further 853 were wounded, but this was exceptional. Captain H. L. Nevill, *Campaigns on the North West Frontier* (London, 1912), p. 301.

28 British Library L/Mil/17/5/3088, A further five cavalry brigades could be deployed with sufficient notice, Indian Expeditionary Force A, War Diary, Simla, October 1914, p. 136.

29 Robert Johnson, "'I Shall Die Arms in Hand, Wearing the Warriors' Clothes': Mobilisation and Initial Operations of the Indian Army in France and Flanders" in *British Journal for Military History*, Vol. 2, No. 3 (February 2016), pp. 111–12.

30 Sir Moore Creagh, the former CiCI, had demanded modern arms and equipment to fulfil Kitchener's planned expeditionary force capabilities, but the government and his successor as CiCI deferred the decision on grounds of cost. Even after six months of war, the Government of India remained on a peacetime footing with regard to military expenditure.

31 Logistics, for example, had to fit into a British army system, with which the Indian Army was unfamiliar. H. Alexander, *On Two Fronts, Being the Adventures of an Indian Mule Corps in France and Gallipoli* (New York: Dutton, 1917), p. 42.

32 Morton-Jack, *Indian Army on the Western Front*, p. 15. He lists the authors endorsing the suffering caused by the climate.

33 Captain R. Grimshaw, *Indian Cavalry Officer, 1914–15* (London, 1986), cited in Trench, *Indian Army*, p. 35.

34 The latter is strongly refuted by Gordon Corrigan, *Sepoys in the Trenches: the Indian Corps on the Western Front, 1914–15* (Stroud: Spellmount, 2006), p. 168 and p. 247. See Nikolas Gardner, *Trial by Fire: Command and the British Expeditionary Force in 1914* (Westport, CT: Praeger, 2003), pp. 177–82.

35 Willcocks, *With the Indians in France* (Constable and Co., 1924), pp. 266–67.

36 Morton-Jack, *Indian Army on the Western Front*, p. 168.

37 *Ibid*, p. 185.

38 John Merewhether and Sir Frederick Smith, *The Indian Corps in France* (London: John Murray, 1919), pp. 462–89; Morton-Jack, *Indian Army on the Western Front*, p. 19 and pp. 162–5.

39 Merewhether and Smith, *The Indian Corps in France*, p. 463; Morton-Jack, *Indian Army on the Western Front*, p. 18.

40 George Morton-Jack refutes the idea that the Indian Corps was withdrawn because of suffering from the northern European climate or operational underperformance. See Morton-Jack, *Indian Army on the Western Front*, p. 157.

41 *Ibid.*, p. 154.

42 Robin Prior and Trevor Wilson, *The Somme,* (New Haven: Yale University Press, 2005), p. 139.

43 M. O'Dwyer, *India As I Knew It, 1885–1925* (London, 1925), p. 225.

44 TNA CP 2275, CAB 24/116, Radcliffe, memorandum, 'The Situation in Mesopotamia, 7 December 1920.

45 R. Holland, "The British Empire and the Great War, 1914–1918" in Judith M. Brown and W. R. Louis (eds), *The Oxford History of the British Empire, Vol. IV: The Twentieth Century* (Oxford: Oxford University Press, 1999), p. 117.

46 Jackson, *The British Empire and the Second World War* (London: Bloomsbury, 2006), p. 143.

47 James Lunt, *Imperial Sunset: Frontier Soldiering in the 20th Century* (London, 1981), pp. 52–53.

48 Andrew Gilchrist, *Bangkok Top Secret: Force 136 At War* (London, 1960); F. S. Chapman, *The Jungle is Neutral* (London, 1949); Jackson, *The British Empire and the Second World War*, p. 434.

49 David Killingray, *Fighting for Britain: African Soldiers in the Second World War* (Woodbridge, Surrey: James Currey, 2010), p. 27.

50 F. A. S. Clarke and A. Haywood, *The History of the Royal West African Frontier Force* (Aldershot, 1964), p. 327.

51 E. R. Elliott, *Royal Pioneers, 1945–1993* (Hanley Swan, 1993); E. H. Rhodes-Wood, *War History of the Royal Pioneer Corps, 1939–1945* (Aldershot, 1960), p. 150.

52 "The Indian Army and the Second World War: A Force Transformed" in Daniel P. Marston and Chandar S. Sundaram (eds), *A Military History of India and South Asia: From the East India Company to the Nuclear Age* (Bloomington, IN: Indiana University Press, 2007), p. 102.

53 *PAIFORCE: The Official History of the Persia and Iraq Command, 1941–1946* (London, 1948); Marston and Sundaram, *A Military History of India and South Asia*, p. 105.

54 British Library, IOR/L/PJ/8/627, Coll. 117/C27/Q Pt 2, India Office Records, Gandhi, 'Quit India' movement and disturbances, calendars of events, narratives, reports and other information compiled in India to assist Secretary of State in replying to Parliamentary Questions (September 1942–April 1943), p. 49.

55 TNA WO 208/819A, 25C, An assessment of the unrest by Congress was intercepted by Military Intelligence.

56 Willcocks, *With the Indians in France*, p. 9.

57 See, for example, Morton-Jack, *The Indian Army on the Western Front*, p. 13; Merewhether and Smith, *The Indian Corps in France*, pp. vii, Chapters 2 and 14.

58 See "Introduction" in Rob Johnson (ed.), *The Indian Army: Virtue and Necessity,* (Cambridge Scholars Press, 2014), pp. 2–3; 10–11.

CHAPTER 9

What Are the Enduring Lessons?

Major General Dr Andrew Sharpe

Armies tend to grow only when public and political appetite coincide with pragmatic need. This book has not been written in an attempt to persuade readers either that armies need to be bigger in general or that their army, specifically, needs to be bigger. It is not, therefore, about whether armies need to grow or even when armies need to grow but, by design, it is about *how* they grow. This is an important distinction to reiterate in this bringing together of the threads contained in the foregoing chapters. The basic assumption of the book is that, regardless of the best intentions of politics, politicians, polities, civil servants and strategic planners of all hues, history shows us that nations have a tendency to reduce their armies in times of perceived peace and, more often than not, to have to expand their armies in a rushed and haphazard manner when threats emerge. And that the conduct of such expansions is often carried out having put off the undesirable for as long as is possible, often until the point where it is either almost or actually too late. The purpose of the studies contained within this book, therefore, is to provide the reader with a better understanding of what is required effectively and efficiently to expand armies in times of need. At best, this would furnish the reader with a recipe for sensible national and military contingency planning and structuring to enable a smoother growth when circumstances so demand. At worst, it provides an insightful reference book into the magnitude of the problem facing the unprepared.

Of the common conclusions of the case studies, first and foremost is that generating, regenerating or expanding armies, especially in times of crisis, is a national problem, not one for the military alone to address. It is widely accepted that the first duty of any government, as articulated by Adam Smith, is to provide security for its people.[1] If this is true, then it would logically follow that the first priority of every government would be to service the needs of their 'first duty', and, therefore, to service the needs of national defence ahead of all other demands upon their attention and resources.[2] But practicality means that this is unlikely to be the case other than in times of clear and immediate threat to the nation's security, and this is likely to be especially so in a democratic society with a well-informed population and an active and free media and active social media. The demands of social and economic needs are much more likely to receive priority and, therefore, resources, than defence.

In the chapter on the Prussian reforms of 1806–14, we saw that the catastrophe of 1806 was not understood as a purely military disaster that merely required military reforms of a technical nature. Rather, in the eyes of the reformers, the events of 1806 had demonstrated fatal flaws in the Prussian state and society, as well as the army, and, furthermore, the participation of the educated strata would tap a vast pool of experience and talent, mobilising intellectual and spiritual forces, which had hitherto been merely engaged in private pursuits, for the benefit of the state. Understanding this background helps us to understand the triangular relationship between the government and politicians, the people and the polity, and the army and its constituent soldiery that Clausewitz described as a central tenet to his philosophy.

Furthermore, against a background of relative disinterest in the utility of land power, in times when terrorism is perceived by both population and government as being the most immediate and dominant threat to public safety and wellbeing, defence priorities become skewed. Terrorism places its first demands on specialist forces and special forces, rather than on more conventional defence. Expertise takes precedence over mass. The most well-trained (and specific-to-task-trained) professionals take precedence over less expert military capabilities. And when public and political pressure demands 'reassurance deployments' by large numbers of military personnel, as has been seen in the second decade of the 21st century in European capitals, such as Brussels and Paris, whatever military capacity is available rapidly becomes used up in patrolling the nation's streets in a policing role, rather than in a military one. This absorbs not only manpower but, importantly, two other vital ingredients of building and maintaining military capability: a real and useable reserve, and the time to train and prepare.

At a NATO summit of army chiefs of staff, held shortly after terrorist events in Paris and Brussels which had led to the deployment of troops onto their respective nations' streets, this author witnessed a conversation between several of the attendees. The French and Belgian generals were discussing the fact that such deployments placed a huge strain on their respective armies' resources. There was little capacity, they argued, for any military activity, including training, for as long as the commitment lasted. And the longer it lasted, the less their armies would be ready or able to conduct more 'normal' defence tasks. A general from a third country remarked that it must have taken great political courage to order such a deployment of troops onto a nation's streets. The French and Belgian generals disagreed with him – on the contrary, they argued, it would take much more courage to order the troops off the streets than it had to order them on. The first order was made in the wake of public demand for action to be taken; it was, they argued, a 'reassurance deployment'. Having set the precedent of deploying troops 'to keep the population safe' in the face of an unpredictable terrorist threat, it would be a much braver politician, they said, who decided that the risk was low enough, and predictable enough, to end the deployment. Thus, incidents that have dramatic and traumatic impact, yet, in the larger strategic context are relatively small, can have disproportionate effects on military capacity and capability. And these effects are not only the short-term ones of the commitment of resource, but also the longer-term ones of preventing armies from training and preparing for their primary roles. Professional armies need to practice if they are to be capable armies. Time to train and free of other commitments, therefore, will always be a measure of actual or potential military capability, whether considering an army in 'normal times' or an army that is required to expand its capacity to deal with an increased threat.

At the same time, from a military point of view, for the Americans and British, and the other nations contributing to the coalitions that have fought in Afghanistan and Iraq in the opening two decades of the 21st century, a string of lessons have been learned in the face of hard-won understanding and intense and visceral experience. But those lessons, as we saw in the chapter concerning the British Army reforms after the Boer War, have provided a skewed education. Between 1902 and 1913, the British Army prepared itself to make sure that it would never make the mistakes of the Boer experience again – next time, they were determined, it would not be like that. And, of course, they were right – next time it would not 'be like that', but not because they had got the lessons right and had learned how to prevail under similar circumstances, but simply because the circumstances were not similar at all. There is considerable evidence that the experience of those armies that went through Afghanistan and Iraq are etched so deeply into the psyche of those who underwent those experiences that it will be hard to get the writers of doctrine and the leaders of reform to shift to prepare for a role that might not even remotely 'be like that' next time around.

The British Army called its preparations for the Afghanistan deployment Operation *Entirety* – a deliberate name choice to make sure that everyone understood that the only thing that mattered was making sure that those who deployed were properly prepared and equipped for the task ahead of them. In short, it sent the message to the army that nothing took priority over success in Afghanistan. This meant that everything else came second; which in turn meant that much else was neglected. When an army becomes sufficiently small, and the task that it faces sufficiently important, it can very quickly turn its entire attention to the problems in hand. Thus, it can forget its need (perhaps 'its duty' is not too strong) to retain, alongside its current commitments, its ability to cope with the unexpected next threats, demands and contingencies that will almost inevitably emerge either concurrent to or shortly after the immediate demands have been addressed. In short, leaders of armies need not only to be the users of capabilities to deal with immediate and patent threats but also to be the curators of capabilities that may be required for latent threats. In this requirement sits one of the foundation stones of good and responsible generalship.

Military skills are not quickly learned and armies, globally, have become increasingly professionalised because short-term conscripts simply don't have the time to acquire the skills required. These skills, once neglected or lost altogether, take a long time to relearn. And those skills are both physical and conceptual. The physical skills include such simple things as weapon handling or basic tactics and fieldcraft but also the use of increasingly complicated equipment or complex procedures, and, at increasing scale, the ability to manoeuvre formations of personnel and equipment in time and space against an actively oppositional enemy. The conceptual ones are harder to articulate, and often take longer to acquire. For example, the requirement to be comfortable with chaos and complexity; the campaign management skills that the military call 'operational art'; or the instinctive and intuitive skills that provide commanders with 'an eye for the ground' and an insight into opponents' minds.

Furthermore, in terms of maintaining an army of appropriate size for the tasks that it faces, the understanding of force ratios to requirements, against a background of political realities, is also hard to articulate and often hard to justify to politicians, civil servants or the public, especially at times of economic or resource pressure. Yet, at the same time, the maintenance of a real reserve (that is to say a capability that is both flexible in the uses to which it may be put and one that has no other demands on its time or commitment other than training and preparation) is a fundamental military principal. A lack of military experience among politicians and civil servants can make the explanation of these requirements difficult. General Sir Rupert Smith relates a story of his time as General Officer Commanding Northern Ireland.[3] He was visited by the then prime minister, Tony Blair. New to government, to the detail of Northern Ireland's problems and to defence issues, the prime minister was at a loss as to why, in his view, the GOC seemingly had three times as many troops at his disposal as the tasks at hand appeared to demand. General Smith tried a number of different ways of explaining why an army on a campaign should always have at least three times as many resources as the immediate campaign tasking seemed to require. On a two-day visit, he failed to convince Mr Blair. Finally, on the drive to the aeroplane to see the prime minister off, he made one last attempt. 'Prime Minister, when your mother sent you off to prep school she would have given the Matron three pairs of underpants for your use: one to be worn, one in the wash, and one to be kept aside in case of accidents – so it is with military campaigns.' 'Ah! Got it!,' replied Mr Blair.

In short, it is not sufficient for armies to work out exactly what they need for an expected requirement (for example, to decide that a single potent modern division or corps would be able to respond to most of both allied and national defence anticipated demands) without understanding that if that capability is committed to operations then another one needs to be 'in the wash' and a prudent nation would have a third kept aside in case of unforeseen 'accidents' or emergencies. If economic and political constraints are such that this sort of three-to-one ratio is deemed to be simply unaffordably extravagant then an understanding of how armies grow is essential; and a set of contingency plans to ensure that they can be grown as rapidly and effectively as circumstances (often unforeseen) may demand is equally essential.

A casual glance at the history of armed conflict reveals that the requirement to grow armies rapidly, in the face of unexpected threats (either in the speed with which they appear and develop, the size of the threat, the nature of the threat or a variety of any or all of the above), is commonplace. Equally evident, however, is the fact that nations, governments and military establishments are more often than not ill-prepared to deal with the demands of rapid expansion, whether in terms of physical capacity, conceptual and intellectual capacity, or depth of national support and capability. From Rome's hurried mobilisation in the Second Punic War to face Hannibal (and lose to him at the battle of Cannae in 216BC after quadrupling the size of the Roman army to meet the threat he posed) to the Napoleonic, and later American and European examples outlined in this book, nations have repeatedly failed to set in place national and military structures, and mindsets that facilitate rapid military expansion when it is required, regardless of policies, notice or other constraints. To fail to understand that this is a pattern of behaviour, and to fail to act to counter it in a modern military or national administration, is to risk only being able to meet defence and security demands for a short period (as long as that single capability remains operational and sustainable – regardless of endurance or casualties). Therefore, a failure to understand this also means that a government may risk repeating the mistakes of history, thus failing in its first duty to its people (which is the provision of security and safety) or, at best, only being able to have a fair chance of succeeding in that duty for a limited period of time.

This, then, is a national effort that requires a national mindset. The evidence of this book makes it clear that the ability to grow an army to meet the nation's needs is not a task for the army alone, or even a defence ministry alone, but a whole-of-nation task. The government, the military, industry and even the strategic husbanding of national manpower would all need to be mobilised in concert with each other. At the most obvious level, there would need to be a wise balance of military requirements against wider war needs. We have seen in the chapters that covered the jingoistic enthusiasm that accompanied the early growth of European and American armies to meet the mobilisation demands of World War I that those who most readily volunteer for armed service in times of national emergency are often those most needed elsewhere. You do not best serve your nation's long-term war needs by allowing large numbers of steel workers and coal miners enthusiastically to volunteer for service in a rapidly expanding army with an urgent short-term view and a voracious appetite for manpower. The balance of military needs against wider national needs requires cross-government coordination, informed by long-term strategic foresight and contingency planning.

But the first requirement, surely, is a national attitude of mind. The mindset that produces a nation in arms (like Napoleonic France or modern-day Israel) is easier to achieve if the nation is located in obvious (geographical) proximity to a national or existential threat. It is easier, for example, to convince an Estonian steel worker that a national effort is required to counteract a Russian threat than it is to convince an American steel worker of the same apparent need. If a nation is protected by geography from threat, as is Britain by the Channel or America by the Atlantic or the Pacific, then the threat appears more distant and the perception of the policy-makers tends to be that such remoteness will allow plenty of warning before drastic steps need to be taken for the defence of the nation. But the perception runs much deeper than in the minds of the policymakers – it pervades the national psyche much more deeply, such that government, government agencies, civil services, businesses and the population at large are much less likely to make, or take an active part in, plans for national defence at scale if the threat feels remote. History has shown us that nations have had to resort to short-term jingoistic exhortation when longer-term national security complacency exists. It has also shown us that such short-term measures are often ill thought out and, therefore, come with undesirable side effects that may later need to be remedied. If defence and security is, indeed, the first duty of a government, then it would perhaps be wise of that government to (gently) remind the national psyche that this is the case, even in times of apparent relative security.

And national psyches (like military and civil-service habits) are deeply ingrained and slow to change. Public moods may be capricious and swift to ebb and flow, or to flare up and die down according to events, but the underlying national outlook is long formed through culture, geography, history and other such long-term building blocks: these tend to remain as a steady foundation to which national opinion and attitudes return regardless of the short-term fickle flow of public opinion. The histories of various countries in expanding their armies, as laid out in this book, explain where those differing habits and attitudes have come from. But the world has changed, and bodies of water are no longer sufficient for keeping nations in safe and splendid isolation. The inter-connectivity of all things, the reach of effects from distant conflict and the complexity of alliance systems all mean that any responsible government would foster a contingency mentality that allowed for a national approach to threats to the nation. And this must be a long-term and measured approach, not one that depends upon short-term reactions to recent turns of events, underpinned by the harnessing of public mood in the face of imminent danger. Such a long-term approach would require, at the very least: a cross-government agreed approach to strategy and strategic contingency policies and planning; a current and contingent national industrial strategy, along with a long-fostered public/private sector relationship; and a national approach to manpower management.

The first of these, then, would be an agreed approach within governments to strategy, policy and planning, including a coordinated approach to contingency planning ahead of crises and emergencies. This is, perhaps, self-evident, and all governments strive to achieve a measure of coordination and forward thinking in this area. But the pressures of modern democracy are such that short-term expediency almost always trumps long-term contingency. Much recent academic debate has commented upon the apparent absence of a strategic approach in modern democratic governments[4]. There is even little agreed understanding in government offices of the term 'strategy' itself. This is particularly the case in 21st century western democracies, where the political management of the immediate normally trumps the long-term strategic and statesman-like balancing of national aims against resources and policies for action.

Many such academic studies have explored the origins of the word 'strategy', and its surrounding terminology, before exploring its application, both recent and historical. Lawrence Freedman offers a particularly effective definition: 'Strategy is about the relationship between (political) ends and (military, economic, political etc.) means. It is the art of creating power.'[5] This makes it clear that the (Clausewitzean) military, civil sector and political relationship is a cornerstone in constructing the required balance between national ends and means. Amongst many other commentators, Beatrice Heuser, for example, does not offer a simple definition herself but comes close to it: 'Strategy is a comprehensive way to try to pursue political ends, including the threat or actual use of force, in a dialectic of wills – there have to be at least two sides in a conflict. These sides interact, and thus Strategy will rarely be successful if it shows no adaptability.'[6] Essentially, she makes the point that the conduct of strategy is a long-term activity, in which not only are immediate resources balanced off against immediate demands but that contingencies are made to deal with the evolution of events, both expected and unexpected. In short, these two definitions help us to understand that governments have a strategic responsibility that transcends short-term political needs but that centres upon contingency planning, long termism and an eye for national resilience.

For some, the term is only truly appropriate when used in respect of the use of military means. In examining strategy and its relationship to war, Hew Strachan offers an insight into both what it is and what it is not

> 'The state therefore has an interest in re-appropriating the control and direction of war. That is the purpose of strategy. Strategy is designed to make war useable by the state, so that it can, if need be, use force to fulfill its political objectives. One of the reasons that we are unsure what war is is that we are unsure about what strategy is or is not. It is not policy; it is not politics; it is not diplomacy. It exists in relation to all three, but it does not replace them'.[7]

In this specific context (i.e. the preparation for and conduct of war), he, again, stresses that strategic activity is long term and as much about the management of contingencies as it is about the management of immediate demands. By inference, therefore, he argues that because of the term's strict relevance to military matters, a nation that genuinely practices 'strategy' will be one that structures itself to react to the demands that may be placed upon its military – be they current and evident, predicted or expected, or unforeseen and distant.

Colin Gray also opens his work, *Modern Strategy*, by examining historic definitions and finds much merit in both Liddell Hart and, of course, Clausewitz. He adapts Clausewitz's words to offer a short and pithy definition of strategy as: 'the use that is made of force and the threat of force for the ends of policy'.[8] Although this definition may, like Strachan's, be quite narrow and focused upon the use of force, rather than other instruments of government, it has merit in its simplicity as an aid to understanding. Having explored the force-centric nature of this definition, Gray offers a much broader thought, which provides a very useful context for the capture of the idea of *strategy*: 'It does not matter precisely which form of words are preferred for a working definition, but the essence of strategy must be identified unambiguously. That essence lies in the realm of the consequences of actions for future outcomes.'[9] In other words, Gray is saying that we certainly need to understand what we are doing things for, but also, again, because consequences can be foreseen or unforeseen, we see that forward-planning and the preparation for contingencies lies at the heart of a truly strategic approach.

If this is so, for a nation to claim that it was taking a genuinely strategic approach to its policy setting, and especially to its national defence contingency planning, it would need to accept, in advance, that it may not be able to predict the time, timing or circumstances of a national emergency that may require it to grow its army well beyond its current capacity. Having accepted that, it would then need to decide, in advance, to draw up contingencies as to how, under varying circumstances it would wish to grow its defence capabilities, in concert with other national requirements, to meet a variety of more or less predictable threats. In simple terms, in acting strategically, we need to hold aside capability and dedicate conceptual effort, alongside the execution of pressing political, policy and event-driven reality because we must prepare ourselves in times of non-crisis for our ability to react when the crisis comes. Because, when it does arrive, it will be, at worst, too late to make such provisions and plans or, at best, it will require a long and risky struggle to recover from the surprise. In short, what this national contingency planning and off-setting should be done for is because it may be too dangerous (and irresponsible) to leave it until later.

And recent history shows that governments, no matter how powerful, cannot afford the luxury of imagining that they can dictate events or even their involvement in events. In an increasingly inter-dependent world, sage policy formers would not fall back on 'ten-year plans' and a blinkered belief that they can dictate national lead times into crises. The implosion of a relatively insignificant state can have knock-on effects that can rapidly and disproportionately affect even the most distant and powerful. Complex alliance systems mean that other people's interests must often be our own interests. Latvia's concerns about Russian expansionism and aggressive behaviour, for example, must be everyone in NATO's concerns – that is the nature of the alliance. The 9/11 attacks reminded us of Trotsky's warning that while you may not be interested in war, war may be interested in you: a small group of men from distant Middle Eastern countries, trained in the remote places of a failed state, took an interest in America that America could not ignore.

Furthermore, the inextricably inter-connected nature of 21st-century global affairs, and especially economies, means that instability anywhere creates instability, to varying degrees, everywhere else: no one is immune to distant problems. States, therefore, no matter how powerful and despite protestations to the contrary, cannot afford to believe that they have absolute choices about where and how they become involved in the affairs of others. This means that not only must national contingency plans be made in advance, in the privacy and secrecy of government departments, but national habits should also be fostered, in advance, that would lead to ingrained behaviour patterns that would allow the more effective execution of those contingency plans.

All of this requires a political determination to 'think long'. Current trends in western democratic politics, however, have shown a politically necessary determination not to be seen to be planning away from published policies or immediate endorsed behaviours. The power of the *project fear* mantra during the 2016 British Brexit referendum campaign showed the ease with which sensible contingency questioning can be easily and aggressively turned into apparent vacillation or negativity, instead of merely sensible enquiry. Such behaviour, while politically logical in the short term, often leads to a directed neglect of contingency planning and structures. Military strategic examples abound: America's determination at the start of World War I to remain nonaligned led to a policy of neutral inactivity that included forbidding contingency planning for fear of such plans being leaked and seen as partisan. In February 2016, an issue of the publication *Ares and Athena* from the British Army-sponsored think tank, the Centre for Historical Analysis and Conflict Research (CHACR), (nearly two years after the annexation of the Crimea) entitled 'Wake up and smell the vodka', was initially described by cautious 'special advisors' in the MoD and FCO as being 'unhelpful' against a short-term background policy of soft-line rapprochement with Russia. 'Imagine the headline, right now, of "British Army thinks Russia is a threat,"!' was the cry, at a time when keeping Russia friendly was the policy. Yet, surely, a more responsible approach would have been: 'imagine the possible headline, in a few years' time, if events turn sour, of "British Army were forbidden from thinking Russia was a threat"'!

So, to summarise these thoughts on the need to view this as a problem with a national perspective: the first duty of government is widely accepted as being to assure the safety of its citizens. This implies that all organs of government should be engaged in, at the very least, contingency planning for the defence of the nation in the event of enhanced foreseen or unforeseen threats. Yet, policy constraints, political realities, media intrusion and, perhaps, even irresponsibility, and aggressive but fickle public opinion are likely to hold sway. Military skill sets and mindsets, and defence priorities are likely to be skewed by events (such as terrorist attacks of limited actual impact but high effect) and lessons of recent conflict that may not apply to future conflicts. Limited resources for all aspects of government are likely to make resources for the military even more constrained. Increasing political ignorance of military realities (such as the real implications of military 'readiness states', of the need for reserves and of the disproportionate effect of defence inflation) is a growing trend.

And in modern democracies, where politics remain alert to 24-hour news feeds and social media opinion formers, short termism and political expediency is likely to trump long-term strategic thinking or action.

Yet, despite all of this, a prudent nation would, at the very least, encourage its military and its civil servants to *think* about these things. The first requirement of a national approach to strategic contingency is, therefore, a mindset that encourages the pursuit of conceptual and physical contingency planning and preparation. Activity being conducted openly where appropriate and in secret when required. In short, step one in engendering a national approach to the problem is the generation of the correct mindset within the corridors of government.

For a nation to be genuinely able to react rapidly to significant threats, however, the mindset, and the contingency capabilities, must be in place well beyond the circles of government. For example, in the UK, the national rail network is not under the nation's control nor are its ship building or aerospace industries; and the UK is now largely dependent upon imports for the raw materials of heavy industry and the materials required to power that industry. The effects of privatisation stretch far beyond the bounds of economics or political philosophy. National industrial capacity, along with the willingness of business owners to moderate the demands of their balance sheets and shareholders against the needs of a nation in (as yet unforeseen) times of crisis, are integral aspects of a nation's capacity to build or expand its military capacity at short notice. It is self-evident, therefore, that the existence, preservation and nurturing of a nation's military industrial complex, in times of perceived reduced need, is a vital aspect of a nation's ability to respond to an increased demand on its military capability. National contingency planning for industry is as important to the military as military contingency planning is to the nation. Furthermore, in the event that a nation's military procurement policies place 'cost effectiveness' above 'national needs', it is also likely that national industries will be put under threat or pressure by competitive pricing from non-national sources. A short-term focus on getting the best deal can lead to a long-term strategic weakening of the nation's ability to fend for itself when it needs to.

As we saw in the chapter on interwar America, shortfalls in national capability are often not just found in the non-existence of tangible or physical things. The establishment in the 1920s of an Army Industrial College was a measure designed not just to teach a few selected army officers about the intricacies of negotiating the military-industrial complex, but rather, with its ever-increasing cohort of attendees and graduates, to make the army as a whole better equipped for interfacing with American industry, both in terms of routine business and in terms of contingency planning and preparation, or in times of crisis or war. As stated earlier in this book: its mission was essentially to train army officers in all aspects necessary to the procurement of all military supplies in time of war and to the assurance of adequate provisions for the mobilisation of materiel and industrial organisation essential to wartime needs. In other words, the function of the college was not just to make routine military-industry relationships work to mutual satisfaction, but also to generate the possession of more intangible things, such as understanding, networking, soft skills, pre-formed relationships, familiarity, trust, behavioural habits and mutual preparedness to act that might allow positive effect at short notice.

This understanding of the depth of the national requirement to have systems and mindsets in place that can allow armies to grow effectively in times of crisis is complex. It goes well beyond simply making sure that a nation's defence industry has capacity and its government and administrators have contingencies in mind and in place. Managing a nation's manpower, or at least being prepared to manage a nation's manpower, with wisdom and foresight is as important as managing the other physical capabilities available. In other words, there needs to be sufficient national foresight not only to have a national mobilisation plan but also one that ensures that the nation does not let all of its engineers, aircraft manufacturers, miners and steel workers enlist in the army in times of need!

Blind reliance on enthusiasm to volunteer often means that nations rapidly lose national capacity for industry or agriculture as people leave vital workplaces to expand the armed forces. This needs management ahead of realisation through it happening. As we saw in the chapters on the British and American stories, when faced with conflict at a huge scale this is a fairly common picture when enthusiasm or jingoism brings a ready supply of eager manpower forward well ahead of an unprepared nation's ability to house, train or equip such a large number of volunteers all at the same time. National moods and the complexity of modern warfare have combined to make large-scale, short-term conscription an increasingly unattractive way of ensuring that large elements of a nation's manpower have an understanding, albeit basic and rusty, of military skills.

That is not to say that there is no appetite at all for a return to conscription as a common tool for both short- and long-term defence capability and capacity. It is of note that after the series of terrorist attacks in France in 2015 there rapidly arose a serious national debate on the merits of conscription, not only to provide a scale of uniformed personnel to defend against the perceived threat, but also to draw in the more peripheral French nationals to imbue a sense of national responsibility and belonging (as opposed to exclusion and remoteness characterised by the ghetto existence of many of those domestically originating terrorists). Conscription, however, sits reasonably comfortably with a French post-revolutionary mindset that established the citizen's duty to defend the state (as opposed to the more commonly accepted version that it is the state's duty to defend the citizen). Such thinking did not sit comfortably, however, for example, with a US mindset as it struggled with the demands of Vietnam, and it remains a mindset that is uncomfortable for much of the world, with an increasing emphasis on the professionalisation of volunteer armed forces.

Regardless of all of the above, in physical terms, if nations are to be self-reliant in enabling their armies to expand rapidly in times of need, they must afford those armies the means of expansion. Armies tend to shrink either because that shrinkage is forced upon them by others (through defeat for example, as we have seen in the German case studies) or through a rebalancing of national priorities (perhaps the threat perception changes, economic circumstances force cutbacks or both). When such reductions occur, especially if, typically, levels of ambition for national influence do not reduce commensurately, defence officials tend to look elsewhere for stand ins to provide the capabilities now absent. This can lead to what is sometimes alliteratively known as 'reliance upon alliance'. In this case, responsible and prudent membership of alliances and defence agreements can be used as a (sometimes irresponsible) substitute for national capability. The USA has long felt, for example, that many European nations abrogate their own responsibilities for national defence by relying on the shelter of a US umbrella. Although such a technique does not 'grow' an army, it can lead to an enhanced effectiveness of that army through its relationship with others. If this is done in a carefully managed way, such as capability sharing where others can be relied upon to deliver capacity that is lacking in one's own army, normally on a quid pro quo basis, then it can be highly effective. If it is done irresponsibly, however, then it can lead to a reliance on others' capabilities that simply do not exist. If a number of cooperating nations, for example, rely on each other to provide ground-based air defence, while at the same time all making savings in that area, the 'reliance on alliance' becomes irresponsible.

We have explored the capabilities that have been provided by colonial or dependency forces and pools of manpower and equipment. France and Britain were both fortunate in the two existential wars of the 20th century in that they were able to call upon considerable resources, in men and materiel, from their respective empires. To maintain perspective, however, it is important to point out that these far-flung empires also put a considerable manpower and materiel bill upon their colonial masters but, on balance, as the conflicts progressed, they also proved to be a vital resource. In the lead-up to World War I, for example, Britain was much more concerned about the threat posed to India by Russia and, therefore, the need to have contingency plans for the reinforcement of the Indian army, than it was about drawing up contingency plans for the Indian Army to be used in the defence either of Britain in Europe or of Britain's other imperial interests in Africa or the Middle East. By the Armistice of 1918, however, nearly one million Indian troops were serving outside India in support of the British war effort. And during World War II, the Indian Army expanded from 200,000 to more than 2.5 million men.

Thus, we have also seen how a reliance on the building of auxiliary, proxy or ancillary forces can build capacity by locum. Armies can also have considerable reach by providing a training core to other armies, building their capacity and hoping to influence their behaviour such that they act in the supporting nation's interests as a local substitute for the deployment abroad of that nation's own assets. When capacity is built in this way using strong ties to the core nation (as was evident, for example, in the British-Indian army of the late-19th and early-20th centuries), the technique can have considerable effect. When the ties are weaker, the results are less certain. In brief, small armies can greatly enhance their effectiveness if they put credible resource into training and influencing the forces of others, but this will rarely be a substitute for the responsibilities of meeting urgent and proximate national threats.

So what steps can an army take, within itself, to develop the capacity to grow? Armies are comprised of three components: the physical, the moral and the conceptual. The physical component concerns those things with which an army fights – its manpower (including numbers and state of training) and its equipment (including numbers and relative sophistication or effectiveness). The moral component concerns those things that generate cohesion and inspire men and women to fight (intangibles such as courage, unit pride, comradeship, trust, discipline, resolution and tenacity). The conceptual component concerns those things that influence how an army fights (tactics, doctrine, cunning, planning, professional knowledge and intuition).

Much of what has been summarised up until this point has covered the physical component of fighting power. It has concerned a nation's ability to provide, rapidly, the manpower and equipment it may require to expand its army's physical capability. In this respect, an army that is behaving responsibly will put energy into identifying those physical shortfalls that will need to be addressed. It will need to identify personnel, equipment and training requirements that may be needed to address various contingencies. It will need to identify and plan for its own ability to absorb those enhancements such that it can grow the physical capacity to fight as effectively and rapidly as possible. It will need to understand how it must be able to restructure itself, sufficiently rapidly, to turn the enhancements into an integral part of the complete military capability. And, as we have seen, it will need to engage the rest of the nation in a discussion so that the mood and physical preparedness of the nation is such that these requirements in terms of personnel and materiel can be met, with enthusiasm and understanding, when required.

Addressing the needs of the moral component, in contingency planning, is not easy. Yet it is a vital component of fighting power, indeed, often, it is *the* vital component. Napoleon is said to have observed that in war the moral is to the physical as three is to one. In this respect, armies understand that, although they may draw their personnel from the population that they represent, the ethos that they require from their people may be somewhat different from the population at large. Armies need discipline and self-discipline in a way that is not normally required from civilian populations. Armies need courage and a sense of selflessness that run contrary to normal human self-preservation. Armies need to balance an instinct for deception against an increased requirement for integrity. None of these complex intangibles can be learned quickly. The circumstances of an army's expansion can go a long way to help but almost always only in the short term. Jingoism, for example, has its place in recruiting personnel and in instilling an initial enthusiasm for the fight, but jingoism has repeatedly proved to be a thin and fragile veneer when hastily built armies are confronted with the visceral and harsh realities of conflict. National temperament has a role to play too, but, as with the physical component already discussed, is only at its most effective if harnessed by design and with deliberate forethought. The two best builders of the moral component of fighting power are, arguably: the effectiveness of military training (especially enhanced by the amount of time spent in training) and a track record of success. Small professional armies can maximise the first and do their best to ensure the second. Rapidly built large armies will always struggle with both. In this respect, time is the key factor – armies need the time to convert the values of their civil society into the moral component values that they need to provide their physical component with the 'three-is-to-one' moral underpinning that gives them fighting effect.

Armies have considerable agency, therefore, in their nation's preparation for the development of both the physical and moral components of their fighting power. But they have absolute control over neither. They can influence how they nurture these capabilities in times of contingency as well as in times of actual need. They can prepare themselves for the absorption and training of these components. The only element of fighting power over which they have almost complete control, however, is the conceptual domain.

In this respect, one clear lesson for military professionals stands out repeatedly in the chapters of this book. Military success has a tendency to lead to hubris – 'it worked last time, so a) we are good at this, and, b) it will probably work next time if we do it the same way'. It is only in the event of heavy defeat that armies have a tendency to really rethink how they think. The Prussian and interwar German chapters have provided real insight into how harsh lessons, followed by imposed necessity, have a way of forcing a genuine transformation in philosophy and the wider conceptual component of fighting power. And armies tend to have complete ownership of how they develop their conceptual component.

Soldiers who understand that it is more often the army that is out-thought that loses, than it is the army that is out-fought, put a premium on professional conceptual competence. Thus, the nurture of the conceptual component of fighting power must always sit at the heart of an army. When armies anticipate that they may need to grow rapidly, either unexpectedly or deliberately, the development of their conceptual component takes on new, and greater, significance. Armies can grow rapidly if the generals who command divisions are, mentally, comfortable with the different demands that would be placed upon them if they were asked to command corps or army groups. Captains who are trained to plan, organise, direct and lead battalions will be able to step up to that mark when asked to do so. Combat officers who are trained to become efficient staff officers, not only understand the mechanics of their trade better but are also capable of stepping up to find relative order in the chaos of conflict. In short, members of an officer corps (and, indeed, a non-commissioned officer corps) who build up a professional knowledge of the detail of their trade and who share not only the same ethos but also, vitally, the same philosophical and practical mental approach are much more likely to succeed than those who do not.

As we see in the chapter on the enlargement of the German army in the interwar period, the Versailles treaty ordered the abolition of the German general staff and of the military academies and schools. This was not a random act but a carefully considered measure to ensure that the conceptual component of Germany's fighting power was being dismantled alongside the physical component. There is little doubt that that the underpinning logic behind the decision to take this course of action was based upon the notion that it is easier to rebuild, rapidly, an army's physical component (i.e. to recruit and train manpower and to equip them with weapons and armaments) than it is to generate the depth of understanding required in the conceptual space (be it the learning and application of tactical doctrine or the grasp of the complexities of operational art) for an army to operate effectively in battle.

Despite the restrictions placed on the Germans during the interwar period, however, they recognised that the maintenance of a strong underpinning conceptual component provides one of the key elements of a foundation for later expansion and effectiveness. And the first step was simply to recognise that, at some stage in the future, expansion would be either desirable, likely or necessary. As we have seen, during the early 1920s, German military thinkers concluded (for a variety of reasons, some political, some practical) that expansion of the German army was either likely or desirable, or both, in the not-too-far-distant future. Thus, logically, the immediate, planned and structured preservation of its conceptual component, as a foundation for the rebuilding of its physical component in the future, was vital.

But, throughout the interwar period, the Germans came to another fundamental conclusion that resonates today. There were threats to German security that needed addressing with what little military resource was available to them. The reduced capacity of German arms meant that what little resource was available (manpower, equipment and time) was needed to dedicate itself to the urgent business of meeting the immediate defence needs of the nation. Yet, tellingly, this was not used as an excuse not to find the time to develop the army's wider conceptual component in the background to their operational activity. This is an object lesson to armies in the 21st century: militaries may be 'busier than ever before with fewer resources than ever before', but this does not excuse them from the professional need to be able to operate, at the very least conceptually, at a different scale and size, in a different manner, and in different contexts from the world of their current commitments.

A universal theme seems to be that of education. The Kriegsakademie (the Germans' interwar programme), Camberley and US professionalisation of military education in the early-20th century: the theme reoccurs throughout this book. It is worth noting that at the Army Staff College in Camberley in the 1980s and 1990s, captains and majors were still learning the art of planning and executing operations at the brigade and divisional level (and even, in a final test exercise, at the corps level). As British military education has become increasingly Joint (in other words, whereas staff training used to be conducted in single-Service isolation, it is now largely brought together, especially at the more senior levels, in a Joint – Army, Navy and Airforce – setting), so the shift has been away from the execution of tactical-level operations (on land in particular, but also in the air and at sea), in favour of a wider education at the operational level, focusing on campaigning and the coordinated efforts of all elements of a modern campaign from a joint defence force, across other government departments and into the wider governmental and non-governmental players of a modern campaign. This switch in educational focus, alongside intense operational experience that gave a very focused understanding of lower-level tactics within a very specific construct of warfare, has perhaps skewed a wider understanding of warfare at a higher tactical level, in British and American army officers at least. It is precisely this level of understanding that is so vital in an army that may seek to expand rapidly in the face of crisis – and it was this capability that enabled the interwar German army to prepare itself for successful rapid expansion in the build-up to hostilities in the late 1930s. As we also saw, the Root reforms at Fort Leavenworth in the early 1900s were not just about better preparing a professional officer corps for its likely war roles but also aimed at establishing a 'brains trust' for the US Army, to ensure that it was capable of operating conceptually on a number of levels.

In all of the foregoing conclusions, two factors spring to the front. First, armies have a duty not just to concentrate on the challenges that immediately face them, no matter how pressing, but also to consider the contingencies of the future. In short, they need to develop not just a willingness, but *a habit* of thinking about, and planning for, warfare on differing scales and with different characteristics from those that immediately face them. Second, having formed the habit, they then need to find that precious commodity: the *time to think* in depth. That time should be spent deliberately and wisely not just on contingency planning, but on the training and education of the leadership core of the army in operations at a scale considerably larger and more threatening than the ongoing circumstances. In this way a virtual cadre of expertise can be laid down, upon which an army can build in times of rapid expansion, providing the newly generated physical component of fighting power with its underpinning conceptual component.

If this book has shown nothing else, it has shown that a prevalent Anglo-American model for growing armies has been characterised by improvisation. It has also shown that such an approach tends to lead to setbacks and problems that bring about urgent and major rethinks. Success in this area, on the other hand, has been found in the approaches taken in the face of defeats or disasters that have forced otherwise complacent militaries (and, indeed, nations) to rethink their structures, philosophies and policies in a much more profound and measured way. They have found the time so to do, whether through a lack of commitments or through a lack of capability that has left them with little to do but think.

In Short

Step one is to recognise that there is not only a need, but rather a responsibility, not just within an army, but within the wider nation, to think about contingent expansion in times of relative peace.

Step two is to find the ever-evasive time within the army to exercise and educate the conceptual component of fighting power, so that military professionals are instinctively able to operate at a different level when national crisis occurs.

At the extreme, to fail to do so is to risk failing, at both a national and an army level, to meet Adam Smith's first requirement of a government in ensuring the safety and security of its own people.

Notes

1 'The first duty of the Sovereign, that of protecting the society from violence and invasion of other independent societies...'; Adam Smith; *Wealth of Nations*; Book V, Chapter 1, Part 1, opening line.

2 Smith's articulation of the first duty of a sovereign has been widely repeated by other statesmen and theorists, see for example 'the chief purpose of government is to protect life. Abandon that and you have abandoned all'. Attributed to Thomas Jefferson. George Grant, *Trial and Error: The American Civil Liberties Union and Its Effect on Your Family* (Wolgemuth and Hyatt, 1989), p. 85.

3 General Sir Rupert Smith KCB, DSO and Bar, OBE, QGM. Commissioned into the Parachute Regiment in 1964 and retired as Deputy Supreme Allied Commander Europe in 2001. Author of, in particular, *The Utility of Force* (London: Penguin, 2005). He served as General Officer Commanding Northern Ireland from 1996 to 1998.

4 In the UK led by individuals such as Professor Sir Hew Strachan, Professor Sir Lawrence Freedman, Professor Beatrice Heuser and Professor Colin Gray.

5 Beatrice Heuser, *The Evolution of Strategy* (Cambridge: CUP, 2010), p. 32.

6 *Ibid.*, pp. 27–28.

7 Hew Strachan, *The Direction of War* (Cambridge: CUP, 2013), p. 43.

8 Colin Gray, *Modern Strategy* (Oxford: OUP, 1999); p. 17.

9 *Ibid.*, p. 18.

Select Bibliography

This select bibliography contains works that are easily accessible for the interested reader.

Barr, Ronald J. *The Progressive Army: US Army Command and Administration, 1870–1914* (London: Macmillan Press, 1998)

Beckett, Ian and Simpson, Keith (eds.). *A Nation in Arms: A Social Study of the British Army in the First World War* (Manchester: Manchester University Press, 1985)

Bond, Brian. *British Military Policy between the Two World Wars* (Oxford: Clarendon Press, 1980)

Bowman, Tim and Connelly, Mark. *The Edwardian Army: Recruiting, Training and Deploying the British Army, 1902–1914* (Oxford: Oxford University Press, 2012)

Broicher, Andreas. *Gerhard von Scharnhorst: Soldat, Reformer, Wegbereiter* (Aachen: Helios, 2005)

Brown, Judith M. and Louis, W. R. (eds.). *The Oxford History of the British Empire, Vol. IV: The Twentieth Century* (Oxford: Oxford University Press, 1999)

Chandler, David and Beckett, Ian, (eds.). *The Oxford History of the British Army* (Oxford: Oxford University Press, 1994)

Clayton, Anthony. *France, Soldiers and Africa* (London: Brassey's, 1988)

Corum, James S. *The Roots of Blitzkrieg: Hans von Seeckt and German Military Reform* (Lawrence, Kansas: University Press of Kansas, 1992)

Crang, Jeremy. *The British Army and the People's War 1939–1945*, (Manchester: Manchester University Press, 2000)

Crépin, Annie. *Défendre la France – Les Francais, la guerre et le service militaire, de la guerre de Sept Ans à Verdun* (Rennes: Presses universitaires de Rennes, 2005)

Davis, Shelby Cullom. *Reservoirs of Men: A History of the Black Troops of French West Africa* (Westport, Conn.: Negro Universities Press, 1970)

Doughty, Robert A. *Pyrrhic Victory: French Strategy and Operations in the Great War* (Cambridge, Massachusetts: Harvard University Press, 2005)

Esdaile, Charles. *Napoleon's Wars – An International History 1803–1815* (London: Penguin, 2007)

Forrest, Alan. *The Legacy of the French Revolutionary Wars – The Nation-in-Arms in French Republican Memory* (Cambridge: Cambridge University Press, 2009)

Fox, Aimée. *Learning to Fight: Military Innovation and Change in the British Army 1914–1918* (Cambridge: Cambridge University Press, 2017)

French, David. *British Economic and Strategic Planning 1905–1915* (London: Allen & Unwin, 1982)
——————. *Raising Churchill's Army* (Oxford: Oxford University Press, 2000)

French, David and Holden Reid, Brian (eds.). *The British General Staff: Reform and Innovation, 1890–1939* (London: Cass, 2002)

Geyer, Michael. *Aufrüstung oder Sicherheit: Die Reichswehr in der Krise der Machtpolitik, 1924–1936* (Wiesbaden: Franz Steiner Verlag, 1980)

Gooch, John. *The Plans of War: The General Staff and British Military Strategy c.1900–1916* (London: Routledge & Keegan Paul, 1982)

Gray, Colin. *Modern Strategy* (Oxford: Oxford University Press, 1999)

Gray, Marion W. *Prussia in Transition: Society and Politics under the Stein Reform Ministry of 1808*, (Philadelphia: American Philosophical Society, 1986)

Gudmundsson, Bruce. *The British Expeditionary Force 1914–15* (Oxford: Osprey, 2014)

Heuser, Beatrice. *The Evolution of Strategy* (Cambridge: Cambridge University Press, 2010)

Hewes Jr, James E. *From Root to McNamara: Army Organization and Administration, 1900–1963* (Washington: Center of Military History, US Army, 1975)

Howard, Michael. *War in European History* (Oxford: Oxford University Press, 1977)

Jany, Curt. *Geschichte der preußischen Armee: Vom 15. Jahrhundert bis 1914*, 2nd revised edition (Osnabrück: Biblio, 1967)

Johnson, Rob (ed.). *The Indian Army: Virtue and Necessity* (Cambridge: Scholars Press, 2014)

Killingray, David. *Fighting for Britain: African Soldiers in the Second World War* (Woodbridge, Surrey: James Currey, 2010)

Kreidberg, Marvin A. and Henry, Merton G. *History of the Military Mobilization in the United States Army 1775–1945* (Washington, DC: Department of the Army, 1955)

Mangin, Charles. *Comment finit la Guerre* (Paris: Plon, 1920)

Marston, Daniel P. and Sundaram, Chandar S. (eds.). *A Military History of India and South Asia: From the East India Company to the Nuclear Age* (Bloomington, IN: Indiana University Press, 2007)

McCartney, Helen. B. *Citizen soldiers: The Liverpool Territorials in the First World War* (Cambridge: Cambridge University Press, 2005)

Militärgeschichtliches Forschungsamt (ed.). *Handbuch zur deutschen Militärgeschichte* (six volumes), Vol. IV, *Wehrmacht und Nationalsozialismus 1933–1945* (Munich: Bernard & Graefe, 1983)

Ministère de la Guerre. *Les Armées françaises dans la Grande Guerre* (Paris: Imprimerie Nationale, 1922–1939)

Mitchinson, K. W. *The Territorial Force at War: 1914–16* (Basingstoke: Palgrave MacMillan, 2014)

Moran, Daniel and Waldron, Arthur (eds.). *The People in Arms – Military Myth and National Mobilization Since the French Revolution* (Cambridge: Cambridge University Press, 2006)

Morton-Jack, George. *The Indian Army on the Western Front: India's Expeditionary Force to France and Belgium in the First World War* (Cambridge: Cambridge University Press, 2014)

Mulligan, William. *The Creation of the Modern German Army. General Walther Reinhardt and the Weimar Republic, 1914–1930* (Oxford: Oxford University Press, 2005)

Müller, Klaus-Jügen (ed.). *The Military in Politics and Society in France and Germany in the Twentieth Century* (Oxford: Berg, 1995)

Nakata, Jun. *Der Grenz und Landesschutz in der Weimarer Republik 1918–1933. Die geheime Aufrüstung und die deutsche Gesellschaft* (Freiburg: Rombach, 2002)

Simkins, Peter. *Kitchener's Army: The Raising of the New Armies, 1914–16* (Manchester: Manchester University Press, 1988)

Spiers, Edward. *Haldane: An Army Reformer* (Edinburgh: Edinburgh University Press, 1980)

Stoker, Donald, et al. (eds.). *Conscription in the Napoleonic Era – A Revolution in Military Affairs?* (London: Cass, 2009)

Stone, David. *Fighting for the Fatherland: The Story of the German Soldier from 1648 to the Present Day* (London: Conway, 2006)

Strachan, Hew. *European Armies and the Conduct of War* (London: George Allen and Unwin, 1983)

——————— . *The Direction of War* (Cambridge: Cambridge University Press, 2013)

Strohn, Matthias. *The German Army and the Defence of the Reich: Military Doctrine and the Conduct of the Defensive Battle 1918–1939* (Cambridge: Cambridge University Press, 2010)

Strohn, Matthias, (ed.). *World War I Companion* (Oxford: Osprey, 2013)

——————— . *1918: Winning the War, Losing the War* (Oxford: Osprey, 2018)

Telp, Claus. *The Evolution of Operational Art: 1740–1813, From Frederick the Great to Napoleon* (London and New York: Frank Cass, 2005)

Walter, Dierk. *Preussische Heeresreformen: 1807–1870, Militärische Innovation und der Mythos der 'Roonschen Reform'* (Munich: Schoeningh, 2003)

Warwick, Peter. *Black People and the South African War, 1899–1902* (Cambridge:Cambridge University Press, 1983)

Wawro, Geoffrey. *The Franco-Prussian War* (Cambridge: Cambridge University Press, 2003)

Weigley Russel F. *The American Way of War: A History of United States Military Strategy and Policy* (Bloomington: Indiana University Press, 1973)

Index